The
English
Ruling
Class

READINGS IN POLITICS AND SOCIETY

GENERAL EDITOR: Bernard Crick

Professor of Political Theory and Institutions,
University of Sheffield

FORTHCOMING VOLUMES

A. J. Beattie, *English Party Politics*
F. W. Bealey, *The Growth and Political Ideas of the British Labour Movement*
J. P. Mackintosh, *The Growth of the Cabinet System*
J. K. Kumar, *Revolution*
William Thornhill, *The Growth and Reform of Local Government*
N. D. Deakin, *The Rise of the Welfare State*
Edmund Ions, *Modern American Political and Social Thought*

Previously published in this series by Routledge & Kegan Paul,

David Nicholls, *Church and State in Britain Since 1820*

The
English
Ruling
Class

Edited and introduced by

W. L. GUTTSMAN

Author of *The British*
Political Elite

HARLAXTON COLLEGE
UNIVERSITY OF EVANSVILLE
GRANTHAM, LINCS.

WEIDENFELD AND NICOLSON
5 Winsley Street London W1

Printed in Great Britain by
Cox & Wyman Ltd, London, Fakenham and Reading

Contents

General Editor's Preface ix

Foreword xi

Acknowledgements xii

Introduction 1

1: THE GENERAL CHARACTER OF THE CLASS

1.1 The Oaks of the Commonwealth (Edmund Burke) 21

1.2 The Lordlies and the Laws of State (Edmund Burke) 21

1.3 Property and Permanence (S. T. Coleridge) 24

1.4 Hereditary Legislators (Benjamin Disraeli) 25

1.5 The Social Virtues of an Aristocracy (E. G. B. Lytton) 27

1.6 The Functions of a Nobility (Walter Bagehot) 29

1.7 A Deferential People (J. S. Mill) 31

1.8 Gentility through Patronage (G. O. Trevelyan) 32

1.9 A Gentlemanly Rule – not a Bureaucratic System
(Charles de Montalembert) 33

1.10 Gentlemen as an Exclusive Social Class (H. Taine) 36

1.11 The Establishment: the Radical Attack (John Wade) 39

1.12 The Genealogy of an Oligarch (Benjamin Disraeli) 42

1.13 A Ruling Family (G. A. Denison) 46

1.14 Hereditary Distinctions are Doomed (J. S. Mill) 47

1.15 The Great Nobles and Their Future (J. L. Sanford
and M. Townsend) 49

1.16 The Changing Gentry (Edmund Burke) 53

1.17 The British Raj (George Orwell) 54

1.18 The Elite and the Transmitters of Culture (T. S. Eliot) 58

2: HONOURS, RANK AND STYLE OF LIFE

2.1 What is a Peer? 60

2.2 True Gentility 61

2.3 Humdrum Castle (Edwin Paxton Hood) 63

2.4   The Ethics of Game   66
2.5   A Ducal Household (G. Ticknor)   66
2.6   The Country House (H. Taine)   68
2.7   A Rate for Rank (J. B. Burke)   71
2.8   On the Dignity of a Peerage   72
2.9   Honours for Sale   76
2.10 Social Sets (Beatrice Webb)   79
2.11 Life at the Top of the Tree of Nobility
          (John, Duke of Bedford)   81

3: LANDOWNERSHIP

3.1   Fruits and Failings of Feudalism (Thomas Carlyle)   83
3.2   Corn Laws and the Burden of Landowners (Lord Milton)   85
3.3   Landlord Interest (Richard Cobden)   87
3.4   Hereditary Landownership   88
3.5   Ownership of Land and its Efficient Use (J. S. Mill)   92
3.6   Virtues and Vices of Landlordism (James Caird)   96
3.7   The English Landowners in Ireland (W. Steuart Trench)   99
3.8   Owning Land and Farming Land   103
3.9   Landownership and Enterpreneurship (James Caird)   105
3.10 Predicaments of Hereditary Landowners (S. G. Osborne)   106
3.11 Ancient Feudalism and Modern Game Preservation   108
3.12 'Bad' Squires (William Stubbs)   110
3.13 The New Domesday (J. Bateman)   111
3.14 'Good' Landlords   116
3.15 The Causes of Sales of Estates   120
3.16 Death in Battle and Death Duties (C. F. G. Masterman)   121
3.17 The Ethos of the Estate and its Future   124
3.18 Taxation and the Burden of Landownership   126

4: INTERESTS, INFLUENCE AND ELECTIONS

4.1   Personal Influence   128
4.2   A Count of the Constituencies (J. W. Croker)   134
4.3   A Local Political Family (J. W. Lowther)   136
4.4   The Unreformed House of Commons (John Wade)   137
4.5   Politicians and their Reward   137
4.6   Ruling Class and Radical Leadership (William Lovett)   139
4.7   Towards a Counter Élite   140
4.8   Squire Rule or Local Democracy (Richard Cobden)   144

4.9 The Territorial Class in Parliament (Bernard Cracroft) 149
4.10 'Inevitable Parliament Men' 159
4.11 Politics and the Power of the Purse 169
4.12 The Consequence of the 'Opening of the Floodgates'
      (Frederic Harrison) 170
4.13 The Political Culture of the Aristocracy
      (Matthew Arnold) 172
4.14 High-born Politicians and Low-born Populace
      (M. Ostrogorski) 176
4.15 Politicians at the End of the Century 178
4.16 The Government of the County and 'The Great Unpaid'
      (F. W. Maitland) 181
4.17 Selection of Justices of the Peace 185
4.18 The Changing Government of the Shires (T. H. S. Escott) 190
4.19 The Inner Circle of Politicians (James Bryce) 191
4.20 Politics and the City (Lord Grantley) 193
4.21 Political Ceremonial (Sir Edward Cadogan) 194

5: EDUCATION

5.1 The Threat of a Comprehensive Education (Samuel Butler) 196
5.2 The Orthodox Education of a Gentleman
      (E. G. Bulwer Lytton) 198
5.3 Cost, Results and Ethos of Education at Eton 201
5.4 Boys of Noble Blood (William Sewell) 205
5.5 Breeding and Education (J. H. Newman) 210
5.6 Social and Intellectual Perversions of University Education 211
5.7 Upper Class Habits at Oxford 212
5.8 Class Distinctions and University Education 214
5.9 Cost of a University Education 216
5.10 Heads of Houses (J. W. Burgon) 217
5.11 Social Selection of the Public School System
      (R. H. Tawney) 218
5.12 Making Public Schools more 'Public' 221

6: THE CIVIL SERVICE

6.1 Placemen and Pensioners (John Wade) 225
6.2 The Rationale of Linking High Office to High
      Status (Sir Henry Taylor) 229
6.3 Birth and Aspiration for Administrative Office
      (J. C. Henderson) 231

6.4   The System of Patronage   231
6.5   Patronage – A Postscript (Anthony Trollope)   234
6.6   The Social Background of Victorian Civil Servants   237
6.7   The Competition Wallah   238
6.8   The Beginnings of Civil Service Reform (T. B. Macauley)   241
6.9   An Open or a Closed Élite   243
6.10 Victorian Diplomats   245
6.11 Prerequisites of a Civil Service Career   249
6.12 'The Outdoor Relief of the British Aristocracy'
        (R. T. Nightingale)   250
6.13 The Closed World of Diplomacy   255
6.14 Selection with a Built-in Bias   261
6.15 Decline in Status and Prestige of the Higher Civil
        Service   262
6.16 Making Your Way (Sir John Arrow Kempe)   264
6.17 Corridors of Powers (Sir James P. Grigg)   266

7: THE ARMY
7.1   The Mid-Victorian Officer Class   266
7.2   The Purchase System and Military Efficiency
        (Sir Charles Trevelyan)   276
7.3   The Social Exclusiveness of Sandhurst   277
7.4   Sandhurst in the Nineteen-Fifties   281
7.5   'Ungentlemanly' Officers? (T. H. Escott)   282
7.6   Influence versus Proficiency   283
7.7   Widening the Field of Selection for Army Officers   284
7.8   The Company of a Crack Regiment (The Duke of Portland)   288
7.9   World War II: the New Army and the Old School Tie   289
7.10 The Representative Function of the Army   290

8: THE CLERGY
8.1   A Wealthy, Worldly Clergy (J. Wade)   293
8.2   The Gulf between Bishops and Clergy (S. G. Osborne)   299
8.3   Clerical Rank and Secular Hierarchy   302
8.4   Bishops as Bulwark of Tradition (James Hurnard)   303
8.5   Parsons as Preservers of Order (Augustus J. C. Hare)   304
8.6   Bishop's Moves (Samuel Butler)   305
8.7   Clerical Justices   307
8.8   The Church and the Crown (Archbishop Lang)   309

General Editor's Preface

The purpose of this series is to introduce students of society to a number of important problems through the study of sources and contemporary documents. It should be part of every student's education to have some contact with the materials from which the judgements of authors of secondary works are reached, or the grounds of social action determined. Students may actually find this more interesting than relying exclusively on the pre-digested diet of text-books. The readings will be drawn from as great a variety of documents as is possible within each book: Royal Commission reports, Parliamentary debates, letters to the Press, newspaper editorials, letters and diaries both published and un-published, sermons and literary sources, et cetera, will all be drawn upon. For the aim is both to introduce the student to carefully selected extracts from the principal contemporary books and docu-ments (the things he always hears about but never reads), and to show him a great range of subsidiary and representative source materials available (the memorials of actors in the actual events).

The prejudice of this series is that the social sciences need to be taught and developed in an historical context. Those of us who wish to be relevant and topical (and this is no bad wish) sometimes need reminding that the most usual explanation of why a thing is as it is, is that things happened in the past to make it so. These things might not have happened. They might have happened differently. And nothing in the present is, strictly speaking, *determined* from the past; but everything is limited by what went before. Every present problem, whether of understanding or of action, will always have a variety of relevant antecedent factors, all of which must be understood before it is sensible to commit ourselves to an explanatory theory or to some course of practical action. No present problem is completely novel and there is never any single cause for it, but always a variety of conditioning factors, arising through time, whose relative importance is a matter of critical judgement as well as of objective knowledge.

The aim of this series is, then, to give the student the opportunity to examine with care an avowedly selective body of source materials. The topics have been chosen both because they are of contemporary importance and because they cut across established pedagogic boundaries between the various disciplines and between courses of professional instruction. We hope that these books will supplement, not replace, other forms of introductory reading; so both the length and the character of the Introductions will vary according to whether the particular editor has already written on the subject or not. Some Introductions will summarize what is already to be found elsewhere at greater length, but some will be original contributions to knowledge or even, on occasions, reasoned advocacies. Above all, however, I hope that this series will help to develop a method of introductory teaching that can show how and from where we come to reach the judgements that are to be found in secondary accounts and text-books.

University of Sheffield   *BERNARD CRICK*

Foreword

The readings published in this book have been culled from the rich store of nineteenth and twentieth century literature which directly or indirectly throws light on the English Ruling Class. In selecting them I have inevitably sifted a much larger volume of material. In editing them I have, of course, made excisions in the texts chosen. I have left out of the extracts here reproduced either material extraneous to the subject or reflections and observations only marginally relevant, but I have not 'edited out' anything which would materially affect the argument presented. What has been reproduced has not been changed in any way – no attempt has been made to correct antiquated spelling or substitute a modern vocabulary for words which have now fallen into disuse. Where only a few words have been left out this is indicated thus . . . and elisions of one line or more by . . . .

I am very grateful to my friend and editor Bernard Crick for encouragement and criticism. I should like to thank my wife for helping me in many ways and my daughter for her assistance with the reading of the proofs. To produce the MS would have been a much more laborious task without the help of facsimile copying machines. I am much indebted to the helpful staff of the British Library of Political and Economical Science who operated them and who assisted with the provision of most of the material used in this collection.

Norwich and London, July 1969   W. L. Guttsman

Acknowledgements

The author and the publisher would like to thank the following for permission to quote from copyright sources:

Edward Arnold Ltd for *Howard's End* by E. M. Forster and *A Speaker's Commentaries* by Viscount Ullswater; University of Chicago Press for *The Spirit of the Age* by J. S. Mill (edited by F. A. Hayek); Burke's Peerage Ltd for *Burke's Landed Gentry*; Miss Sonia Brownell and Secker and Warburg Ltd for 'Shooting an Elephant' by George Orwell (in *New Writing*, 1st series, No. 2); Faber and Faber Ltd for *Notes Towards the Definition of Culture* by T. S. Eliot; London School of Economics and Political Science for *Our Partnership* by Beatrice Webb; Cassell and Company Ltd for *Silver-Plated Spoon* by the Duke of Bedford; Times Newspapers Ltd for *The Times*, 19 May 1920; the Country Landowner's Association for *Quarterly Circular* of the Country Landowner's Association; B. T. Batsford Ltd for *The Croker Papers* (edited by B. Pool); William Blackwood and Sons Ltd for *Lord John Manners and His Friends* by C. Whibley; the Estate of the late Lady Gwendolyn Cecil for *Life of Robert, 4th Marquis of Salisbury* by Lady Gwendolyn Cecil; J. G. Lockhart and Hodder and Stoughton Ltd for *Cosmo Gordon Lang* by J. G. Lockhart; University of Michigan Press for 'The Popular Education of France' by Matthew Arnold in *Complete Works*, II; Hutchinson Ltd for *Memories* by Walter Long; John Murray Ltd for *Before the Deluge* by Sir Edward Cadogan; Allen and Unwin Ltd for *The Radical Tradition* by R. H. Tawney; W. Heffer and Sons Ltd for *The Statesman* (edited by H. J. Laski); Oxford University Press for *An Autobiography* by Anthony Trollope; the Executors of the Estate of Sir James Grigg for *Prejudice and Judgment* by Sir James Grigg; Cambridge University Press for *The Setting Sun* by James Hurnard (edited by R. Hamilton); The Fabian Society for *The Personnel of the British Foreign Office* by R. T. Nightingale; Longmans Green and Company for *Thomas George, Earl of Northbrook, A Memoir* by B. Mallett and *Life of the Duke of Devonshire* by B. Holland; The Macmillan Company of New York for *Democracy and the Organisation of Political Parties* by M. Ostrogorski; the Estate of the seventh Duke of Portland for *Men, Women and Things* by the Duke of Portland; the Estate of the late Lord Grantley for *Silver Spoon* by Lord Grantley.

Introduction

What is a Ruling Class? Did it ever exist and, if so, how and why did it decline? Today, as a hundred years ago, certain institutions, Parliament, Cabinet, the Civil Service, the Judiciary, the Armed Forces, Public Schools and Universities, shape the lives of ordinary people in varying degrees. Others, such as landownership, or the Established Church, have lost much of their ancient influence and new centres of power have arisen: the Press, the entertainment industry and, above all, the boardrooms of private industry and of the public corporations.

There can be little doubt of the reality of the power exercised by the men who occupy such positions in our society. Technological advances, greatly improved methods of communication and continuing and accelerating processes of amalgamations, have vastly extended the effects and the consequences of the decisions taken by bureaucrats, boards and governing élites in general; and those who are subject to their command are puny by comparison.

The readings brought together in this book are concerned not so much with topical problems as with how the present has been shaped by the past. They throw light on the 'Men at the Top' who used to govern us and who in some measure still do so today. They also deal with the vehicles and instruments of their rule. However, as the documentation presented here is selected from the public debates, controversial literature, memoirs, reports and investigations of the period covered, these extracts invariably illuminate also the relationship between the governing and the governed.

It is the changing nature of the latter which above all exemplifies the differences between the situation today and that of mid-Victorian England. Today an individual has, at least formally, power over his rulers: if he is a puppet he can, at least, claim that he has chosen his manipulators or the rules of the game in which he plays a part. We may see the constellation of power in modern industrialized societies as composed of a set of interlocking and intercommunicating directorates which, as C. Wright Mills has persuasively argued, may – and in times of crisis will – make major and possibly fatal decisions pertaining in the last resort to matters of national survival. Or we may agree with J. K. Galbraith that the functioning of modern society is best understood in terms of a pluralistic concept of countervailing powers, so that the struggles and agreements between the institutionalized representation of such powers as Capital and Labour tend to become substitutes for the battle between parties on the legislative plane. In neither case do we assume any strict congruence between the holders of offices and a definite and narrowly circumscribed social group. While Mills' 'Power Élite' is largely composed of men of high social origin and prestigious and prominent positions, it is not exclusively recruited from their ranks. It is rather the ethos which prevails among its members and the criteria which make for acceptance, promotion or rejection which help to weld these men into a socially homogeneous group.[1]

In this respect too there has been a break with the past, a movement from a society where position in the élite was based on what has been termed 'ascribed' status towards one where 'achieved' status has become increasingly important. Conversely, we have moved from a society where those who occupied leading positions were united by family ties and by a common ethos to others of the same class who shared in the exercise of power, towards one where affinities and lines of communication between members of the élite no longer proceed entirely along class lines and where the

[1] J. K. Galbraith, *American Capitalism, the concept of countervailing power*, rev. ed. 1961.
C. Wright Mills. *The Power Élite*, 1956, espec. pp. 280–1.

attitudes of a class-conscious upper class may actually be in conflict with sections of the élite.[2]

It is in the context of such analytical considerations that I am using the concept of an English Ruling Class as a paradigm for the illustration of the English upper class in its prime and in its decline and for the illustration of the growth, change and occasional decline of the institutions through which this rule was apparent. I look at these institutions not in respect of their formal structure but in terms of the men who occupied leading positions, their background and attitudes, and in terms of the ideas and pre-suppositions which governed their recruitment.[3]

Taken in its contemporary setting, the existence of an English Ruling Class was less subject to doubt in the nineteenth century than it would be if approached today with the vastly refined tools of modern sociological analysis.[4] The techniques which have recently been successfully employed in the quantitative analysis of élites and élite behaviour are manifold: social mobility studies can illustrate the actual movement between élite and non-élite occupations; the life-history approach can illuminate background, recruitment patterns and *cursus honorum* of élite groups; studies of decision-making processes within an institutional setting, say a legislature, seek to refine the analysis of the power structure. All help in this analysis.[5]

Some of the documents reproduced in this book refer directly, and in quantitative terms, to the composition of different leader-ship groups [3·13, 2·1, 2·9, 2·15, 6·5, 6·11, 7·4]. It would however be

[2] This is illustrated in C. P. Snow's writings, espec. *The New Men* and *The Corridors of Power*.

[3] For a comparison see the descriptive account of a ruling class and its decline in E. Digby Baltzell, *Philadelphia Gentlemen*, 1958, republished (paper back) as *An American Business Aristocracy*, 1962.

[4] Cf. P. Young, *Scientific Social Surveys and Research*, 4th ed. 1966.

A. V. Cicourel, *Method and Measurement in Sociology*, 1964.

R. Dahl, *Modern Political Analysis*, 1964.

Karl W. Deutsch, *The Nerves of Government, models of political communication and control*, 1966.

[5] See the essays in Marwick, Dwaine (ed.), *Political Decision Makers*, 1961, and S. M. Miller, *Social Mobility*, Current sociology, 9, 1960.

[6] For modern social analyses of segments of the English Ruling Class and British Élite Groups in general see a.o.

H. Jenkins and D. C. Jones, 'Social Class of Cambridge Alumni', *British Journal of Sociology*, vol. I (1950).

3

P. 90

claiming too much to say that this amounted to a full justificatiom of the use of the term 'the English Ruling Class'. Paradoxical though it may seem, this concept was more widely accepted and understood, approved or vilified as the case may have been, in the middle of the nineteenth century than it would be today: the protagonists as well as the antagonists of the Victorian 'landed and gentlemanly class' had little doubt about the reality of the phenomenon which they were describing. No one claimed that the British oligarchy was a closed élite, or that the aristocracy could, or should, be a closed group. A limited penetration of new groups into the ruling class was welcome, if it was regulated and if absorption of the newcomers guaranteed. The protagonists of the old order defended it because of the social stability inherent in an accepted hierarchical order [1·2] or because of the solid, commonsense approach to matters of public administration by those who had, it was thought, almost imbibed the technique at their fathers' knees when administering their estates [1·4.] The Reform of 1832 was a compromise but one which in the eyes of Earl Grey, its author, would strengthen rather than weaken the position of the aristocracy. The opposition referred to oligarchic privileges and material benefits arising from it, which accrued to its members [1·11, 4·7] it attacked the system of patronage and nepotism with its attendant inefficiencies in the administration of country and county [4·8, 6·4].

Outside observers were generally agreed on the virtues – or vices – of the social-political system which governed Britain. De Montalembert saw in the predominance of aristocracy, coupled with limited but fixed political rights for everybody, a guarantee of political stability [1·9]. Karl Marx, the author of the very term 'Ruling Class', writing in the midst of the Crimean War crisis, half expected a breakdown of 'that antiquated compromise, called the British Constitution, between a class that ruled officially – namely

T. Bishop and R. Wilkinson, *Winchester and the Public School Élite*, 1967.

R. K. Kelsall, *Higher Civil Servants in Britain from 1870 to the Present Day*, 1955.

T. Lupton and C. Shirley Wilson, 'The Social Background and Connections of Top Decision Makers, *The Manchester School*, January 1959.

Noel Annan, 'The Intellectual Aristocracy', in J. H. Plumb (ed.), *Studies in Social History*, 1955.

W. L. Guttsman, *The British Political Élite*, 1963.

the aristocracy – and a class that ruled non-officially, i.e. the Middle Class'. He thought that under the impact of war and the shattering blow to official prestige which was the result of apparent military and administrative muddle, 'the aristocracy which, subject to general principles laid down by the middle class rules supreme in the Cabinet, the Parliament, the Administration, the Army and the Navy has now been obliged to sign its own death-warrant'.[7]

De Tocqueville, who at the same time was engaged in his studies of French society in the eighteenth century and of the causes that led to revolution, was naturally drawn into a comparison of the *'ancien régime'* – with its rigid class structure and the perpetual striving for status – with the more open web of English society and its aristocracy which he had observed during his repeated stays in England. He noted the absence of caste-like distinctions despite the notable degree of snobbery among the aristocracy, and he thought he could discern the gradual widening of the concept and connotation of the 'gentleman'. He also noticed the absence of widespread hostility between middle class and aristocracy not because the latter 'kept open house as that its barriers were ill-defined, not so much that entrance was easy as that you never knew when you got there'.[8] Yet it was clear to Tocqueville – as it must be to us – that if in this society 'the power and spirit of the aristocracy was still paramount' it was so not in the least for the reason that the English nation, in Bagehot's famous phrase, was a deferential nation. We can assume that the 'removable barriers' which governed movement between the layers of the social hierarchy became for many self-imposed obstacles, while others deliberately avoided crossing them and sought to establish their own counter-élite, or to achieve the triumph of their own class.[9]

The contemporary analysis of the Victorian ruling class must of course be seen in the context of a political struggle for which it formed a major target, and the views held by protagonists and

[7] Karl Marx and Friedrich Engels, *On Britain*. A modern selection 1953, pp. 410–11 (from Karl Marx, 'The Crisis in England and the British Constitution', *New York Daily Tribune*, 1855).

[8] Cf. A. de Tocqueville, *The Old Régime and the Revolutions*, (L'ancien régime et la révolution, 1856) 1955, pp. 88–9 and *Journeys to England and Ireland*, ed. J. P. Mayer, 1955, espec. pp. 59–61 and 66–74.

[9] For Bagehot's view on Victorian social structure, see his Essay on Sterne and Thackeray, 1864, in *Collected Works*, vol. IV.

antagonists were undoubtedly coloured by this and were in consequence less than objective. Today we are no longer so concerned in this country with the direct defence of formal privileges and prerogatives or with long and sustained attacks on entrenched positions buttressed by legal enactments and social conventions. Our analysis of our own society can therefore be more objective.

At the same time we must realize that the meaning of the concept of a ruling class and popular attitudes to it have altered in the course of time. What constitutes privilege or conversely the rights of citizenship, is in itself a changing concept and one whose boundaries have been drawn more widely since the *Cornhill Magazine* asserted as indisputable truth that 'there must always be an intellectual distinction between the higher and lower classes corresponding to that distinction between classes themselves' [2·2].

The radical attack on aristocratic rule and on the power of the state was driven home largely on the political and legal front. The cries were those such as universal franchise (or perhaps only manhood or householders'), voting by ballot, the right of association, better local administration, a more humane poor law, payment of M.P.s and the curtailment of the power of the House of Lords to veto legislation. Only gradually, in part, and very largely without the participation of the working class, did the attack extend to the wider range of institutions which flanked and supported the social and political power of the ruling class: the Armed Services, the Bureaucracy, the Judiciary, the Established Church and the educational system.

Throughout this period the central institution which supported this class – the ownership of by far the largest part of the nation's land and the rent rolls which these acres produced – was seriously threatened only in Ireland where the crassest form of exploitation coupled with poor arable conditions and primitive agricultural technology brought about the most violent class struggle and showed English landlordism at its most feudal [3·7]. Apart from the violent anti-landlordism which showed itself in Ireland in the second half of the nineteenth century, the movements against the land-holding system were few and far between, showing themselves in such minor eruptions as O'Connor's National Land Company, the Land and Labour League, and later the agitation for agricultural smallholdings, and the small band of followers of

Henry George – eruptions which found some belated echoes in the Liberal Land Reform proposals of the 1920s. The decline of English landed wealth which expressed itself in the rapid decrease in the size and number of estates from 1890 onwards was the result of factors extraneous even to the British polity: the decreasing profitability of farming in the face of competition from cheap imported corn and the ever-higher levels of taxation which were the results of the First World War. This involuntary process of liquidation was no doubt more strongly felt as the individual victims felt less responsible for it. With their decline died an institution, and the contemporary comments have the quality of a dirge even though today we may no longer be moved by them [3·16, 3·17].

The strength of the English Ruling Class in the heyday of its power cannot, however, be measured solely in terms of its economic power as a class of landowners and leaders of agriculture. In 1867 Baxter estimated that the income from agriculture amounted to approximately 14 per cent of the total national income, and by 1900 this had dropped to 6 per cent. At the time of the 'New Domesday' survey in 1873 the rent of all estates with holdings of more than 3,000 acres or a rental of not less than £3,000 was in the region of £15–20,000,000 and it thus formed only a fraction of all incomes.[10] The significance of landownership lies not in its overall economic strength but in the large individual and unearned income which was enjoyed by a small group of inter-related families [3·13]. Their power was rather a kind of penumbra which extended from this base of rentierdom and caused its membership to permeate the Army, the Church, the Civil Service, the professions and the universities. Rent rolls laid the foundations for social eminence in the area – often a large part of a county – where a family's estates were paramount [2·5]. Landownership was the platform for leadership in philanthropic enterprise or agricultural advance [3·6, 3·14]. Above all it was an essential precondition of political power and it was often sought with that object in mind [4·3, 4·14]. Until 1886 when the agricultural workers received the vote, landownership in a large number of

[10] For a historical survey of agricultural income see J. R. Bellerby, a.o. *Agriculture and Industry : Relative Income*, 1956. For general data on the British National Income see P. Deane and W. A. Cole, *British Economic Growth, 1868–1955*, 1962.

constituencies still spelt direct power at the hustings, or at least a weighty counter in the electoral struggle.[11] And prior to the disappearance of many of the smaller boroughs following the Reform of 1867, the proprietary politics of the large landowner were even more obvious.[12]

Whether the practice of entail weakened English agriculture in the long run (and through that hastened the decline of landlord power itself) is difficult to ascertain. The attack on the system of settling estates was made partly on economic grounds, but there lurked behind it an understandable desire to break the monopoly of a class. In broad social terms its effects were undoubtedly harmful but in the short term and as an instrument of maintaining family power it was probably a good system. One of its most important functions in our context was the fact that it forced younger sons – and their sons and descendants – to seek employment and fortune elsewhere. Until the Civil Service Reforms following the Northcote-Trevelyan Report of 1854, this class had a virtual monopoly of the Public Service. Though deprived of a patrimony, they were not forced into the world friendless and penniless. They were often supported by an endowment or settlement or were aided by a provident marriage. Above all, they had their family to fall back upon, both as a 'pied-à-terre' and as a means of support and influence. Though forced out into the world they did not go naked and there was therefore no need to take just any kind of job however little 'standesgemäss' or *infra dig*.

Before 1914 members of this class if they were sufficiently introspective could say with the heroine of E. M. Forster's *Howard's End* that they 'stand upon money as upon islands. It is so firm beneath our feet that we forget its very existence . . . and most of the others are down below the surface of the sea. I stand each year upon six hundred pounds, and Helen upon the same, and Tibby will stand upon eight, and as fast as our pounds crumble away into the sea they are renewed from the sea, yes from the sea. And all our thoughts are the thoughts of six hundred pounders, and all our speeches . . .'.

A qualitative analysis of the English Ruling Class at its apogee in the mid-Victorian era would have to start from such a network of families, numbering perhaps not more than five thousand, and

[11] H. J. Hanham, *Elections and Party Management*, 1959.
[12] M. Gash, *Politics in the Age of Peel*, 1953.

trace the occupation of the living adult male cousinhood totalling possibly twenty thousand to thirty thousand. No doubt we would find some men who had become thoroughly assimilated into commercial occupations merged with the lower middle class, or even become proletarianized, and a similar investigation of the same subjects' descendants carried out fifty years later would conceivably show an even greater degree of '*déclassement*'. Conversely, if we look at the institutions which form the basis for the careers acceptable to the children of the gentry (to use this short-term expression) we find a widening basis of recruitment as we progress in time and as one century gives way to the next.[13] But it is equally important to realize the slowness of this change – and the resistance to it – which is one of the main themes of the documentation presented in the following pages.

Much of this documentation has been chosen to illuminate certain institutional themes and to apply the concept of the ruling class to those specific areas where it came regularly into conflict with other considerations and ideas.

There is, above all, the significance of the hereditary system and the importance of titles and honours. The titular aristocracy is both an external symbol of the British Ruling Class and, as we have already noted obliquely with reference to primogeniture in the inheritance of landed property, an indication of its relative social fluidity. A title could make a parvenu respectable or at the lowest make his offspring acceptable. At the same time we must realize that until the latter part of the nineteenth century ennoblement rarely conferred what did not already exist. Much as we may enjoy the description of ennoblement which Disraeli has given [1·12] reality was frequently different. Pitt's plebeian aristocracy, so vividly described in *Sybil*, was largely a figment of Disraeli's imagination.[14]

In the conferment of titles some economic criterion in respect of size of income and particularly source of income entered clearly into the considerations governing the award, and the debate on the proposed introduction of peerages for life in 1857 shows us some

[13] Cf. Guttsman, *The British Political Élite*; R. K· Kelsall, *Higher Civil Servants*; J. M. Lee, *Social Leaders and Public Persons, a study of county government in Cheshire*, 1963.

[14] Cf. A. S. de Turberville, *The House of Lords in the 18th Century*, 1927, and *The House of Lords in the Age of Reform*, 1958.

of the considerations which people thought applied [2·8]. A generation later Beer Barons and Shipping Peers, Press Lords and other successful large entrepreneurs in general were launched on the political world in increasing numbers and not many seem to have raised an eyebrow. Their rank was often closely related to the size and openness of their purses as measured by contributions to party funds. This kind of thing had undoubtedly happened in the past but, by the turn of the century and especially after the large-scale creation of wartime honours, the blatant character of such transactions began to give rise to misgivings and eventually to outright opposition [2·9].

If a kind of tariff did indeed exist – as has been suggested[15] – then it would, of course, correspond to some sort of economic hierarchy in the nobility as such. There were a large number of non-titled landed families of great distinction whose wealth exceeded that of many members of the peerage, but it is generally true to say that 100 years ago dukes were not only richer than dustmen but also, on the average, wealthier than mere barons [1·15]. However, the debate which eventually led to the scrutiny of honours, and thus did away with the most flagrant abuses of the system, no longer showed any concern with the status aspect of hereditary titles. Not that the peerages created in the twentieth century, which now constitute over half of the entire Roll of the Peerage, were a cross section of the population – there are few 'poor peers' today even on the Labour benches, and when we occasionally read of the corporation labourer or the smallholder who inherits a title, he will often be the scion of an ancient house.

In my book *The British Political Élite* I wrote at length about the close connection between the 'Ruling Class' and the political leadership. The predominance of aristocrats and those from closely allied groups in Parliament and consequently in the Cabinet is as much due to the slow development of liberal and open political institutions – especially the persistence of constituencies open to direct influence by a few socially or economically powerful individuals – as to the character of party organization. It owes much to the fact that the non-payment of M.P.'s restricted selection; and it was helped by the continuing deference shown by constituents for their social superiors. This deference and the slow development of strong class cohesion on the part of lower

[15] G. Macmillan, *Honours for Sale*, 1955.

social strata is essential for the understanding of aristocratic power, and we need a better explanation for it than Bagehot's psychologism. It ought to be traced to the electoral behaviour at the constituency level and to the establishment of a set of hierarchical relationships in many constituencies, helped perhaps by the selection of tenants according to religious and political persuasions, and elucidated through the canvass preceding an election.[16]

However, Parliament is only one of our governing institutions which demonstrates the staying power of a ruling class. Even in local government representative institutions, today by far the most democratically recruited of governing bodies, its influence was apparent until well into the nineteenth century. Until the Municipal Corporation Act of 1835, local administration was largely in the hands of appointed Justices of the Peace, except where it was vested specifically in Boards or Commissions set up on an *ad hoc* basis. Even afterwards the local magistrates performed many administrative functions outside the municipal boroughs until their responsibility was taken over by the County Councils under the provision of the 1887 Act. And these local magistrates were predominantly recruited from the group of squires and parsons, and once appointed they held their office generally for life so that change, even if sought, was slow. The selection of magistrates was of course governed by the requirement that the J.P. had freehold property of at least £100. Landowners and clergymen apart, few could qualify for this. Cobden attacked the traditional power of the magistracy in a vigorous pamphlet [4·8] and Maitland pronounced a panegyric at its demise [4·16]. The devotion and disinterestedness of many of these men in many of their tasks, acting within the moral framework of their class, need not be doubted, but neither should their identification with the need to protect property, when they read the Riot Act and called in the local militia to fight bread riots or Chartist agitation. Their stern narrow-mindedness speaks to us in the critical account of their doings by a member of their own class, Sir Charles Napier, who commanded the Northern Army in the 1830s.[17] Successive

[16] D. C. Moore, 'Social Structure, Political Structure and Public Opinion in Mid-Victorian England', in *Ideas and Institutions of Victorian England, Essays in Honour of G. Kitson Clark*, 1967.

[17] Sir William Napier (ed.), *Life and Opinions of Sir Charles James Napier*, 4 vols. 1857, vol. II.

legislative measures did away with the restrictive rules for the appointment of magistrates; it first removed clergymen from the roll and then abolished the property qualification.[18] But even when the formal obstacles to a more widely based selection had been removed the selection became anything but democratic. Although today most walks of life are represented on the bench the higher social groups still have the lion's share. Magistrates have, on the other hand, almost entirely lost their administrative function and thus the link between the respect of justice – or the lack of it – and the consequent respect for the landed and propertied class has declined.

In the town the representation established as the result of municipal reform showed little connection with the representation of the ruling class. In the agricultural counties, on the other hand, its members have from the beginning played a part in county administration – as Maitland foresaw and as Escott describes [4·18] – and to some extent they are still doing so today.[19] Here, as in Parliament, the persistence of the English Ruling Class is only partly the result of legal advantages, social privileges and inward drive. The lack of adequate political organization on the local government level, especially in the shires, for long worked against the effective selection and possible representation of other classes: the members of the 'County' set had an easy passage if they sought to take part in county government.

The tenacious hold of the ruling classes on the senior appointments in the Civil Service has frequently been described.[20] Even after the crass power of patronage which the ruling class exercised widely in its own favour was abolished and, indeed, far into the examination era, these ties continued [6·10–13]. It is interesting to recall that the changes in the methods of recruitment came about less as the result of democratic pressure or in an attempt to widen the area of individual rights than as the consequence of a pressure towards greater efficiency and the need to recruit talent rather than rely on tradition. And this pressure arose as much from inside the service as from without: many heads of the departments felt this to be of paramount importance if the service was to cope with the

[18] There is no good general survey of the Magistracy but see: Frank Milton, *The English Magistracy*, 1967.

[19] Cf. J. M. Lee, *Social Leaders and Public Persons*.

[20] Kelsall, *Higher Civil Servants*.

growing complexity of bureaucratic operation [6·4]. The opponents of innovation fought a rearguard action by attempting to pour ridicule on the idea that the qualities which the service demanded were indeed amenable to such tests and by poking fun at some of the questions asked in the examinations [6·7]. In some respects, and shorn of its 'class-bias', the argument advanced contains germs of truth and in a curious way opposition to examinations and the whole 'mandarin' system was to come back into the discussion and to lead to the system of internal promotion which more than the public examination entries accounted for the rise to the top of men from the slums and the Board Schools.

No selection system can be fully free from a built-in bias. This may be the result of the type and range of papers and questions set in the written examination or other hidden factors. Thus applicants from Oxbridge with good honours degrees do better than candidates with similar degrees from other universities.[21] Or it may flow, unconsciously no doubt, from the mental framework in which the selectors work [6·14]. They may arise from an institutional framework and, given the assumptions of it, particularly the role expected of the administrator, a selection-process may then be rationally devised to serve them – even if the institutions themselves are wrongly conceived. Foreign representation and colonial administration are cases in point. Bagehot spoke of the Ambassador being not only the servant of his country but also 'a public spectacle', and an account reproduced here, though hostile, underlines this point [6·10]. An inside account of the system of recruitment to the colonial service speaks of the *arcanae imperii* which must not be divulged.[22] Given such national 'aims', it may have made sociological sense to recruit to the foreign service on a more narrow basis than for the Home Civil Service. Even if the former was in the twentieth century no longer the 'outdoor relief' of the British aristocracy, it continued to be more narrowly recruited than the rest of the British Civil Service [6·12] and the rule which until 1928 demanded of its prospective members the possession of an independent income of £300 per annum made it the preserve of a minority.

That biases still exist today cannot be doubted, but the basis for

---

[21] Cf. Royal Commission on the Civil Service (Fulton Commission), Appendices 3 and 4.

[22] Sir R. Furse, *Aucuparius, Recollections of a Recruiting Officer*, 1962.

the long-continued self-recruitment of the English Ruling Class lies in any case buried in its educational system. This is not to suggest that the older public schools or the ancient universities were in any legal sense élite institutions; only dissenters were excluded as a matter of custom or as the result of specific entrance requirements. Only in the last decades of the nineteenth century did Oxford and Cambridge do away with the old barriers and attendance at chapel remained compulsory at most colleges until after the First World War. The strong identification of the public schools with the established church generally continued to put off practising non-conformists, and their curriculum did little for those interested in scientific and modern subjects.

Equally important as a factor limiting entry to these institutions was the cost – less in respect of fees than with regard to the incidental but necessary expenses arising out of this education [5·3, 5·9]. At the bottom of this was the expected pattern of life of the country house. The reformers sought to limit the expenses, not only to widen the intake but also to improve the academic character of the training [5·6]. As we progressed selection became somewhat stricter, discipline more rigorous and the formal distinctions in the status of undergraduates with the special privileges granted to men of aristocratic lineage were abolished. Only after the First World War do we find the beginning of a concerted attack on the privileged position and range of economic opportunities which fell to those who attended either schools like Eton, Rugby or Winchester, or studied in the ancient universities [5·11].[23]

There can be little doubt of the gradual and progressive widening of the area of educational opportunity; yet at the same time it is clear that the élite institutions were least affected by it. The admission of new social groups into the sphere of secondary and higher education proceeded largely through the creation of new institutions, such as the grammar schools, founded first by the more progressive local authorities and later throughout the country or in the civic universities. The clientele of the Clarendon schools and of Oxbridge has changed character only to a limited extent.[24]

Yet formal and informal restrictions apart, the public schools

[23] Cf. Brian Simon, *Education and the Labour Movement*, 1965.

[24] Bishop and Wilkinson, *Winchester and the Public School Élite*. Committee of Vice-Chancellors and Principals, *Applications for Admission to Universities*, 1957, Report of the Committee on Higher Education (Robbins Report), Appendix 2B.

and the ancient universities tended to instil in those who passed
through them a sentiment of superiority and a belief in predestined
roles as the nation's leaders [5·2]. In doing so they may equally
well have sought to instil the ideal of service and the duty of charity
towards the less fortunate, but through this they did not really
reduce the gulf between their members and the rest of the population, or at least the 'lower orders' [5·4].

The differences in ethos produced by the educational system of
the establishment, on the one hand, and of the state educational
system, on the other, prevented the rise of a genuinely national
culture and inhibited the process of political socialization of the
newly emancipated classes. The expression of such a division of
the nation was subtle. It links up with the choice of occupation on
the one hand, and with the use of leisure on the other. With regard
to the former, I have already pointed both to the status-value of
the choice of career and to the resistance within the bureaucracy to
anything which might devalue 'gentlemanliness' in personal
conduct in favour of 'mere' competence, intellectual acumen and
technical skill. These sentiments were even more apparent in the
army. Here the strict separation between officers and men enhanced general social distinctions. Moreover in peacetime, especially, the primary role of the officer was thought to demand skill in
the exercise of authority rather than technical proficiency. Given
this underlying idea, it was not surprising that until its abolition in
1871, entry into the officer class was generally governed by the
purchase system. This was essentially linked to the peacetime army,
for what was bought was not the financial return of an investment
nor a succession of annual salaries – as in the assessment of the
reversionary value of a clerical living – but a down payment for
status and prestige derived from the post [7·1]. If it dropped sharply in wartime this was not so much because of the possible drop in
the period of the annuity purchased but rather because the job had
lost its attractiveness [7·1]. In war, however, technical competence
and the ability for constructive strategic thinking was of increasing
importance. After the Crimean débâcle there was an upsurge of
doubt about the usefulness of the purchase system and about the
value of the education which the aspiring officer received. At the
same time wars brought their crop of officers recruited from the
ranks to make up for the shortages created by war. The presence
of men of lower social origins in the officer corps gave rise to social

antagonism [7·2, 7·3, 7·5]. In any case, opposition to the abolition of the purchase system was vigorous, as it was to any change in the curricula of the military training establishments which sought to place greater emphasis on intellectual training and achievement. But the distrust by the traditional officer caste of those born on the other side of the track was echoed by the latter not in words but in deeds. Faced with the image of upper-class selectiveness and snobbishness, the grammar school boy which the army sought to recruit failed generally to respond and if current army recruitment policy is anything to go by, the authorities are still looking for him. The statistics of Sandhurst entrants and of officers commissioned confirm the continued identification of much of the officer corps with the older ruling class.

The equation of the officer corps with the membership of an established social and traditional élite is, naturally, a widespread phenomenon. Indeed, a democratically-recruited officer class is almost confined to new states. The clergy, on the other hand, has generally been recruited from a wider social field and the ministry provided traditionally a vehicle for upwards social mobility. Many of the incumbents of English parish livings have, of course, come from humble beginnings and have generally continued in humble circumstances all their lives. On the other hand we had, throughout most of the nineteenth century, a lower and an upper clergy. The latter owed their livings often to purchase or the selective preferment – if not outright nepotism – which characterized the ladder of clerical advancement. And it is hardly surprising that with the right of presentation vested generally in the hands of the landowning class or the government the choice fell so often on the members of the cousinhood, or that it provided convenient provision for needy relatives or faithful camp followers or their sons or nephews [8·1]. Thus a part of the clergy was closely identified with other sections of the English Ruling Class through ties of family and friendship [1·13]. Another connection existed on the plane of office through the movement of the clergy to appointments to Public Schools' headmasterships, University Chairs or headships of Oxbridge Colleges. And, as we have seen, clergymen were often included in the roll of the Justices of the Peace [8·7]. The clergy thus extended their influence further than their spiritual career. It would, however, be entirely erroneous to assume that membership of the professions was exclusively self-recruited: there was upward movement from the middle class and with the growth of the bureaucracy and of the armed services an increasing number of 'new men' found their way into positions of power and influence. But such a movement was specific and individual; no organized movement of public protest demanded radical changes in recruitment. The acquisition of political power by the working class did not lead to widespread demands for a change in the methods of recruitment to the Civil Service or in the selection of the holders of key positions, although there were certain rumblings in the wings.[25] When Ernest Bevin as Foreign Secretary substituted the 'Country House Method' of selection by interview and practical tests for the traditional examination procedure, some thought that paradoxically this might diminish rather than enhance the working-class boy's chances of entering the Foreign Service.

In the selection for documentation of economic and professional groups, such as landowners, politicians, the army, the Church and the bureaucracy, I was not only concerned with the fact that these have constituted the preferred occupations of the British upper class, but also with their place in the process of government considered in a wider sense. They held the central power; they translated government decisions into everyday administrative action; they wielded the sword and they propagated the word.

I have thus approached the problem of the British Ruling Class empirically: I have looked at men whom we know to have been influential, even powerful, both as types and by virtue of the institutions to which they belonged and I have sought to illuminate the related changes which these institutions have undergone. I have attempted to adduce some proof of the underlying hypothesis that membership of such groups, or the right of access to them, though customary rather than legal, does in some real measure identify the ruling class as a social class and separate it from other classes in society.

I have not sought to answer the question as to the ultimate location of power, either in terms of an economic system or in the ideological sense of a group of men seeking power for selfish or unselfish reasons. In other words, I have deliberately neglected in the construction of my analytical framework two major streams of sociological theory which more than any other have been connected

[25] Cf. H. J. Laski, *Parliamentary Government in England*, 1938.

with the discussion of the ruling class: the Marxist theory and the theories of Mosca and Pareto.

The élite theories of the latter are, however, singularly unsuggestive for detailed historical analysis. The theory of the circulation of élites tells us little about who will emerge successfully in the struggle for power and under what conditions, nor does it tell us about the time-span of the change. In as far as there are alterations between psychological types, the material available for an analysis is rarely detailed enough to permit the establishment of a genuine cycle. The changes in the types of skills found in the members of governing groups are more easily observable, and such a model has been used with some success in the series of studies of political élites in various countries carried out under the direction of H. D. Lasswell.[26] In the context of the British political élite we can also observe changes from landowner/rentier politicians to professional ones, especially lawyers and members of the intelligentsia.[27] But this development, though linked to changes in the task and organization of government, is part of a wider phenomenon. The class allegiances and fortunes of political parties changed at the same time and new ideologies drew on the support of new sections of the population. The ruling élite model is either a truism developed with great sophistication or it is a suggestive hypothesis for the analysis of global changes over long periods of time. For our task it fails because it lacks anchorage in social structure or in distinct ideological systems.

In the Marxist model the political system, like the social, takes its character from the organization of production and the modern state is an expression of the capitalist system, 'nothing more than a committee for the administration of the consolidated affairs of the bourgeois class as a whole'.[28] The bourgeois innovator and accumulator, profiteer and ruthless exploiter, is at the same time the hero and the villain of Western society's development and its emancipation from its feudal shackles. England, where the lines quoted above were written, had seen Marx's apotheosis in its purest and most developed form. Formal political power had passed to the entrepreneurial middle class in 1832. Thirty years

[26] Cf. D. H. Lasswell, a.o. *The Comparative Study of Élites*, Stanford, 1952, and books on the Politbureau and the Nazi élite, etc.

[27] Cf. Guttsman, *British Political Élite*, espec. pp. 87–97 and 195–221.

[28] *Communist Manifesto*, ed. D. Ryazanoff, 1930, p. 28.

later Marx could write that 'the power that used to be concentrated in the hands of Asiatic and Egyptian kings or Etruscan theocrats and the like [had] in modern society been transferred to the capitalist – it may be to individual capitalists; or it may be to collective capitalists as in joint-stock companies'.[29]

It was as clear to Marx as it must be to us that the capitalist entrepreneur does not rule in person and the Marxist ruling class, which occupies such a central thought in his thinking, is not confined to those who directly or indirectly wield economic power. It includes those who administer the state and its subordinate organs, and, as we saw, he recognized that the latter may be a different group of people, remnants of the old dominant feudal classes who, in the phrase referred to, 'rule officially'. This gulf between those who hold ultimate power and those who rule the state is, however, according to this view more apparent than real because both alike are imbued by an ideology which derives from the material conditions and provides them with an intellectual justification and legitimation.[30]

There is no reason to assume that those who occupied positions of formal power in nineteenth- and early twentieth-century Britain, even if socially differentiated from the cotton-spinners and shipbuilders, colliery managers and surveyors who frequently voted them into office, were deeply antagonistic to the economic claims of the capitalist system. Nor did the protagonists of the latter show much desire to exchange profits, often combined with real power locally, for the prestige of office, epaulettes or pulpit.

This is not to deny the existence of genuine social antagonism or of real areas of conflict between the two sections of the ruling class: wasteful panoplies of power, the efficiency of administration, access to higher education, were all matters of concern to the middle classes and I have sought to highlight these issues. But on major matters the 'antiquated compromise' withstood the test of time. Over the repeal of the Corn Laws, a substantial section of the landowning element in Parliament supported free trade; and over Home Rule for Ireland, Whig and Tory landowners and Nonconformist businessmen combined and underpinned what otherwise might have tottered. The traumatic experience of the Crimean

[29] Karl Marx, *Capital*, I (trans. Eden and Cedar Paul), p. 350, quoted in R. Tucker, *Philosophy and Myth in Karl Marx*, 1961.
[30] Cf. Marx & Engels, *The German Ideology*, Pt. I: section on the ideology.

wars shook the alliance and changed it, but did not destroy it. Perhaps Mosca was right when he claimed that the fact that England survived the nineteenth century without revolution was due to 'the greater energy, the greater political wisdom, the better political training that her ruling class possessed'.[31]

The strength and tenacity of the traditional English ruling class clearly owes not a little to the pragmatic approach, good sense, personal moderation and feelings of responsibility with which its members carried out their task. But equally important was the ideological strength of its position. The ruling class and the middle class, sharing a large number of fundamentals, interacted and supported each other over a wide field until they came increasingly to merge; so that in the constellation of power today the two are hardly separable.

As with the aristocracy of old, this class is not hermetically closed but I think that today we no more have than we ever had in the past a genuinely 'open' élite. After a century of increasingly powerful working-class organization in the industrial and political fields, this is a phenomenon of great significance.

[31] G. Mosca, *The Ruling Class*, 1939, p. 119.

I The general character of the class

1·1 THE OAKS OF THE COMMONWEALTH

From Edmund Burke, A Letter to the Duke of Richmond (*1772*) *in* Works and Correspondence, *8 vols. 1852, I, p. 190.*

You people of great families and hereditary trusts and fortunes are not like such as I am, who, whatever we may be by the rapidity of our growth and even by the fruit we bear flatter ourselves that, while we creep on the ground, we belly into melons that are exquisite for size and flavour yet still we are but annual plants that perish with our season, and leave no sort of trace behind us. You, if you are what you ought to be, are in my eye the great oaks that shade a country, and perpetuate your benefits from generation to generation.

1·2 THE LORDLIES AND THE LAWS OF STATE

From Edmund Burke, Letter ... to a Noble Lord on the attacks made upon him and his pension in the House of Lords by the Duke of Bedford and the Earl of Lauderdale, *1796, pp. 37–9; 51–4.*

Burke mercilessly attacks the pretensions and prejudices of an individual aristocrat while defending vigorously the basis of the system on which aristocratic power rests.

The crown has considered me after long service: the crown has paid the Duke of Bedford by advance. He has had a long credit for any service which he may perform hereafter. He is secure, and long may he be secure, in his advance, whether he performs any services or not. But let him take care how he endangers the safety of that Constitution which secures his own utility or his own insignificance, or how he discourages those who take up even puny arms to defend an order of things which, like the sun of heaven, shines alike on the useful and the worthless. His grants are ingrafted on the public law of Europe, covered with the awful hoar of innumerable ages. They are guarded by the sacred rules of prescription, found in that full treasury of jurisprudence from which the jejuneness and penury of our municipal law has by degrees been enriched and strengthened. This prescription I had my share, a very full share, in bringing to its perfection. The Duke of Bedford will stand as long as prescriptive law endures – as long as the great, stable laws of property, common to us with all civilized nations, are kept in their integrity, and without the smallest intermixture of the laws, maxims, principles, or precedents of the Grand Revolution. They are secure against all changes but one. The whole Revolutionary system, institutes, digest, code, novels, text, gloss, comment, are not only not the same, but they are the very reverse, and the reverse fundamentally, of all the laws on which civil life has hitherto been upheld in all the governments of the world. The learned professors of the Rights of Man regard prescription not as a title to bar all claim set up against old possession, but they look on prescription as itself a bar against the possessor and proprietor. They hold an immemorial possession to be no more than a long continued and therefore an aggravated injustice.

Such are *their* ideas, such *their* religion, and such *their* law. But as to *our* country and *our* race, as long as the well-compacted structure of our Church and State, the sanctuary, the holy of holies of that ancient law, defended by reverence, defended by power, a fortress at once and a temple, shall stand inviolate on the brow of the British Sion – as long as the British monarchy, not more limited than fenced by the orders of the state, shall, like the proud Keep of Windsor, rising in the majesty of proportion, and girt with the double belt of its kindred and coëval towers, as long as this awful structure shall oversee and guard the subjected land – so long the mounds and dikes of the low, fat, Bedford level will have nothing to fear from all the pickaxes of all the levellers of France. . . .

The Duke of Bedford conceives that he is obliged to call the attention of the House of Peers to his Majesty's grant to me, which he considers as excessive and out of all bounds.

I know not how it has happened, but it really seems, that, whilst his Grace was meditating his well-considered censure upon me, he fell into a sort of sleep. Homer nods, and the Duke of Bedford may dream; and as dreams (even his golden dreams) are apt to be ill-pieced and incongruously put together his Grace preserved his idea of reproach to *me* but took the subject-matter from the crown grants *to his own family*. This is 'the stuff of which his dreams are made'. In that way of putting things together his Grace is perfectly in the right. The grants to the House of Russell were so enormous as not only to outrage economy, but even to stagger credibility. The Duke of Bedford is the leviathan among all the creatures of the crown. He tumbles about his unwieldy bulk, he plays and frolics in the ocean of the royal bounty. Huge as he is, and whilst 'he lies floating many a rood' he is still a creature. His ribs, his fins, his whalebone, his blubber, the very spiracles through which he spouts a torrent of brine against his origin, and covers me all over with the spray, everything of him and about him is from the throne. Is it for *him* to question the dispensation of the royal favour?

I really am at a loss to draw any sort of parallel between the public merits of his Grace, by which he justifies the grants he holds, and these services of mine, on the favourable construction of which I have obtained what his Grace so much disapproves. In private life I have not at all the honour of acquaintance with the noble Duke; but I ought to presume, and it costs me nothing to do so, that he abundantly deserves the esteem and love of all who live with him. But as to public service, why, truly, it would not be more ridiculous for me to compare myself, in rank, in fortune, in splendid descent, in youth, strength, or figure, with the Duke of Bedford, than to make a parallel between his services and my attempts to be useful to my country. It would not be gross adulation, but uncivil irony, to say that he has any public merit of his own to keep alive the idea of the services by which his vast landed pensions were obtained. My merits, whatever they are, are original and personal: his are derivative. It is his ancestor, the original pensioner, that has laid up this inexhaustible fund of merit which makes his Grace so very delicate and exceptious about the merit of all other grantees of the crown.

1·3 PROPERTY AND PERMANENCE

From S. T. Coleridge, On the Constitution of Church and State (*1830*) *4th ed. by H. N. Coleridge, 1852, pp. 26–8.*

Coleridge contrasts the sense of permanence and stability, which he connects with possession of transmissable landed property, with the progress in civilization and the arts, which to him are connected with entrepreneurial and professional elements in society.

Now, in every country of civilized men, acknowledging the rights of property, and by means of determined boundaries and common laws united into one people or nation, the two antagonist powers or opposite interests of the State, under which all other State interests are comprised, are those of permanence and of progression.

It will not be necessary to enumerate the several causes that combine to connect the permanence of a state with the land and the landed property. To found a family, and to convert his wealth into land, are twin thoughts, births of the same moment, in the mind of the opulent merchant, when he thinks of reposing from his labours. From the class of the *novi homines* he redeems himself by becoming the staple ring of the chain, by which the present will become connected with the past, and the test and evidence of permanency be afforded. To the same principle appertain primogeniture and hereditary titles, and the influence which these exert in accumulating large masses of property, and in counteracting the antagonist and dispersive forces, which the follies, the vices, and misfortunes of individuals can scarcely fail to supply. To this, likewise, tends the proverbial obduracy of prejudices characteristic of the humbler tillers of the soil, and their aversion even to benefits that are offered in the form of innovations. But why need I attempt to explain a fact which no thinking man will deny, and where the admission of the fact is all that my argument requires?

On the other hand, with as little chance of contradiction, I may assert that the progression of a State in the arts and comforts of life, in the diffusion of the information and knowledge, useful or necessary for all; in short, all advances in civilisation, and the rights and privileges of citizens, are especially connected with, and derived from, the four classes, the mercantile, the manufacturing, the distributive, and the professional.

1·4 HEREDITARY LEGISLATORS

From Benjamin Disraeli, A Vindication of the English Constitution, *1835, republished in Disraeli's* Whigs and Whiggism: Political Writings, *1913, pp. 199–201.*

This pamphlet, published in December 1835, was dedicated by Disraeli to Lord Lyndhurst to whose political star he had hitched his wagon. Disraeli had a little earlier written a series of vituperative articles in the *Morning Post* in support of Lyndhurst's diehard opposition to the Municipal Corporation Bill and of ultra-Toryism in general. In this pamphlet Disraeli praises the aristocrats' role in the constitution and extols the House of Lords in a more systematic form than in his earlier attacks.

Political institutions must be judged by their results. For nearly five centuries the hereditary Peerage, as at present constituted, has formed an active and powerful branch of our legislature. Five centuries of progressive welfare are good evidence of the efficient polity of the advancing country. No statesman can doubt that the peculiar character of the hereditary branch of our legislature has mainly contributed to the stability of our institutions, and to the order and prosperous security which that stability has produced. Nor can we forget that the hereditary principle has at all times secured a senate for this country inferior in intelligence to no political assembly on record. . . .

I do not think, my Lord, that anyone will be bold enough to assert – or, if bold enough to assert, skilful enough to maintain – that the late Reform, which was to open the doors of the House of Commons to all the unearthed genius of the country, has indicated as yet any tendency to render this rivalry on the part of the

Peers of England a matter of greater venture. If in old times the hereditary senate has at least equalled in capacity the elective chamber, no impartial observer at the present day can for a moment hesitate in declaring that, not only in the higher accomplishments of statesmen, in elevation of thought and feeling, in learning and in eloquence, does the hereditary assembly excel the elective, but, in truth, that for those very qualities for the possession of which at first sight we should be most disposed to give a House of Commons credit, that mastery of detail and management of complicated commonplaces which we style in this country 'business-like habits', the Peers of England are absolutely more distinguished than the humbler representatives of the third estate.

But the truth is, my Lord, that the practical good sense of this country has long ago disposed of the question of the principle of hereditary legislation, even if its defence merely depended on its abstract propriety. For if we examine the elements of the House of Commons with a little attention, we shall soon discover that hereditary legislators are not confined to the House of Lords, and that the inclination of the represented to make representation hereditary is very obvious and very natural. The representative of a county is selected from one of the first families in the shire, and ten years after the son of this member, a candidate for the same honour, adduces the very circumstances of his succession to his father as an increased claim upon the confidence of the constituency. Those who are versed in elections know that there is no plea so common and so popular. Such elections prove that, far from holding the principle of hereditary legislation absurd, public opinion has decided that the duties of an English legislator are such as, on an average of human capacity, may descend from sire to son; and that, while there is nothing to shock their reason in the circumstance, there is much at the same time to gratify the feelings and please the associations of an ancient people, who have made inheritance the pervading principle of their social polity, who are proud of their old families and fond of their old laws.

1·5 THE SOCIAL VIRTUES OF AN ARISTOCRACY

From E. G. Bulwer Lytton, England and the English *(1833), 1887, pp. 29–31.*

By comparing the British aristocratic system with that of the Continent Lytton brings out the fluidity of the nobility in Britain compared with its castelike character in France and Germany. [See also 5·2]

The supposed total of constitutional power has always consisted of three divisions; the king, the aristocracy, and the commons: but the aristocracy (until the passing of the Reform Bill), by boroughs in the one house, as by hereditary seats in the other, monopolized the whole of the three divisions. They ousted the people from the commons by a majority of their own delegates; and they forced the king into their measures by the maxim, that his consent to a bill passed through *both* houses could not with safety be withheld. Thus, then, in state affairs, the government of the country has been purely that of an aristocracy. Let us now examine the influence which they have exercised in social relations. It is to this, I apprehend, that we must look for those qualities which have distinguished their influence from that of other aristocracies. Without the odium of separate privileges, without the demarcation of feudal rights, the absence of those very prerogatives has been the cause of the long establishment of their power. . . .

The social influence of the aristocracy has been exactly of a character to strengthen their legislative. Instead of keeping themselves aloof from the other classes, and 'hedging their state', round with the thorny, but unsubstantial barriers of heraldic distinctions; instead of demanding half a hundred quarterings with their wives, and galling their inferiors by eternally dwelling on the inferiority, they may be said to mix more largely, and with more seeming equality, with all classes, than any other aristocracy in the savage or civilized world. Drawing their revenues from land, they have also drawn much of their more legitimate power from the influence it gave them in elections. To increase this influence they have been in the habit of visiting the provinces much more often than any aristocracy in a monarchical state are accustomed to do. Their hospitality, their field sports, the agricultural and county meetings they attend, in order 'to keep up the family interest', mix them with all classes; and, possessing the usual urbanity of a court, they have not unfrequently added to the weight of property, and the glitter of station, the influence of a personal popularity, acquired less, perhaps, by the evidence of virtues, than the exercise of politeness.

In most other countries the middle classes rarely possessing the riches of the nobility, have offered to the latter no incentive for seeking their alliance. But wealth is the greatest of all levellers, and the highest of the English nobles willingly repair the fortunes of hereditary extravagance by intermarriage with the families of the banker, the lawyer, and the merchant: this, be it observed, tends to extend the roots of their influence among the middle classes, who, in other countries, are the natural barrier of the aristocracy. It is the ambition of the rich trader to obtain the alliance of nobles; and he loves, as well as respects, those honours to which himself or his children may aspire. The long-established custom of purchasing titles, either by hard money or the more circuitous influence of boroughs, has tended also to mix aristocratic feelings with the views of the trader; and the apparent openness of honours to all men, makes even the humblest shopkeeper, grown rich, think of sending his son to College, not that he may become a wiser man or a better man, but that he may *perhaps* become my lord bishop or my lord chancellor. . . .

By this intermixture of the highest aristocracy with the more subaltern ranks of society, there are far finer and more numerous grades of dignity in this country than in any other. You see two gentlemen of the same birth, fortunes, and estates – they are not of the same rank, – by no means! – one looks down on the other as confessedly his inferior. Would you know why? His *connexions* are much higher! Nor are connexions alone the dispensers of an ideal, but acknowledged consequence. Acquaintanceship confers also its honours: next to being related to the great, is the happiness of knowing the great: and the wife even of a *bourgeois*, who has her house filled with fine people, considers herself, and is tacitly allowed to be, of greater rank than one, who, of far better birth and fortune, is not so diligent a worshipper of birth and fortune in others; in fact, this lady has but her own respectable rank to display – but that lady reflects the exalted rank of every duchess that shines upon her card-rack.

These mystic, shifting, and various shades of graduation; these shot-silk colours of society produce this effect: That people have no exact and fixed position – that by acquaintance alone they may rise to look down on their superiors – that while the rank gained by intellect, or by interest, is open but to few, the rank that may be obtained by fashion seems delusively to be open to all. . . . As wealth procures the alliance and respect of nobles, wealth is affected even where not possessed; and, as fashion, which is the creature of an aristocracy, can only be obtained by resembling the fashionable; hence, each person imitates his fellow, and hopes to purchase the respectful opinion of others by renouncing the independence of opinion for himself.

1·6 THE FUNCTIONS OF A NOBILITY

From W. Bagehot, The English Constitution, *1904 ed., pp. 89–94.*

Bagehot saw the House of Lords, and indeed even the whole of the nobility, as an important element in the dignity of the Constitution. The positive social function which he ascribes to it and which he illustrates by comparisons with Continental countries has often been overlooked.

The office of an order of nobility is to impose on the common people – not necessarily to impose on them what is untrue, yet less what is hurtful; but still to impose on their quiescent imaginations what would not otherwise be there. The fancy of the mass of men is incredibly weak; it can see nothing without a visible symbol, and there is much that it can scarcely make out with a symbol. Nobility is the symbol of mind. It has the marks from which the mass of men always used to infer mind, and often still infer it. A common clever man who goes into a country place will get no reverence; but the 'old squire' will get reverence. Even after he is insolvent, when every one knows that his ruin is but a question of time, he will get five times as much respect from the common peasantry as the newly-made rich man who sits beside him. . . .

The order of nobility is of great use, too, not only in what it creates, but in what it prevents. It prevents the rule of wealth – the religion of gold. This is the obvious and natural idol of the Anglo-Saxon. He is always trying to make money. . . . He has a 'natural instinctive admiration of wealth for its own sake'. And within good limits the feeling is quite right. So long as we play the game of industry vigorously and eagerly . . . we shall of necessity respect and admire those who play successfully, and a little despise those who play unsuccessfully. . . But the admiration of wealth in many countries goes far beyond this; it ceases to regard in any degree the skill of acquisition; it respects wealth in the hands of the inheritor just as much as in the hands of the maker; it is a simple envy and love of a heap of gold as a heap of gold. From this our aristocracy preserves us. There is no country where a 'poor devil of a million-naire is so ill off as in England'. The experiment is tried every day and every day it is proved that money alone – money *pur et simple* – will not buy 'London Society'. Money is kept down, and, so to say, cowed by the predominant authority of a different power.

But it may be said that this is no gain; that worship for worship, the worship of money is as good as the worship of rank. . . . But it is not true that the reverence for rank – at least, for hereditary rank – is as base as the reverence for money. As the world has gone, manner has been half-hereditary in certain castes, and manner is one of the fine arts. . . . In reverencing wealth we reverence not a man, but an appendix to a man; in reverencing inherited nobility, we reverence the probable possession of a great faculty – the faculty of bringing out what is in one. . . .

There is a third idolatry from which that of rank preserves us, and perhaps it is the worst of any – that of office. The basest deity is a subordinate *employé*, and yet just now in civilised governments it is the commonest. In France and all the best of the Continent it rules like a superstition. It is to no purpose that you prove that the pay of petty officials is smaller than mercantile pay; that their work is more monotonous than mercantile work; that their mind is less useful and their life more tame. They are still thought to be greater and better. They are *decorés*; they have a little red on the left breast of their coat, and no argument will answer that. In England, by the odd course of our society, what a theorist would desire has in fact turned up. The great offices, whether permanent or parliamentary, which require mind now give social prestige, and almost only those. An Under-Secretary of State with £2000 a year is a much greater man than the director of a finance company with £5000, and the country saves the difference. But except in a few offices like the Treasury, which were once filled with aristocratic people, and have an odour of nobility at second-hand, minor place is of no social use. A big grocer despises the exciseman; and what in many countries would be thought impossible, the exciseman envies the grocer. Solid wealth tells where there is no artificial dignity given to petty public functions. A clerk in the public service is 'nobody'; and you could not make a common Englishman see why he should be anybody. . . .

The social prestige of the aristocracy is, as every one knows, immensely less than it was a hundred years or even fifty years since. Two great movements – the two greatest of modern society – have been unfavourable to it. The rise of industrial wealth in countless forms has brought in a competitor which has generally more mind, and which would be supreme were it not for awkwardness and intellectual *gêne*. Every day our companies, our railways, our debentures, and our shares, tend more and more to multiply these *surroundings* of the aristocracy, and in time they will hide it. And while this undergrowth has come up, the aristocracy have come down. They have less means of standing out than they used to have. Their power is in their theatrical exhibition, in their state. But society is every day becoming less stately. As our great satirist has observed, 'The last Duke of St David's used to cover the north road with his carriages; landladies and waiters bowed before him. The present Duke sneaks away from a railway station, smoking a cigar, in a brougham.' The aristocracy cannot lead the old life if they would; they are ruled by a stronger power. They suffer from the tendency of all modern society to raise the average, and to lower – comparatively, and perhaps absolutely, to lower – the summit. As the picturesqueness, the featureliness, of society diminishes, aristocracy loses the single instrument of its peculiar power.

1·7 A DEFERENTIAL PEOPLE

From J. S. Mill, Letters, *2 vols, 1910, ed. by H. S. R. Elliot, vol. I, p. 205.*

Deference is the obverse of dignity. Bagehot looked at it approvingly, Mill rather despairingly. The letter quoted was addressed on 15 April 1858 to Mazzini, who had proposed the formation of an international society for political objects.

The English, of all ranks and classes, are at bottom, in all their feelings, aristocrats. They have the conception of liberty, and set some value on it, but the very idea of equality is strange and offensive to them. They do not dislike to have many people above them as long as they have some below them, and therefore they have never sympathised and in their present state of mind never will sympathise with any really democratic or republican party in other countries. They keep what sympathy they have for those whom they look upon as imitators of English institutions – Continental Whigs who desire to introduce constitutional forms and some securities against personal oppression – leaving in other respects the old order of things with all its inequalities and social injustices; and any people who are not willing to content themselves with this, are thought unfit for liberty.

1·8 GENTILITY THROUGH PATRONAGE

From G. O. Trevelyan (ed.) Life and Letters of Lord Macaulay, *new ed. 2 vols, 1878, vol. I, pp. 338–9.*

Macaulay, writing to his sister in 1833 about an obviously dim and rather distant relative's claims for office, castigates the snobbery and the desire to emulate an upper crust which permeated English society.

My father is at me again to provide for P—. What on earth have I to do with P—? The relationship is one which none but Scotchmen would recognise. The lad is such a fool that he would utterly disgrace my recommendation. And, as if to make the thing more provoking, his sisters say that he must be provided for in England, for that they cannot think of parting with him. This, to be sure, matters little: for there is at present just as little chance of getting anything in India as in England.

But what strange folly this is which meets me in every quarter people wanting posts in the army, the navy, the public offices, and saying that, if they cannot find such posts, they must starve! How do all the rest of mankind live? If I had not happened to be engaged in politics, and if my father had not been connected, by very extraordinary circumstances, with public men, we should never have dreamed of having places. Why cannot P— be apprenticed to some hatter or tailor? He may do well in such a business: he will do detestably ill as a clerk in my office. He may come to make good coats: he will never, I am sure, write good despatches. There is nothing truer than Poor Richard's saw: 'We are taxed twice as heavily by our pride as by the state.' The curse of England is the obstinate determination of the middle classes to make their sons what they call gentlemen. So we are overrun by clergymen without livings; lawyers without briefs; physicians without patients; authors without readers; clerks soliciting employment, who might have thriven, and been above the world, as bakers, watchmakers, or innkeepers. The next time my father speaks to me about P—, I will offer to subscribe twenty guineas towards making a pastry-cook of him. He had a sweet tooth when he was a child.

1·9 A GENTLEMANLY RULE – NOT A BUREAUCRATIC SYSTEM

From Charles de Montalembert, The Political Future of England, *1856, pp. 85–97.*

Another comparison between England and France links aristocracy with the character and quality of the administration, especially at the local level. Montalembert's assessment of the value of the practice of agricultural succession as symbolized by entail is interesting in view of the general tendency in discussing this to cite the French experience as evidence for the virtue of a free trade in land.

The true strength of the English Aristocracy and nationality abides in many thousands of families of Landed Proprietors, and who, in virtue of their property, are the magistrates, and, to use our French phrase, *administrators of the country*. They do not disdain, as the old French nobility did, to accept administrative, legislative, and judicial functions. Far from it – they have almost monopolised them, and by so doing have maintained themselves at the head of all the developments of society. Men without names and without fortune often arrive at great political employment, sometimes even to the supreme management of public affairs, just as might happen in republics or in absolute monarchies. It happens sometimes also, but with more difficulty, and rarely, that such men obtain consideration in a small or even a large town, where they may not have acquired property. But as a general rule, the higher positions, the Lords-Lieutenant, Sheriffs, and Justices of the Peace, the Grand

33

Jurors, the Commissioners of roads, the Conservators of public edifices – in fact, all that in France is done by the salaried servants of our variable Government, which is seldom today what it was yesterday or will be tomorrow – all this, I say, is in England executed by the class of Country Gentlemen, who, while they continue to live at home, regulate the finances and administer justice in their respective localities, spontaneously, gratuitously, and with an admirable degree of perfection.

Independent of the Court and the Cabinet, exempt, as far as men living in society can be, from personal interests, and safe from the intrigues, affronts, and trammels of a system of centralization and *bureaucracy*, which are everywhere the headquarters and standing army of democracy, the English Country Gentlemen exhibit in their position, their habits, and their vigorous and useful existence, the only example of a real and influential aristocracy that Europe possesses.

All this, I think, is evident; but it is perhaps less so how this *Gentry* has had the good fortune to escape the jealousy or the hatred of those either above or below them. This success is owing to the Gentry's being, like the peerage, and still more than the peerage, accessible to all.

Every man who makes his fortune, be it in industry, commerce, the bar, or in the medical or any other profession, aspires to become a landed proprietor. He becomes so sooner or later, and then immediately begins to think, like a true Englishman, of founding a family and consolidating an estate. He thus becomes a member of that great corporation of Gentry which guides, governs, and represents the country. . . . After, at latest, one generation this new family is received on a perfect equality with the most ancient of the country. . . . No exterior distinction shows the difference of origin and antiquity between the modern and the ancient gentry – no useless title, uselessly lavished – not even that indefinable euphony of names which, with us, attaches itself to the origin of the nobility, which still constitutes its only *prestige*. . . .

The large landed fortunes do not, as some fancy, and as is often repeated, prevent there being in England, as elsewhere, many small proprietors. . . . Landed property is accessible to everybody in England, and, everything considered, is, on the whole, cheaper than in France. But the English system has a double advantage: on one hand the laws of inheritance prevent a ruinous subdivision of the soil and an indefinite increase of small proprietors, while on the other the small proprietors are not incited to any political opinions antagonistic to those of the great proprietors, round whom they, as it were, naturally group themselves, generally adopting their ideas, passions, and quarrels, willing and even proud to be their active, intelligent, and voluntary clients. Here is then an Aristocracy constituted on the most solid basis, that of services rendered to the public, and of the permanent exercise of an independent, and till these days uncontested authority. It has preserved all that Aristocracy could and ought to preserve, since the invention of gunpowder and the maintenance of regular armies have deprived it of the exclusive privilege of fighting for the community. It has remained free and powerful. How has it escaped the fate of Continental aristocracies, the unpopularity, the degradation which have become the common lot of the nobility in almost all the other nations of Europe?

... The English Aristocracy has escaped political prostration and royal despotism by the honest and courageous exercise of parliamentary government. . . . It has saved itself by invoking and exerting the powers of right and of reasoning – the conflict of thought and speech – while at the same time it studied and cultivated with an indefatigable solicitude the general interests, commerce, agriculture, manual industry, and arts, through the medium of the individual responsibility of its representatives exercised in the free and public discussions of parliament. . . .

It renounced in good time all the rights, the dues, the suits and services, the privileges that were necessary and beneficial consequences of the feudal system in the middle ages, but which had lost that double character in the transformations of modern society. . . .

We had formerly in France a social *régime* in which some men were everything and others nothing – a *régime* by which, to gratify the pride of a few, we humiliated the many. We thought to remedy this state of things by inventing a *régime* in which no individual whatever is of any account, but all are equally abased. England alone has created and for centuries maintained a social system which oppresses and humiliates no one, and permits every Englishman to walk erect, and to say for himself, as well as the King, *Dieu et mon droit!* . . .

Such is also the reason of the affectionate veneration which the rural population entertain for the landed aristocracy. Daily in contact one with another, these two classes live in the best intelligence; and this, let it be well understood, is the strongest safeguard of England against revolutions, and the true bulwark of her constitution against the encroachments of democracy. So long as the agricultural classes in a country are not pervaded with the revolutionary spirit, its victories are but ephemeral, and have no root whatever. . . .

There is not yet in England on this point any sign of dissension or of serious dissatisfaction. It is not certain that even now the working classes do not ask in their hearts whether the Aristocracy be not their natural ally against the abuses of industrialism. By making the best use of its *prestige* – by renouncing in time divisions and distinctions formerly useful and fruitful, but now obsolete, in order to concentrate its solicitude and its efforts on the more important social questions, the English aristocracy (of which many of its members have already taken this line) would probably acquire the first place in the esteem and the confidence of the working masses. However that may be, the career is open, and the prize will be awarded to the most zealous and the most deserving.

1·10 GENTLEMEN AS AN EXCLUSIVE SOCIAL CLASS

From H. Taine, Notes on England (Notes sur l'Angleterre), *1957 (1872) translated by E. Hyams, pp. 142–5.*

Here is another contrast of French and English Society, which castigates English snobbery and perceives the subtle gradations within the English upper crust. Taine visited Britain first in 1859 and returned in 1871. Sections of his book appeared first in an English translation in the *Daily News* in the 1870s.

Naturally, a class of this kind is a closed society and its limits are strictly maintained. Aristocratic institutions have, like others, their disadvantages. The system is one of social enclosures, and of efforts made by those of a lower class to get in and by those of the upper class to keep them out. For example a person like the elegant and intelligent farmer's wife of whom I was writing is not in society: she is not invited to 'archery meetings', and several ladies B— has named to me and whom, on this score, he disapproves of, avoid greeting her in order to stop, in advance, all access to a possible familiarity. Doubtless those English people who have lived abroad and have open minds are above such wretched manifestations of false pride, and they frankly recognize its folly and [condemn its] excesses.

But as regards the rest, under a cover of reserve, it is always perceptible. In their heart of hearts and perhaps without even admitting it to themselves, they believe, or are inclined to believe, that a tradesman, a financier, a man of business, constantly obliged to think of profit and details of profit all day long, is not a gentleman and never can be. He has not the requisite education, ideas or language. 'What should a tradesman or a farmer talk of if not of matters to do with his trade? The mind, engaged in coarse occupations and set in coarse habits, itself becomes coarse.' According to this opinion, feelings, also, become debased: the man who deals in money or business is inclined to selfishness; he has not the disinterestedness, the large and generous views, proper to the leaders of a nation; he is unable to forget his own small interest and think of the great public ones. And only on those terms has one any right to command. Consequently, and until he has proved the contrary to be true, the tradesman, the business man is made to keep his distance, and his family cannot be received by the reigning families.

... When a rich man buys an estate it is not his place to put himself to the expense of entertaining or to inform the neighbourhood. If, in mind, character, and manners, he is a gentleman, this will be known within a fortnight and the neighbouring families will then call on him. But even when adopted he will not yet have the privileges of the others: for instance he would not be elected as Member of Parliament and if he were to stand as a candidate the public would say 'He is too new he does not yet belong here.' He is planted, as it were, but has not taken root. His son perhaps, or his grandson, might be adopted, but not himself. To represent a constituency it is necessary to be attached to it by every interest and every habit, to have been involved in it for several generations. The primary condition of recognized leadership is long-established residence, and all strong aristocracies are local. . . .

I have been trying to get a real understanding of that most essential word 'a gentleman'; it is constantly occurring and it expresses a whole complex of particularly English ideas. The vital question concerning a man always takes this form: 'Is he a gentleman?' And similarly, of a woman 'Is she a lady?' In both cases what is meant by a positive reply is that the person in question belongs to the upper class. This class is fully recognized as a fact: a workman, a peasant, or a shop-keeper would not try to cross the line of demarcation. But how do you recognize that a person belongs to the upper class? In France we have not got the word because we have not got the thing. . . . The gentry, the squires, barons, feudal chiefs did not, as under Louis XV, become simply privileged individuals, ornamental parasites, troublesome, unpopular, odious, proscribed and then later maintained in the State rather as a tolerated memorial of the past than as an effective element. No; here they kept in touch with the people, opened their ranks to talent, recruited to their number the pick of the rising commoners; and they have remained the ruling class, or at least the most influential class in both parish and State. To that end they have adapted themselves to their time and their new role. They have made themselves into administrators, patrons, promoters of reform and good managers of the commonwealth; they have become well-informed and well-educated men, men who apply themselves to work and who, as citizens, are the most enlightened, the most independent and the most useful of the whole nation.

On this pattern has the idea 'gentleman' been formed, a very different thing to the idea *gentilhomme*. Gentilhomme evokes thoughts of elegance, style, tact, finesse; of exquisite politeness, delicate points of honour, of a chivalrous cast of mind, of prodigal liberality and brilliant valour: these were the salient features of the French upper class. Similarly, 'gentleman' expresses all the distinctive features of the English upper class, in the first place the most apparent, those which appeal to the simpler minds – for example, a large private fortune, a considerable household of servants, a certain outward appearance and bearing, habits of ease and luxury; often enough in the eyes of the common people and especially of the servant class, these outward semblances are all that is necessary. Add to them, for more cultivated minds, a liberal education, travel, information, good manners and ease in society.

But for real judges the essential quality is one of heart; . . . a real 'gentleman' is a truly noble man, a man worthy to command, a disinterested man of integrity, capable of exposing, even sacrificing himself for those he leads; not only a man of honour, but a conscientious man, in whom generous instincts have been confirmed by right thinking and who, acting rightly by nature, acts even more rightly from good principles.

In this idealized portrait you will recognize the accomplished leader. To it must be added specifically English features – complete self-mastery, constantly maintained *sang-froid*, perseverance in adversity, serious-mindedness, dignity of manners and bearing, the avoidance of all affectation or swaggering. You will then have the model which, copied as nearly as possible or at least aspired to, produces the man who commands obedience here.

1·11 THE ESTABLISHMENT: THE RADICAL ATTACK

From John Wade, The Extraordinary Black Book, an Exposition of Abuses in Church and State, *1835, pp. 277; 284–5 and 272–3.*

The Black Book, *together with its successor* The Extraordinary Black Book, *was a kind of Speaker's Handbook of the early Radicals. The ammunition which it provided to Reformers was drawn from sound authorities and official sources and examples of abuses will be given under individual headings. The extracts given below state the anti-aristoctatic feelings of the Radicals. (The table giving the income of different classes of the community is derived from Patrick Colquhoun's* Treatise of the Resources of the British Empire, *1814).*

CLASSES AND INCOMES

Different Classes of Society, and their respective Incomes

DESCRIPTION OF PERSONS	Number	Income £
ROYALTY	300	501,000
NOBILITY	13,620	5,400,000
GENTRY, including baronets, knights, country gentlemen, and others having *large* incomes	402,535	53,022,590
CLERGY: Eminent clergymen	9,000	1,080,000
Lesser ditto	87,000	3,500,000
Dissenting clergy, including itinerant preachers	20,000	500,000

STATE AND REVENUE, including all persons employed under government	114,500	6,830,000
PENSIONERS, including those of Greenwich, Chelsea, and Kilmainham Hospitals ..	92,000	1,050,000
LAW: Judges, barristers, attorneys, clerks, &c.	95,000	7,600,000
PHYSIC: Physicians, surgeons, apothecaries, &c.	90,000	5,400,000
AGRICULTURE: Freeholders of the better sort	385,000	19,250,000
Lesser Freeholders	1,050,000	21,000,000
Farmers	1,540,000	33,600,000
TRADE: Eminent merchants	35,000	9,100,000
Shopkeepers, and tradesmen retailing goods	700,000	28,000,00
Innkeepers and publicans, licensed to sell ale, beer, and spirituous liquors	437,000	8,750,000
WORKING CLASSES: Agricultural labourers, mechanics, artizans, handicrafts, and all labourers employed in manufactures, mines, and minerals	7,497,531	82,451,547
Paupers, vagrants, gypsies, rogues, vagabonds, and others supported by criminal delinquency	1,548,500	9,871,000

The magnitude of the territorial revenues of the Aristocracy is not such as to be in extreme disproportion with the incomes of many others in a community of great commercial opulence, and forms not any portion of the vice of their institution. Whether some noble lords have augmented their rental out of the spoils of the Church and the Crown is a question merely of historical curiosity and can never be of any practical utility: it is occasionally adverted to as a set-off to oligarchical pride and pretension; beyond which it has no available application. By the law of England, the quiet possession of an estate for *sixty years* gives a clear and valid title; and we believe there are few noblemen who cannot adduce legal proof of the undisturbed enjoyment of their parks and mansions for a much longer period. So far, then, as the *acres* are concerned they are perfectly safe; whatever political changes may intervene – and great ones are impending – the legitimate incomes of the peerage can never be endangered, unless they blindly and pertinaciously oppose a regeneration which the wants of the age render indispensable; unless they emulate, in fatuity and crime, CHARLES CAPET and his guilty accomplices.

Aristocratic monopoly and abuse do not result from enormous landed revenues, but from hereditary rights of legislation, from primogeniture and entail-laws, and from nomination boroughs. None of these, however, are essential constituents of an upper chamber; only two-thirds of the nobility are entitled, by birth, to seats in parliament; primogeniture and entails are feudal barbarisms void of utility in modern society; and the usurpation of the franchises of the people is such a manifest subversion of constitutional immunities, so inimical to the general freedom and prosperity, that it cannot be defended on any pretext of justice or expediency. Abolish these corruptions, and all things will work together for good, without spoliation, without civil convulsion; and the Devonshires, the Landsdownes, and Northumberlands enjoy, undisturbed, their widespread domains, and retain, without murmur or complaint, their social distinction and supremacy.

The great fount of evil has been the decayed boroughs; these have been the Pandora's box, from which have flowed national calamities, desolating wars, lavish expenditure, and the monstrous debt and dead weight. They have been the obstacles to every social melioration – civil, commercial, legal, and ecclesiastical. By means of them, the nobility have been enabled to double their private revenues, appropriating to themselves the dignities and livings of the church; pensions and grants out of the public purse; and filling, with their connexions and dependants, every lucrative office in the army, navy, and public administration. There are only two descriptions of offices, namely, those requiring talent and industry, the duties of which cannot be discharged by deputy, that the boroughmongers have denied themselves. Unfit for the higher stations in courts of law, they have condescended to fill the profitable situations of clerk, registrar, messenger, usher, or receiver, and carry bags and wands in the trains of those whose ability alone made them their superiors, and to whom they were compelled to pay this homage as a penalty for their own indolence and cupidity.

In consequence of the boroughs, all our institutions are partial, oppressive, and aristocratic. We have an aristocratic church, aristocratic bar, aristocratic taxation, aristocratic corn-laws, aristocratic laws of property, and, till recently, aristocratic game-laws;

in short, the aristocratic spirit pervades every thing – all is privilege, prescription, monopoly, association, and corporation. But why, it may be asked, has it so long continued, – why did not a wealthy, spirited, and enlightened community exert itself long before to abate the general oppression? The chief reason was this – we had also an ARISTOCRATIC PRESS! By this little key-stone was the entire Gothic arch of antiquated abuse and imposture upheld. . . .

It is not civil distinctions, but the nuisance of civil usurpations the just and enlightened wish to see abated. An aristocracy of office, of acquirement, and desert, is a natural aristocracy; but an aristocracy of birth is a feudal barbarism which honours the shadow in place of the substance, and dissevers merit from its just reward. Hereditary right to property we can comprehend, but hereditary right to be legislators, bishops, post-captains, military commanders, and secretaries of state, shocks common sense. One is a private immunity, transmissible from father to son; the other are public functions, which can never be alienated to any order of men; they belong to the living, and cannot be bequeathed and regulated by the dead; they are adjuncts to the present not to a past generation. . . .

It is neither the mansions nor parks of the peerage that excite popular cupidity; it is the hereditary monopoly – not by constitutional right, but usurpation – of the political franchises of the people which begets hostile feelings; because it enables the privileged legislators to tax others and not themselves – to engross all public honours, offices, and emoluments – in a word, to make all the great social interests of a vast community, of which, in number, intellect, and even wealth, they constitute a most insignificant portion, subservient solely to the purposes of their own vanity, folly, indulgence, and aggrandizement. Here is the national grievance; and let us inquire whether, from the adventitious circumstance of property, they have any claim to inflict this great wrong on society.

1·12 THE GENEALOGY OF AN OLIGARCH
From Benjamin Disraeli, Sybil, Chapter 3.

Disraeli's account of the rise of the Egremonts, like that of the Earls de Mowbray, although fictitious and coloured by his aversion to the Whigs, is a good synoptic description of 'aristocratic evolution'.

Egremont was the younger brother of an English earl, whose nobility, being of nearly three centuries' date, ranked him among our high and ancient peers, although its origin was more memorable than illustrious. The founder of the family had been a confidential domestic of one of the favourites of Henry VIII, and had contrived to be appointed one of the commissioners for 'visiting and taking the surrenders of divers religious houses'. It came to pass that divers of these religious houses surrendered themselves eventually to the use and benefit of honest Baldwin Greymount. The king was touched with the activity and zeal of his commissioner. Not one of them whose reports were so ample and satisfactory, who could baffle a wily prior with more dexterity, or control a proud abbot with more firmness. Nor were they well-digested reports alone that were transmitted to the sovereign: they came accompanied with many rare and curious articles, grateful to the taste of one who was not only a religious reformer but a dilettante; golden candlesticks and costly chalices; sometimes a jewelled pix; fantastic spoons and patens, rings for the fingers and the ear; occasionally a fair-written and blazoned manuscript: suitable offering to the royal scholar. Greymount was noticed; sent for; promoted in the household; knighted; might doubtless have been sworn of the council, and in due time have become a minister; but his was a discreet ambition, of an accumulative rather than an aspiring character. He served the king faithfully in all domestic matters that required an unimpassioned, unscrupulous agent; fashioned his creed and conscience according to the royal model in all its freaks; seized the right moment to get sundry grants of abbey lands, and contrived in that dangerous age to save both his head and his estate.

The Greymount family having planted themselves in the land, faithful to the policy of the founder, avoided the public gaze during the troubled period that followed the reformation; and even during the more orderly reign of Elizabeth, rather sought their increase in alliances than in court favour. But at the commencement of the seventeenth century, their abbey lands infinitely advanced in value, and their rental swollen by the prudent accumulation of more than seventy years, a Greymount, who was then a county member, was elevated to the peerage as Baron Marney. The heralds furnished his pedigree, and assured the world that, although the exalted rank and extensive possessions enjoyed at present by the Greymounts had their origin immediately in great territorial revolutions of a recent reign, it was not for a moment to be supposed that the remote ancestors of the Ecclesiastical Commissioner of 1530 were by any means obscure. On the contrary, it appeared that they were both Norman and baronial, their real name Egremont, which, in their patent of peerage, the family now resumed.

In the civil wars the Egremonts, pricked by their Norman blood, were cavaliers, and fought pretty well. But in 1688, alarmed at the prevalent impression that King James intended to insist on the restitution of the church estates to their original purposes, to wit the education of the people and the maintenance of the poor, the Lord of Marney Abbey became a warm adherent of 'civil and religious liberty', the cause for which Hampden had died in the field, and Russell on the scaffold, and joined the other whig lords, and great lay impropriators, in calling over the Prince of Orange and a Dutch army, to vindicate those popular principles which, somehow or other, the people would never support. . . .

The great deliverer King William III, to whom Lord Marney was a systematic traitor, made the descendant of the Ecclesiastical Commissioner of Henry VIII an English earl; and from that time until the period of our history, though the Marney family had never produced one individual eminent for civil or military abilities, though the country was not indebted to them for a single statesman, orator, successful warrior, great lawyer, learned divine, eminent author, illustrious man of science, they had contrived, if not to engross any great share of public admiration and love, at least to monopolise no contemptible portion of public money and public dignities. During the seventy years of almost unbroken whig rule, from the accession of the House of Hanover to the fall of Mr Fox, Marney Abbey had furnished a never-failing crop of lord privy seals, lord presidents, and lord lieutenants. The family had had their due quota of garters and governments and bishoprics; admirals without fleets, and generals who fought only in America. They had glittered in great embassies with clever secretaries at their elbow, and had once governed Ireland, when to govern Ireland was only to apportion the public plunder to a corrupt senate.

Notwithstanding, however, this prolonged enjoyment of undeserved prosperity, the lay abbots of Marney were not content. Not that it was satiety which induced dissatisfaction. The Egremonts could feed on. They wanted something more. Not to be prime ministers or secretaries of state, for they were a shrewd race who knew the length of their tether, and notwithstanding the encouraging example of his grace of Newcastle, they could not resist the persuasion that some knowledge of the interests and resources of nations, some power of expressing opinions with propriety, some degree of respect for the public and for himself, were not altogether indispensable qualifications, even under a Venetian constitution, in an individual who aspired to a post so eminent and responsible. . . . What they aimed at was promotion in their order; and promotion to the highest class. They observed that more than one of the other great 'civil and religious liberty' families, the families who in one century plundered the church to gain the property of the people and in another century changed the dynasty to gain the power of the crown, had their brows circled with the strawberry leaf. And why should not this distinction be the high lot also of the descendants of the old gentleman-usher of one of King Henry's plundering vicar-generals? Why not? True it is, that a grateful sovereign in our days has deemed such distinction the only reward for half a hundred victories. True it is, that Nelson, after conquering the Mediterranean, died only a Viscount! But the house of Marney had risen to high rank, counted themselves ancient nobility; and turned up their noses at the Pratts and the Smiths, the Jenkinsons and the Robinsons of our degenerate days; and never had done anything for the nation or for their honours. And why should they now? It was unreasonable to expect it. Civil and religious liberty, that had given them a broad estate and glittering coronet, to say nothing of half-a-dozen close seats in parliament, ought clearly to make them dukes.

1·13 A RULING FAMILY

From G. A. Denison, Notes of My Life, 1805–1878. Oxford, 1878, pp. 1–3.

Denison's father was John Denison, a Nottinghamshire landowner. He himself became a clergyman of an extreme High Church persuasion. He engaged actively and as a controversialist in the field of elementary education rejecting any form of governmental control.

I was born, Dec. 11, 1805, at Ossington, in Nottinghamshire: one of a family of fourteen children, nine sons, five daughters, living to man's and woman's estate; the nine sons, and three of the daughters, my mother's children. My dear father died in 1820, aged 62; he sat in Parliament, I think, for Colchester; afterwards for Minehead: my dear mother died in 1859, aged 82. Two sons, one daughter, are still living; I am the eldest survivor. . . .

Six of us were at Eton; one at Harrow; one was brought up for the navy: he died at the age of thirty-one, loved and valued by all who knew him. Six were at Oxford, as Undergraduates; four at Ch[rist] Ch[urch], one at Oriel, one at Balliol.

My eldest brother, John Evelyn, Viscount Ossington 1872; married, 1827, Lady Charlotte Bentinck, third daughter of the Duke of Portland; and after some thirty years of Parliamentary life, became Speaker of the House of Commons, 1857; resigned, 1872. Died, 1873.

Edward, First Class in Classics, Fellow of Merton, became Bishop of Salisbury in 1837; married, 1839, Louisa Mary Ker Seymer, 2nd Hon. Clementina Hamilton, 1845. Died, 1854.

William, went from Eton to Woolwich, then into the Engineers; married, 1838, Caroline Hornby. After employments at home and abroad, he became in 1846 Governor of Van Dieman's Land; Governor-General of Australia, K.C.B., 1855; Governor of Madras, 1861. After Lord Elgin's death, he acted for some months as Governor-General of India. Died, 1871.

Henry, Double-first Class, Fellow of All Souls. Was paralysed by an injury received in Australia; returned to England, 1841, and after many years of great suffering, died, 1858.

Stephen, First Class in Classics, Stowell Fellow of University;

married Susan Fellowes, 1845; was for many years Deputy Judge Advocate. Died, 1871.

Frank was the Sailor. Died, 1841.

Alfred, after some twenty years of laborious, honourable, and successful life in Australia, returned finally to England, 1859, and became Private Secretary to the Speaker.

Charles was in the 52nd Regiment, and became Colonel in it. He had sundry Staff employments in India; and afterwards, till he was compelled by failing health, caused by sun-stroke, to retire from active life, was Chief Commissioner of Civil Service at Madras. Died, 1877.

I was First Class in Classics, Fellow of Oriel, and gained the Chancellor's Prizes for Latin, and English Essay, 1828, 1829. Married, 1838, Georgiana, eldest daughter of the Rt. Hon. J. W. Henley.

My sister Charlotte, daughter of my father's first marriage, married Charles Manners Sutton, then Judge Advocate General; afterwards, for seventeen years Speaker of the House of Commons, and Viscount Canterbury.

Matilda, the second sister of the first marriage, married Thomas Smith, Esq.

Julia married the Rev. Henry des Voeux; Henrietta, John Henry Jacob, Esq. My surviving sister, Charlotte, is the wife of the Right Hon. Sir Robert Phillimore.

1·14 HEREDITARY DISTINCTIONS ARE DOOMED

From J. S. Mill, The Spirit of the Age, ed. by F. A. Hayek, Chicago, 1942, pp. 50–6. [A collection of essays originally published anonymously in The Examiner in 1831 and issued in book form for the first time in the above edition.]

Writing under the influence of Comte and Saint Simon, to whose writings he had been introduced by Gustave d'Eichthal and with whom he was to establish personal contact, Mill put the hereditary ruling caste into a perspective very different from that presented by Coleridge and Disraeli.

It is not necessary for me to point out that until a comparatively recent period, none but the wealthy, and even, I might say, the hereditarily wealthy, had it in their power to acquire the intelligence, the knowledge, and the habits, which are necessary to qualify a man, in any tolerable degree, for managing the affairs of his country. It is not necessary for me to show that this is no longer the case, nor what are the circumstances which have changed it: the improvement in the arts of life, giving ease and comfort to great numbers not possessed of the degree of wealth which confers political power: the increase of reading: the diffusion of elementary education: the increase of the town-population, which brings masses of men together, and accustoms them to examine and discuss important subjects with one another; and various other causes, which are known to every body. All this, however, is nothing more than the acquisition by other people in an inferior degree, of a few of the advantages which have always been within the reach of the higher classes, in a much greater degree: and if the higher classes had profited as they might have done by these advantages, and had kept their station in the vanguard of the march of improvement, they would not only at this moment have been sure to retain in their hands all the powers of government, subject perhaps to severer conditions of responsibility, but might possibly even have continued for a considerable time longer to retain them on the same footing as at present. . . .

But the higher classes, instead of advancing, have retrograded in all the higher qualities of mind. In the humanizing effects of civilization they have indeed partaken, and, to some extent, in the diffusion of superficial knowledge, and are so far superior to their predecessors: but those predecessors were braced and nerved by the invigorating atmosphere of a barbarous age, and had all the virtues of a strong will and an energetic active mind, which their descendants are destitute of. For these qualities were not the fruits of an enlightened education skilfully pointed to that end, but of the peculiar position of the holders of power and that position is no longer the same. . . .

But the virtues which insecurity calls forth, ceased with insecurity itself. In a civilized age, though it may be difficult to *get*, it is very easy to *keep:* if a man does not earn what he gets before he gets it, he has little motive to earn it thereafter. The greater the power a man has upon these terms, the less he is likely to deserve it. Accordingly, as Mr HALLAM has remarked, Great Britain has had since WILLIAM III. no monarch of more than ordinary personal endowments; nor will she ever more, unless the chapter of accidents should open at a page inscribed with very singular characters. We may add, that the House of Peers has produced, since the same epoch, hardly any remarkable men; though some such have, from time to time, been aggregated to the order. As soon as these facts became manifest, it was easy to see a termination to hereditary monarchy and hereditary aristocracy: for we never shall again return to the age of violence and insecurity, when men were forced, whatever might be their taste for incapacity, to become men of talents in spite of themselves: and mankind will not always consent to allow a fat elderly gentleman to fill the first place, without insisting upon his doing something to deserve it. I do not undertake to say in what particular year hereditary distinctions will be abolished, nor do I say that I would vote for their abolition, if it were proposed now, in the existing state of society and opinion: but to the philosopher, who contemplates the past and future fortunes of mankind as one series, and who counts a generation or two for no more in marking the changes of the moral, than an age or two in those of the physical world, the ultimate fate of such distinctions is already decided.

1·15 THE GREAT NOBLES AND THEIR FUTURE

From J. L. Sanford and M. Townsend, The Great Governing Families of England, *2 vols. 1865, pp. 8–9, 14–20.*

Even a generation later not all would have agreed with Mill. The following analysis and the prophecy with which it ends are from the introduction to a collection of histories of thirty-one major noble houses.

The existence of a real and permanent aristocratic power in English politics, wielded by men whose numbers are by no means very great, is, I conceive, as certain as that of the people or the throne. With its merits or demerits I have at present nothing whatever to do. . . . The present purpose is analysis, and not argument, – to point out that even now, whatever a few thinkers may assert, the power of the aristocracy is still the most direct and constant of the five influences – the landlords, commerce, the priesthood, the press, and the population – which in quiet times direct the internal and external policy of Great Britain. It is, then, perhaps, worth while to define what the English 'aristocracy' really means. It is, I conceive, only another word for the greater owners of land. It has little to do with office, though that in England has been, and is, rarely held by very poor men. Still less has it to do with pedigree, though ancient birth may increase the influence which primarily belongs to property. The possession of estates by one house through a long series of years indefinitely increases the authority of that house, but it is from the influence of habit, not from any reverence paid to blood. . . . There is no pedigree in England, and very few in Europe, which can vie with that of the Earls of Devon – and, unlike most, it is not of heralds' manufacture – but an additional five thousand acres would represent five times the political influence derived from that descent. . . .

From the Act of Settlement to 1831, English history is but the record of the intrigues of the governing families; and when in 1832 the people deprived them of the legal autocracy they and their cousins possessed through their majority in Parliament, they bided their time, secure that in 'the long-run the influence of property was sure to tell'. It did tell. During the long peace which followed 1832 their property increased enormously; the ability the class has always displayed led them to take the lead in all productive enterprise; they reformed agriculture, opened mines, built great harbours, planted forests, cut canals, accepted and profited by the railway system, and built the faubourgs of the great cities. Able and audacious, still regarded with curious liking by the people, and full of that individuality, that sense of personal right, which is the strength of an aristocracy, they again threw themselves into politics, and speedily regained nearly their ancient monopoly of power. They alone could afford to follow politics from boyhood as a profession, and that fact gave and gives them a twenty years' start of all competitors. They alone have as a class that instinct of control given to able individuals in all classes, and they therefore speedily monopolised high offices. Above all, they alone had as a class not to be made known to the people. Smith must serve before a constituency knows who Smith is, but a Seymour's* name tells the same constituency all about him, his antecedents and his connections, his fortune and his tone. . . . So powerful has been the

* *Family name of the Dukes of Somerset.*

action of these circumstances, so engrained is in England the preference for these houses, that the thirty-one families whose histories we have related supply at this moment one clear fourth of the English House of Commons, the ultimate power in the State. A careful analysis shows that the thirty-one families at this moment supply one hundred and ten members, or a clear working fourth of the English section of the representation. . . . I believe it to be beyond all shadow of doubt that when we have added the great Irish and the great Scotch proprietors, it will be found that sixty families supply, and for generations have supplied, one-third of the House of Commons, one-third of the ultimate governing power for an Empire which includes a fourth of the human race. . . . The great houses have been, and to a large extent still are, to our political system what bones are to the body. Unseen, they have given strength and firmness to what might else have been a gelatinous mass. No king, or demagogue, or soldier has been able to mould the mass according to his own fancies because of these hard substances. . . . It is the disadvantage of aristocracy that all political ability not immediately connected with rank has a double task to perform – first to rise to the aristocratic level, then to persuade the people. It takes an able man twenty years to obtain from the nation the consideration these families obtain from birth, to put Jones at forty-five on a level with Cavendish at twenty-one. This is true not only of Parliament but of the services; and the consequence is, that three-fourths of the ability and courage and genius of the people is lost to the service of the State. A Wellesley is a general at thirty, a Havelock or Campbell wastes his life in rising to the point at which men think of making him a general. The consequence is, that unless England happens at any one moment to find a genius in the highest rank, she must either do without one, or content herself with one who comes from the mass, and has wasted half his power in raising himself above them. But for the fact that the great families sometimes adopt a man of striking ability, as they adopted Burke, Pitt, Peel in part, Sir Cornewall Lewis, and may yet adopt Mr Gladstone, this evil would, in the long-run, outweigh all the advantages of their power. . . .

Will the influence of these great families endure? The answer of most thinkers is that it will not – that the steady growth of the democratic idea has pulverised influences greater than theirs, and must ultimately pulverise them. I cannot feel so certain – cannot blind myself to the facts, that after Caesarism had crushed the Roman world to one uniform level of slavery, the patriciat had still a monopoly of regular administration; that in modern France the Faubourg St Germain still rules society; that in modern America it is a real help to a man to be born Adams, or Randolph, or Winthrop; that in this England of ours the abolition of the Upper House would instantly fill the Lower one with great Peers. Let the suffrage be universal, and Earl Derby stand for Lancashire, does any one know any Hodgson who would have a chance? . . . We are probably but on the threshold of commercial success, and of that vast enterprise it is they who always reap the first-fruits. No trade can flourish that for every pound does not pour a shilling into the treasury of a Grosvenor or a Bentinck, a Russell or a Stanley, a Neville or a Gower. They own the soil, and rental rises with wealth, as the surface of a field rises from successive deposits of guano. Every year, too, the pedestal on which they stand, the greatness of the Anglo-Saxon race, rises and spreads wider. In another hundred years these thirty-one families will be the marked and ticketed families among two hundred millions of English-speaking men, the only persons possessed of advantages to which ordinary men cannot attain, the only figures higher than that increasing crowd. A Percy, say, was great under the Tudors – that is, among two millions of half-civilised men. He is less now comparatively, but positively he stands socially above sixty millions of wholly civilised men, who are racking nature to find him means of gratification. His political power may decline, but his social power must increase. . . . Dukedoms may be abolished by the year 2000, – we pretend to no opinion on that point – perhaps no man save John Stuart Mill could give us even a reasonable prophecy: but of this we feel assured, that if they are not abolished an English Dukedom will in that year be a prize beyond all social compare – a prize such as the Throne is now – a position of the ultimate goal of all that is great, or ambitious or rich among a race which will by that time be ruling directly or indirectly over half the world.

1·16 THE CHANGING GENTRY

From Burke's Landed Gentry, *1952, Preface.*

Burke's Landed Gentry, the genealogical record of the British
Gentry for over 100 years, continued in 1921 to give the pedigrees
of families who during or after the First World War had sold their
estates. In subsequent editions its scope widened even further.
In doing so it was only taking account of the social changes which
had taken place.

When the first edition of the *Landed Gentry* was published in 1837,
it was described on the title page as the history of the 'Commoners
of Great Britain and Ireland enjoying territorial possessions or
high official rank but uninvested with heritable honours'. In his
preface the founder, John Burke, stated 'that in these pages will be
found the lineage of nearly four hundred families, enjoying in the
aggregate probably a revenue of two millions sterling, and deriving,
many of them, their territorial possessions from William of Nor-
mandy'. Every part of this statement has been changed by succeeding editors. There are now between four and five thousand
families in these pages, but only the tiniest minority of these
possess property derived from ancestors traceable at the Norman
Conquest.

The property qualification, however, remained unchanged up
to and including the 1914 edition. In the twelve editions between
1837 and 1914, no family was entered in the book unless it had a
considerable country estate. In the 1921 edition, on the other hand,
there are a number of entries in which the family is described as
'late of' or 'formerly of' their property. The First World War
caused national expenditure to jump from hundreds to thousands
of millions; those who held agricultural land and who had no
other financial resources were hit hardest by taxation and forced to
sell their estates. It seemed very inequitable that the loss of an
estate for economic reasons outside the owner's control should
exclude an interesting pedigree from the *Landed Gentry*. Once this
principle was established it received great extension in subsequent
editions. In 1937, perhaps a third of the entries were for families
which no longer owned land; in the present edition this proportion
may have risen to half.

Families which have recently acquired a landed estate are still coming into the *Landed Gentry* in large numbers. Any estate agent who deals with country properties can tell of properties ranging from 200 to 2,000 acres which often change hands. The whole attitude towards landed estates has changed. Whereas in John Burke's day the successful business man acquired an estate so that he might settle there, and his children and children's children after him, now an estate is bought purely for the benefit of the actual present owner. People do not look to posterity, present taxation will not let them.

Yet each of the recent editions has been larger than its predecessor, and the present volume extends to nearly 3,000 pages. It follows therefore that the book is becoming largely a pedigree record. There are few entries in the present edition in which the family is not traced beyond three generations. There has been a great awakening of genealogical interest in England in the last generation – it always existed in Scotland, Wales and Ireland – and it seems that pedigree-making is likely to extend now far beyond the old exclusive ranks of the county families.

1·17 THE BRITISH RAJ

From George Orwell, 'Shooting an Elephant', New Writing, 1st Series, No. 2, 1936 and reprinted in Selected Essays, Penguin Books, 1957, pp. 91–6.

There is a direct link between the squires and politicians of England a hundred years ago and the Burmese Police Officer forced to kill an elephant, formerly enraged but now no longer dangerous, in order to save face.

SHOOTING AN ELEPHANT

In Moulmein, in Lower Burma, I was hated by large numbers of people – the only time in my life that I have been important enough for this to happen to me. – I was subdivisional police officer of the town, and in an aimless, petty kind of way anti-European feeling was very bitter. No one had the guts to raise a riot, but if a European woman went through the bazaars alone somebody would probably spit betel juice over her dress. As a police officer I was an obvious target and was baited whenever it seemed safe to do so. . . .

All this was perplexing and upsetting. For at that time I had already made up my mind that imperialism was an evil thing and the sooner I chucked up my job and got out of it the better. Theoretically – and secretly, of course – I was all for the Burmese and all against their oppressors, the British. As for the job I was doing, I hated it more bitterly than I can perhaps make clear. . . . I was young and ill-educated and I had had to think out my problems in the utter silence that is imposed on every Englishman in the East. I did not even know that the British Empire is dying, still less did I know that it is a great deal better than the younger empires that are going to supplant it. All I knew was that I was stuck between my hatred of the empire I served and my rage against the evil-spirited little beasts who tried to make my job impossible. With one part of my mind I thought of the British Raj as an unbreakable tyranny, as something clamped down, in *saecula saeculorum*, upon the will of prostrate peoples; with another part I thought that the greatest joy in the world would be to drive a bayonet into a Buddhist priest's guts. Feelings like these are the normal by-products of imperialism; ask any Anglo-Indian official, if you can catch him off duty.

One day something happened which in a roundabout way was enlightening. It was a tiny incident in itself, but it gave me a better glimpse than I had had before of the real nature of imperialism – the real motives for which despotic governments act. Early one morning the sub-inspector at a police station the other end of the town rang me up on the phone and said that an elephant was ravaging the bazaar. Would I please come and do something about it? I did not know what I could do, but I wanted to see what was happening and I got on to a pony and started out. I took my rifle, an old .44 Winchester and much too small to kill an elephant, but I thought the noise might be useful *in terrorem*. Various Burmans stopped me on the way and told me about the elephant's doings. It was not, of course, a wild elephant, but a tame one which had gone 'must'. . . . It had already destroyed somebody's bamboo hut, killed a cow and raided some fruit-stalls and devoured the stock; also it had met the municipal rubbish van, and, when the driver jumped out and took to his heels, had turned the van over and inflicted violences upon it.

The Burmese sub-inspector and some Indian constables were waiting for me in the quarter where the elephant had been seen. It was a very poor quarter, a labyrinth of squalid bamboo huts, thatched with palm-leaf, winding all over a steep hillside. I remember that it was a cloudy, stuffy morning at the beginning of the rains. We began questioning the people as to where the elephant had gone, and, as usual, failed to get any definite information. That is invariably the case in the East; a story always sounds clear enough at a distance, but the nearer you get to the scene of events the vaguer it becomes. Some of the people said that the elephant had gone in one direction, some said that he had gone in another, some professed not even to have heard of any elephant. I had almost made up my mind that the whole story was a pack of lies, when we heard yells a little distance away. . . . I rounded the hut and saw a man's dead body sprawling in the mud. He was an Indian, a black Dravidian coolie, almost naked, and he could not have been dead many minutes. The people said that the elephant had come suddenly upon him round the corner of the hut, caught him with its trunk, put its foot on his back and ground him into the earth. This was the rainy season and the ground was soft, and his face had scored a trench a foot deep and a couple of yards long. He was lying on his belly with arms crucified and head sharply twisted to one side. His face was coated with mud, the eyes wide open, the teeth bared and grinning with an expression of unendurable agony. . . . As soon as I saw the dead man I sent an orderly to a friend's house near by to borrow an elephant rifle. I had already sent back the pony, not wanting it to go mad with fright and throw me if it smelt the elephant.

The orderly came back in a few minutes with a rifle and five cartridges, and meanwhile some Burmans had arrived and told us that the elephant was in the paddy fields below, only a few hundred yards away. As I started forward practically the whole population of the quarter flocked out of the houses and followed me. They had seen the rifle and were all shouting excitedly that I was going to shoot the elephant. They had not shown much interest in the elephant when he was merely ravaging their homes, but it was different now that he was going to be shot. It was a bit of fun to them, as it would be to an English crowd; besides they wanted the meat. It made me vaguely uneasy. I had no intention of shooting the elephant – I had merely sent for the rifle to defend myself if necessary – and it is always unnerving to have a crowd following you. I marched down the hill, looking and feeling a fool, with the rifle over my shoulder and an ever-growing army of people jostling at my heels. At the bottom, when you got away from the huts, there was a metalled road and beyond that a miry waste of paddy fields a thousand yards across, not yet ploughed but soggy from the first rains and dotted with coarse grass. The elephant was standing eight yards from the road, his left side towards us. He took not the slightest notice of the crowd's approach. He was tearing up bunches of grass, beating them against his knees to clean them and stuffing them into his mouth.

I had halted on the road. As soon as I saw the elephant I knew with perfect certainty that I ought not to shoot him. It is a serious matter to shoot a working elephant – it is comparable to destroying a huge and costly piece of machinery – and obviously one ought not to do it if it can possibly be avoided. And at that distance, peacefully eating, the elephant looked no more dangerous than a cow. . . . I did not in the least want to shoot him. I decided that I would watch him for a little while to make sure that he did not turn savage again, and then go home.

But at that moment I glanced round at the crowd that had followed me. It was an immense crowd, two thousand at the least and growing every minute. It blocked the road for a long distance on either side. I looked at the sea of yellow faces above the garish clothes – faces all happy and excited over this bit of fun, all certain that the elephant was going to be shot. They were watching me as they would watch a conjurer about to perform a trick. They did not like me, but with the magical rifle in my hands I was momentarily worth watching. And suddenly I realized that I should have to shoot the elephant after all. The people expected it of me and I had got to do it; I could feel their two thousand wills pressing me forward, irresistibly. And it was at this moment, as I stood there with the rifle in my hands, that I first grasped the hollowness, the futility of the white man's dominion in the East. Here was I, the white man with his gun, standing in front of the unarmed native crowd – seemingly the leading actor of the piece; but in reality I was only an absurd puppet pushed to and fro by the will of those yellow faces behind. I perceived in this moment that when the white man turns tyrant it is his own freedom that he destroys. He becomes a sort of hollow, posing dummy, the conventionalized figure of a sahib. For it is the condition of his rule that he shall spend his life in trying to impress the 'natives', and so in every crisis he has got to do what the 'natives' expect of him. He wears a

57

mask, and his face grows to fit it. I had got to shoot the elephant. I had committed myself to doing it when I sent for the rifle. A sahib has got to act like a sahib; he has got to appear resolute, to know his own mind and do definite things. To come all that way, rifle in hand, with two thousand people marching at my heels, and then to trail feebly away, having done nothing – no, that was impossible. The crowd would laugh at me. And my whole life, every white man's life in the East, was one long struggle not to be laughed at.

1·18 THE ÉLITE AS THE TRANSMITTERS OF CULTURE
From T. S. Eliot, Notes Towards the Definition of Culture, *1947, pp. 46–9.*

A late and sophisticated argument justifying a functional aristocracy as guardians of culture and tradition.

I have, in the preceding paragraphs, been speaking mainly of the 'governing class' and the 'governing élite'. But I must remind the reader again that in concerning ourselves with class *versus* élite, we are concerned with the total culture of a country, and that involves a good deal more than government. We can yield ourselves with some confidence to a governing élite, as the republican Romans surrendered power to dictators, so long as we have in view a *defined purpose* in a crisis – and a crisis may last a long time. . . . But, if we are looking for a way to select the right people to constitute every élite, for an indefinite future, by what mechanism are we to do this? If our 'purpose' is only to get the best people, in every walk of life, to the top, we lack a criterion of who are the best people; or, if we impose a criterion, it will have an oppressive effect upon novelty. The new work of genius, whether in art, science or philosophy, frequently meets with opposition.

All that concerns me at the moment is the question whether, by education alone, we can ensure the transmission of culture in a society in which some educationists appear indifferent to class distinctions, and from which some other educationists appear to want to remove class distinctions altogether. . . . In the society desired by some reformers, what the family can transmit will be limited to the minimum, especially if the child is to be . . . manipulated by a unified educational system 'from the cradle to the grave'. And unless the child is classified, by the officials who will have the task of sorting him out, as being just like his father, he will be brought up in a different – not necessarily a better, because all will be equally good, but a different – school environment, and trained on what the official opinion of the moment considers to be 'the genuinely democratic lines'. The élites, in consequence, will consist solely of individuals whose only common bond will be their professional interest: with no social cohesion, with no social continuity. They will be united only by a part, and that the most conscious part, of their personalities; they will meet like committees. The greater part of their 'culture' will be only what they share with all the other individuals composing their nation.

The case for a society with a class structure, the affirmation that it is, in some sense, the 'natural' society, is prejudiced if we allow ourselves to be hypnotised by the two contrasted terms *aristocracy* and *democracy*. The whole problem is falsified if we use these terms antithetically. What I have advanced is not a 'defence of aristocracy' – an emphasis upon the importance of one organ of society. Rather it is a plea on behalf of a form of society in which an aristocracy should have a peculiar and essential function, as peculiar and essential as the function of any other part of society. What is important is a structure of society in which there will be, from 'top' to 'bottom', a continuous gradation of cultural levels: it is important to remember that we should not consider the upper levels as possessing *more* culture than the lower, but as representing a more conscious culture and a greater specialisation of culture. I incline to believe that no true democracy can maintain itself unless it contains these different levels of culture. The levels of culture may also be seen as levels of power, to the extent that a smaller group at a higher level will have equal power with a larger group at a lower level; for it may be argued that complete equality means universal irresponsibility; and in such a society as I envisage, each individual would inherit greater or less responsibility towards the commonwealth, according to the position in society which he inherited – each class would have somewhat different responsibilities. A democracy in which everybody had an equal responsibility in everything would be oppressive for the conscientious and licentious for the rest.

2 Honours, rank and style of life

2·1 WHAT IS A PEER?

A poem, originally puplished in the Northern Star, *7th May, 1842*

WHAT IS A PEER?

What is a peer? A useless thing;
A costly toy, to please a king;
   A bauble near a throne;
A lump of animated clay;
A gaudy pageant of a day;
   An incubus; a drone!

What is a peer? A nation's curse –
A pauper on the public purse;
   Corruption's own jackal:
A haughty, domineering blade;
A cuckold at a masquerade;
   A dandy at a ball.

Ye butterflies, whom kings create;
Ye caterpillars of the state;
   Know that your time is near!
This moral learn from nature's plan,
That in creation God made man;
   But never made a peer.

2.2 TRUE GENTILITY

From 'Gentlemen', Cornhill Magazine, *1862, pp. 330–5.*

Whilst not insisting on a legal or genealogical definition of the word 'gentlemen', the anonymous author was convinced that agreeable social conduct, refined feeling and intellect are inevitably bound up with upper and middle class occupations and a degree of economic independence.

The characteristic moral distinctions by which society is as it were divided into two halves, are summed up in the one word 'Gentleman'. The division between those who are, and those who are not entitled to this appellation, is as real and important as it is indefinite. It may, therefore, be worth while, in the first place, to examine the proper meaning of the word. The original meaning of the word gentleman, which it has never entirely lost, was nearly, if not quite, the same as that of its French equivalent *gentilhomme*. It denoted the fact that the person to whom it was applied was a member of one of a certain set of families, or the holder of a certain definite official or professional rank. As these families and officials were supposed to be distinguished from the rest of the world by the degree in which they possessed particular qualities, physical, moral, and intellectual, the word came by degrees to denote the combination of the two sets of distinctions; and as people came to perceive that the moral and intellectual qualities were far the most important and distinctive, they learned to attribute to the word a moral rather than a personal meaning. Hence, in the present day, the word implies the combination of a certain degree of social rank with a certain amount of the qualities which the possession of such rank ought to imply; but there is a constantly increasing disposition to insist more upon the moral and less upon the social element of the word, and it is not impossible that in course of time its use may come to be altogether dissociated from any merely conventional distinction. . . .

Like many other words, the word gentleman, considered merely in its personal sense, is used upon a tacit assumption which must become express if its full meaning is to be understood. This tacit assumption is that the persons to whom the word applies form a body associated together for the sake of the pleasure which is to be derived from each other's society, and not for those more serious purposes which great associations of men, such as states, churches, armies, legislative and political bodies, and the like, are intended to promote. A man whose personal qualities fit him to take his place in such a society may properly, or at least intelligibly, be described as a gentleman, whatever else he may either have or want. It would be difficult, if not impossible, to give a complete list of the qualities which such a position implies, but they may be ranged under three great heads: some of them are artistic, some moral, and some intellectual: and of these the artistic qualities are the most definite, the most easily ascertained, and the most universally required. Thus it is equally inconsistent with the character of a gentleman to blow one's nose with one's fingers, to tell gross lies, or to be unable to read; but of the three offences the first is most obviously and most fundamentally irreconcilable with the character in question. Indeed the two others are ungentlemanlike principally, if not entirely, because of their inartistic nature. . . . Hence it follows that when we speak of a gentleman we do not mean either a good man, or a wise man, but a man socially pleasant and we consider his goodness and wisdom, his moral and intellectual qualities as relevant to his claims to be considered a gentleman only in so far as they contribute to his social pleasantness. . . .

It is a mere dream to suppose that so long as the differences of rank, which Mr Roebuck rightly considers essential to society continue to exist, there will not be an immense and indelible intellectual difference between the upper and the lower classes of society. It is just as absurd to suppose that the average labourer or mechanic will ever be intellectually equal to the average gentleman, as to suppose that the average gentleman will ever have the muscles of a man who works with his hands ten hours a day. The brain of a barrister in full practice will be as much more fully developed than the brain of a blacksmith, as the arm of the blacksmith will be better developed than the arm of the barrister. This distinction is by no means confined to the more intellectual professions, such as politics, the bar, or medicine. It extends to most of the social positions which, in common language, are described as conferring the rank of a gentleman, as compared with those which do not confer it. Whatever may be the faults of the comfortable classes in our community, no reasonable person will accuse them, as a body, of want of energy. There is hardly to be found amongst us such a thing as a really idle class. A country gentleman, for example, hunts and shoots, goes to magistrates' meetings, and to the quarter sessions, and finds an immense variety of occupations in the management of his estate and affairs. He is almost sure to be something of a lawyer, something of a farmer, and, in these days, very probably he is something of a soldier as well. At all events, as the head of a family, he has, like the Centurion, servants under him, and says 'to one man come, and he cometh, and to another go, and he goeth'. To this it must be added, that he has generally been educated up to the age of twenty-two or twenty-three at school or college. That such a person should not be intellectually superior to a man of the same natural gifts, who was taken from a school where he just learned to read and write, and to do elementary sums, at eleven or twelve years of age, and who since that time has passed his life in shoemaking or carpentering, is absurd. . . .

A man whose intellect is highly cultivated will, by that circumstance alone, be enabled to see more clearly the moral relation and significance of different actions, and to appreciate more fully the artistic merits of particular courses of conduct, than one who does not enjoy similar advantages. Hence the intellectual superiority which the higher ranks of society must always enjoy over the lower, will involve a corresponding superiority in reference to moral and artistic matters. A gentleman, as such, will probably have more delicate moral perceptions and better taste than the members of other classes, for this simple reason, that the superior cultivation of his understanding will have increased the strength and delicacy of all his perceptions, moral, intellectual, or artistic.

For these reasons there must always be an intellectual distinction between the higher and lower classes, corresponding to that distinction between the classes themselves which Mr Roebuck admits to be indispensable to the general welfare of society. . . .

2·3 HUMDRUM CASTLE

From Edwin Paxton Hood, The Age and Its Architects, *1850, pp. 182–6.*

A fictionalized account of life in and under the shadow of the manor.

I will confess, that as I have stepped through the chambers of Humdrum Castle, a feeling of awe for the antiquity of the spot has crept over me. As I have passed down its stately corridors and long galleries, and looked at the pictures of the fair and faultless ladies of the illustrious house, and the noble, stern, and richly clad men to whom they had given birth, I am not certain that it was a very democratic feeling that crept over me; and then the politeness, the courtesy of the heads of the house, these have very frequently almost converted me from my radical propensities. Very well do I remember once waiting on his lordship, with a note of introduction in reference to some matters of business. A tall handsome man stepped out from the breakfast room to meet me, and introduced me to the countess: I was invited to a vacant place and instantly made to feel myself at home. . . . Around me in the room were several selected portraits of some men who had spent their boyhood and youth there; – from that room had gone forth the men who had become bishops in the church, generals in the army, admirals in the navy, and chancellors on the bench. In my ignorance, I had imagined all lords to be ogres, with stars on their breasts, and all countesses to be sneering, scornful, stately beauties. That morning effected a great change. Listening with all deference to me, and inducing me to talk, before I left I had nearly made up my mind that it was possible for lords and ladies to be possessed of some humanity, and that generosity and gentleness might be found even among some of the members of the house of Humdrum. I was young then, and have learned to feel differently, and to prize innate humanity more. But I have often thought since, when I have heard some very loud in their vehement protestations of attachment to democracy, 'Ah friend, I wonder how *you* would feel if the Earl of Humdrum asked you to breakfast!' The most note-worthy circumstance in the town of Humdrum, and in its castle and family too, is the spirit of nogoishness. . . . Things go on very happily; the people do not desire that they should be different; the tradesmen find it to their advantage to hold their tongues; indeed, they are bound over by their half-yearly and annual accounts, to keep the peace, to hold no strange doctrines, to say no unpleasant things, to read no books at all, or only books without souls, to read no newspapers unless it be the 'Conservative Graball', or the 'Independent Fudge'. . . .

Allied to the family of Humdrum is, 'A gentleman and nobleman of the old school', the Earl of Fitzsham, retaining as much of the Squire Western about him as is possible in such a day as ours. He still boasts of being on easy and friendly terms with all the people on his estates: that is, he looks on his villages as kennels, where he keeps his dogs, and prides himself on spending a good part of the year (in all about three months,) on his estates in the country. To do him all justice, he is not pompous in his equipage or furniture, save on great occasions, when he makes an extraordinary glitter; but he is proud of his blood and his birth, and has more regard for the poorest peer, whose ignoble blood

'Has crept through scoundrels ever since the flood,'

than for the richest railway king whose father was a draper or a barber. He has an instinctive abhorrence and jealousy of all trade, tradesmen, manufacturers, or merchants; he looks on them askance, as if he thought them very suspicious characters, and somewhat unconstitutional. As to his religion, it is derived from the state, the only party he thinks that has any business to interfere with such matters. ... He hates mechanics' institutes, and the printing-press and newspapers almost as much, though he does sometimes subscribe for 200 or 300 copies of the 'Fitzsham Advertiser', or the 'Independent Fudge', when either has reported and re-edited his speech at the 'Agricultural Show', or the 'Annual Meeting of the Gentlemen of the Hunt'. He was educated at Oxford, where he learned to 'drink, tie cravats, and drive a tandem'. He is a magistrate, and thinks it incumbent upon him to make especial example of poachers. He is now and then in the House, but thinks it a 'confounded bore'; never doubts for a moment that the country is in a most awful state, and believes we don't know the mischief that those railways are doing to the agricultural interests. He has sense enough to know, that at any rate they are downright levellers. The place where he lives has for ages borne the beautiful and appropriate name of Fitzsham! situated in the county of Dumdrudge. When his lordship is at home the banner is seen flying from the castle turret. Dumdrudge gives the name to his lordship's eldest son, the young Lord Dumdrudge; and it is the boast of the family, that from time immemorial, Dumdrudge has given bishops to the church, generals to the army, admirals to the navy, lawyers to the bench, and ministers to the state.

2·4 THE ETHICS OF GAME

From the 13th Report *of the Commissioners of Inland Revenue* (*covering the period 1856–69*) *Vol. I, p. 66* (*Parliamentary Papers 1870, vol. XX*).

The duty for Game Licences in the year ended the 31st March, 1861, being that in which the rates of duty were reduced and the licences transferred to the Excise amounted to £129,841 and for this year ended the 31st March, 1869, to £168,448. The increase amounting to 30 per cent in the intervening period is, so far, satisfactory, but we regret to say that the evasion of this duty is very general, even among those, who, from their station in life, should be the first to discountenance such a violation of the law. The penalties attaching to pursuit of game without a certificate are made use of largely to punish poachers and we have no lack of information against that class of persons, but although we know as a fact that vast numbers of the better classes shoot without certificates, we rarely obtain evidence necessary for proceedings against them.

2·5 A DUCAL HOUSEHOLD

From G. Ticknor, Life of W. H. Prescott [*1863*], *1906, pp. 420–4.*

Prescott, the American historian, visited England in 1850. In a letter to his daughter he described a visit to Alnwick, the seat of the Duke of Northumberland.

The dining-room is very large, as you may imagine, to accommodate so many persons. There was a multitude of servants, and the liveries, blue, white, and gold, of the Duke were very rich. We had also our own servants to wait on us. The table was loaded with silver. Every plate was silver, and everything was blazing with the Northumberland arms. The crest is a lion, and you see the lion carved on the stone-work displayed in sugared ornaments on the table, in the gilt panelling of the rooms, &c. As you enter the town of Alnwick, a stone column some sixty feet high is seen, surmounted by a colossal lion, and four monsters of the same family in stone lie at its base. . . . After dinner, which was a great London dinner over again, we retreated to the drawing-room, where a concert was prepared for us, the musicians having been brought from London, three hundred miles distant. The room was hung round with full-length portraits of the Duke's ancestors, some of them in their robes of state, very showy. I went to bed in a circular room in one of the towers, with a window, shaped something like a rose, set into a wall from five to six feet thick. In the morning I waked up, and heard the deep tones of the old clock announcing seven. . . . As I looked out of the window, I saw myself to be truly in an old baronial fortress, with its dark walls, and towers gloomily mustered around it. On the turrets, in all directions, were stone figures of men, as large as life, with pikes, battle-axes, &c., leaning over the battlements, apparently in the act of defending the castle, – a most singular effect, and to be found only in one or two fortresses. . . .

At a quarter past nine the whole household assembled for prayers in the chapel, to the number, it might be, of over a hundred. Services were performed by the Duke's chaplain, and at parts of them every one knelt. Prayers in this way are read every morning in the English houses that I have seen, and, where there is no chaplain, by the master. It is an excellent usage, and does much for the domestic morals of England. From prayers we go to the breakfast-table, – an informal meal. After the breakfast the company disperses to ride, to walk, to read, &c. . . .

At seven o'clock again came the dinner, for which we dress as much as in town. One day we all dined – the men – at a public dinner of all the great tenant farmers in the county. The building was of boards and sail-cloth, and lighted with hundreds of gas-lights. There were about a thousand persons, and the Duke and his guests sat at a long table, raised above the others, and, as it ran crosswise also to these, it commanded the whole hall. It was an animated sight, especially as the galleries were filled with the ladies of the Castle and the County. I luckily had laid in a good lunch; for as to eating in such a scramble, it is hopeless. There was a good deal of speaking, and, among others, Lawrence did credit to himself and his country. . . .

On returning to the castle we found an informal dinner prepared for us, and in another room a superb dessert of cakes, ices, and

confectionery. The tables, both at breakfast and lunch, are orna-
mented with large vases of flowers of the most brilliant colours,
with clusters of white and purple grapes of mammoth size, pine-
apples, peaches, &c. . . .

Another day we went in to see the peasantry of the great tenants
dine, some sixteen hundred in number, or rather we saw them for
half an hour after dinner. The Duke and Duchess took the head
of the hall; and I thought the people, dressed in their best, to
whom the dinner was given, as they drank off healths to their
noble hosts, would have gone mad with enthusiasm. I nearly did
so from the noise. The Duke, on allusion to his wife, brought her
forward; and she bowed to the multitude. It was altogether a
pretty sight. Persons in their condition in England are obliged to
be early accustomed to take part in these *spectacles*, and none do
it better than our excellent host and hostess. They are extremely
beloved by their large tenantry, who are spread all over the County
of Northumberland.

The Duke has shown the greatest desire to promote the education and comfort of his peasantry. 'He wants us all to be comfortable', one of them said to me; and the consequence is he is universally beloved by them. Both he and his wife visit the poor
cottages constantly; and she has a large school of her own, in
which she assists in teaching the children. One of the prettiest
sights was the assembly of these children in one of the Castle
courts, making their processions in the order of their schools; that
of the Duchess being distinguished by green jackets. The Duke
and Duchess stood on the steps, and the little children, as they
passed, all made their bows and courtesies, a band playing all the
while. Afterwards came the feasting. It was a happy day for the
little urchins, – a visit to the Castle; and I am told there was no
such thing as getting any study out of them for days previous; –
and I will answer for it there will be none for days to come. . . .

2·6 THE COUNTRY HOUSE

From H. Taine, Notes on England *1957 (1872) pp. 147-50.*

Taine visited England in 1859 and again in 1871.

We have visited seven or eight gentlemen's parks, large or medium
sized, almost all very fine and two or three really admirable. The

perfect meadows shine under the sun and are richly covered with buttercups and daisies. The oaks are ancient and often enormous. Embanked and cared-for streams run in the little valleys and are made to form small lakes on which swim exotic ducks. Here and there, surrounded by a belt of gleaming water, rise small islands covered with rhododendrons flaunting their rose-pink sprays of flowers. Along the walls rabbits start from beneath our feet and, at every turn is a new vista of the undulating plain, dotted with clumps of trees, its whole scale of greens softening towards the blue of the horizon. . . .

The one which covers seven hundred acres has trees in it which two or even three men could not encompass with outstretched arms, oaks, limes, planes, cypresses [sic], yews, which have freely developed the fullness of their growth and forms. Isolated or in groups on the soft, rich meadowland they stand, their opulent pyramidal shapes or vast domes given ample room to spread, and often drooping to the very grass with a breadth and freedom which must be seen to be believed. They have been cared for like children of rich parents; they have always had full liberty to grow, all their needs catered for, nothing has ever checked their growth or hindered their luxuriance; they breathe the air and consume the soil like rich noblemen to whom that air and soil belong by right. . . .

The house itself is a huge mansion, indifferently pleasing, massive, the interior modernised. The furniture of the ground and first floors, recently bought to replace the old furniture, cost £4000. Three drawing-rooms, sixty feet long and twenty high, are furnished with tall looking-glasses, good pictures, some excellent engravings, and bookcases. In front of the house is a conservatory where they spend the afternoons in bad weather and where, even in winter, there is an illusion of spring-time. The rooms for any young girls among the house guests are fresh, light, virginal, papered white or blue, each with an assortment of pretty, feminine knick-knacks and delicate engravings, well suited to the amiable tenants of these rooms. For the rest, feeling for the picturesque in decoration and the overall plan and arrangement is less developed than with us: for instance, less attention is paid to matching of colours and articles of furniture. But grandeur and simplicity are not wanting, and there is no taste for overcrowding or bric-à-brac. They like large, bare surfaces and empty space, and the eyes are rested, there is room to breathe and walk about without fear of knocking into articles of furniture.

Great attention has been given to comfort, notable in all that concerns sleeping, washing and dressing accommodation. In my own room there is a carpet covering the whole floor, oil-cloth before the wash stand, matting along by the walls. Two dressing-tables, both with two drawers, the first provided with an adjustable looking-glass, the second with a large pitcher, a small one, and a medium-sized one for hot water, two porcelain basins, a brush rack, two soap-dishes, a carafe and glass and a bowl and glass. Below this a third toilet table, very low, with a pail, another basin and a large shallow zinc basin for one's morning ablutions. In a cupboard, a towel rail with four different kinds of towel, one very thick and fluffy.

Another, and indispensable cupboard or cabinet in the room, which is a marvel. Linen mats under every vessel or utensil; these alone, in an occupied house, must entail a permanent laundry. Three pairs of candle-sticks and candles, one set fixed to a small portable table. Wax and paper spills in pretty little tubs, pin-cushions full of pins, porcelain candle extinguishers and metal candle snuffers. Every attribute of the bed white, downy, perfect.

A servant waits on you in the room four times a day. In the morning to draw the curtains and blinds and open the inside shutters, take away shoes and clothes, and bring a large jug of hot water, and a linen mat for standing on; again at noon and at seven in the evening to bring water and so forth, so that the guest can wash for luncheon and dinner; and at night to shut the windows, turn down the bed, prepare the wash-stand, replace towels and other linen. It is all done with gravity, silence and respect. . . .

A number of these great houses* are historical: only by seeing them can one realise what inheritance from generation to generation can accumulate in the way of treasures, in a great family. I have been told of one in which, by a clause in the entail,† the owner is obliged to spend several thousand pounds a year on silver ware. After having crammed all the sideboards, they resorted to having the banister of the staircase made of solid silver. In the late Exhibition I saw a whole museum of valuable curios and *objets*

---

* Taine calls them *châteaux*. E.H. [Edward Hyams, translation.]

† *Une clause de l'institution*: literally 'in the appointment (of the heir)'. Whatever is meant, perhaps *entail* will serve. E.H.

d'art loaned by Lord Hertford. In 1848 the same nobleman, talking to a Frenchman who was a friend of his and was in serious difficulties, said,

'I have a place in Wales which I have never seen but they tell me it's very fine. A dinner for twelve is served there every day, and the carriage brought round to the door, in case I should arrive. It's the butler who eats the dinner. Go and settle down there; as you see, it will not cost me a farthing'.

. . . But I am forgetting myself. . . . The conclusion I have been aiming at is that these great hereditary fortunes are as if designed to preserve these and all treasures of beauty. After a number of generations a great house and park become a casket of gems.

2·7 *A RATE FOR RANK*

From J. B. Burke, Vicissitudes of Families. *2nd Series, 1860, pp. 6–7.*

In the two series published under the above title the genealogist gives pen-sketches of declining aristocratic family fortunes. In the preface he suggests means of preventing such sad occurrences.

I am inclined to think, that, in modern times, the main cause of the misery and deplorable fate that have happened to some of our most eminent families may be discovered in that part of the law of inheritance which, in the absence of direct heirs male, allows the estates to pass to an heiress, while the title to which they belong devolves on a collateral branch that may be equally devoid of wealth or education; in other words, the property goes to one line, and the dignity to another, incapable of supporting it.

I have always considered that it would be of infinite advantage if means could be devised for remedying the evil in some way or other. But for the immense difficulty of rendering, even by legislative enactment, real property perpetually inalienable, it might be well that the crown made it a *sine qua non* that every recipient of an hereditary title of honour should be required, before his patent could pass, to *endow* the dignity granted to him with a landed estate which could never afterwards be detached from it. A Baronet's qualification might be fixed at £500 a year in land, a Peer's at £2000. At any rate, a scheme like the following might be adopted. Each Peer or Baronet should be compelled, by statute, to contribute to government a proper sum (to be arrived at by actuarial estimate), so that out of the aggregate of such contributions, the administration of the day, or some public functionary, say the Lord Chancellor or Lord President, could allocate such annual payments, as it might be competent to pay, to Peers and Baronets in reduced circumstances, *for the maintenance of their dignity*. The great difficulty of all such legislation is to reconcile certainty of payment to, and enjoyment by, persons who are in debt, and whose property, whether in globo or annual, would, of necessity, be liable to claims of their creditors. There appears, however, a way of conscientious reconcilement arising from the consideration of the nature of public dignities, and the requirement of the public service. It has been held in numerous cases, that such stipends, the enjoyment of which is necessary *for the maintenance of the public dignity*, or for the furtherance of the public service, cannot be taken by the creditors of the holders. Consequently, all that need be assumed as an argument for such legislation is, that it is due to the public service and dignity that Peers and Baronets should always, as such, have the right to receive out of a fund, constituted as suggested above, such annual income for the maintenance of their respective rank and position. The statute might provide for this, by an enactment following out the understanding already admitted by the law.

In cases where honours have been won by personal achievement, and where the distinguished men, to whom such honours are given, have not the means to provide the required contributions, a power might be vested in the crown, to authorize a sufficient sum to be paid out of the exchequer to assist or enable a grantee of a peerage, or baronetcy conferred for *great public services*, to contribute the necessary sum to the fund.

2·8 ON THE DIGNITY OF A PEERAGE

From Hansard, *3rd Series, vol. 40, columns 291–4, 353–4, 355–9.*

The following extracts are taken from the debate in the House of Lords on the 'Wensleydale Peerage' case – the legality of the 'peerage for the duration of his life' which the government had decided to confer on Sir James Parke, a Judge of the Exchequer Court. Parke was old and childless and the limitation of his

Barony was deliberately meant to be a test case. The legal aspects of the case are irrelevant here, but it is interesting to see the light thrown by the debate on the character of a hereditary peerage. What possessions were needed to sustain it? How much did it raise the status of the family and not just the individual? If numbers of lawyers were to enter the House of Peers other groups would follow – as they surely did – and what would be the consequences?

The Government was defeated over this measure and Parke received an ordinary Peerage.

Earl Granville:

Let me illustrate my position, without making any invidious allusions, by the case of the noble and learned Lord I now see in his place [Lord Campbell]. Without making any impertinent inquiries as to his wealth, it is impossible to be unaware that my noble and learned Friend enjoyed a large and lucrative practice; that he possesses very extensive estates in Ireland; that he enjoys the advantage of having one of the few large houses in this town which has the aristocratic appendages of a court and a garden; and that he also has a son who has not shrunk from occupying a prominent position in public life. But imagine the converse of this. At the present moment – and such a fact would not detract in the least from his eminence as a lawyer and his greatness as a judge – my noble and learned Friend might have had no other resources than his salary as a judge; and if his son entertained a distaste for public life – as might possibly be the case, it would have been a hard thing upon Sir John Campbell, and a still harder thing upon this House, if we had been deprived of the advantage of his presence here. And now, my Lords, allow me to refer to the argument which the noble and learned Lord [Lord Lyndhurst] based upon the alleged dependence of this House upon the Crown should life peerages be created. Such an argument seems to me to require very little answer. The noble and learned Lord said that the subjects of such a creation would be subservient to the Crown, because they would be always looking to the Minister of the time being for an hereditary peerage. Now, if these individuals possessed fortune enough to sustain the dignity of an hereditary peerage – and without such a fortune any man must be a fool to wish for it – they would have an undoubted right to look for an advancement of this kind. But is this necessarily to render them servile in their character? Is there no similar influence at work in this House at this moment? Will any one tell me that there is not now in this House one single Lord who wishes to be a Viscount – no Viscount who wishes to be an Earl – no Earl who does not wish to be a Marquess, or Marquess a Duke? Is there not a single Duke who would like to have the knighthood of the Garter, or who would not feel rather hurt if the Lord Lieutenancy of his county were not given to him? And, then, will anybody pretend that those fair objects of ambition make Peers dependent upon a Ministry, or subservient to the Crown? . . .

Lord Campbell:

My Lords, I think it would be well to view the imperfections of this House with some tenderness, to recollect what it has done for public liberty, and not to endanger its existence till you are sure that a better can be found to supply its place.

My Lords, all who concur in these sentiments ought to condemn this measure. The power now claimed of making Peers for life cannot be confined to lawyers with a view to the decision of appeals. Before long it must necessarily be abused by unscrupulous ministers; and even what might be considered the legitimate use of it must inevitably put an end to the non-elective branch of the Legislature. If persons of merit from all classes, military, naval, mercantile, literary, and scientific, who cannot conveniently obtain seats in the other House, are to be introduced here, the selection of them will not, and I think ought not, to be left to the Minister of the day; the public would loudly and justly call out for another organic change by which the Members of the House of Lords might be elected by the people. How long would the Monarchy survive? It has been said, that we who deny this power are attacking the Prerogative and weakening the Throne. Let those who hold such language recollect the saying of Lord Bacon, 'To depress the nobility may make a King more absolute, but less safe'. . . .

If the proposed life-peerage system is established, henceforth no lawyer, however eminent he may have been as an advocate, whatever services he may have rendered to the state in the House of Commons, whatever fame or fortune he may have acquired, can aspire to an hereditary peerage, or to become the founder of a family. To make a distinction between the Chancellor and the Chief Justice – between one Chancellor or Chief Justice and another, when coming into this House, as to the tenure of their honours, would be intolerable. All must be under the same rule – 'no sons of theirs succeeding'. If this rule were to have a retrospective operation, about one-third of the present nobility of England, including Earls, Marquesses, and Dukes, would be degraded. But, my Lords, what I regard more is, that the change is an injustice to the middling and humbler ranks of society, to whom a prospect has hitherto been held out of mixing with the ancient nobility through the profession of the law. My Lords, by the favour of the Crown, for which I am most grateful, I am beyond any interest in this question for my own family; but I should have thought that I acted a sordid part if I had been contented with joining the band to whom hereditary honours are secured, delighting in the monopoly we are to enjoy, – and if I had assisted to kick down the ladder by which I myself have risen. . . .

Earl Grey:

There are two things which this House has to fear. One is, that its benches may become overcrowded by Peers not possessing adequate means for the maintenance of their rank; the other, that it may sometimes want among its Members a sufficient proportion of those who have raised themselves to the dignity of the peerage by their own talent and industry. It is absolutely essential to the continuance of the high character of this House that a certain number of those who obtain an hereditary seat in it should be raised to the dignity of the peerage for their services to the State; it is of the utmost importance that we should have men in the House of Lords who have distinguished themselves by their personal services. But I by no means think that this distinction should be exercised in favour of lawyers only. I think other descriptions of services – naval, military, and political – ought to be so rewarded – in my view the distinction should be extended to men who have distinguished themselves in every walk of life. . . . There may be men who are well fitted to take their places in this House who may have large families and small fortunes, quite sufficient for themselves, but who are nevertheless unable, with justice to their families, to leave such a fortune to the person who is to succeed to the peerage as might be desirable for the due maintenance of its rank and dignity. Yet that they are often so excluded is proved conclusively by the letter of Lord Eldon, which has been read this evening, which shows that an hereditary peerage has often proved an injury to the individual, and to the public. Men whom it is desirable to bring into this House may often possess means amply sufficient to support their rank during their own life, but from having only a life income or a numerous family to be provided for may be unable to accept an hereditary peerage, without injury to their family. In such cases, it would be most desirable to grant peerages for life only. I may be asked, are we then to refuse to grant hereditary honours as heretofore to those who have rendered distinguished services to their country? By no means. Those services have frequently been rendered by men who have acquired a fortune quite sufficient to make a provision for the peerage. In other cases, Parliament may be justified in making a sufficient provision for the person who receives the honour, and for his descendants. In all such cases, it is desirable that an hereditary peerage should be granted. It is of advantage that the titles of Marlborough, of Nelson, and of Wellington, should recall to distant generations the achievements of the great men by whom they were won, and of the glory they have gained for their country. But will any man tell me that it does not often happen that an hereditary peerage cannot be granted to persons who have a fair claim to it, because they have not sufficient means to maintain its dignity, while the Government of the day do not feel justified in asking Parliament to make a permanent provision for their descendants? In these cases, is it not an evil that admission to this House should be denied to them? The effect of creating peerages for life would be the more easily to open the doors of this House to men who it is desirable should be admitted.

2·9 HONOURS FOR SALE

From Hansard, *4th Series, vol. 156, columns 1791–4, 1815–8 (Debate of 17th July, 1922).*

The groups of industrialists, businessmen and *nouveaux riches* who were elevated to the peerage in increasing numbers from the 1880s onwards often owed their elevation not only to public munificence and charitable benefactions but also to more direct contributions to the coffers of one of the political parties. The borderline between selfless generosity and corruption is not always easy to draw and there is now little doubt that honours, particularly after the war, were increasingly 'for sale'. Parliament debated this issue repeatedly from the 1890s onwards. The following extracts are from the debate which finally led to the institution of a system of much stricter control over the award of political honours.

Lord Robert Cecil:

Let us be quite clear what it is that we are discussing today. We are discussing the popular belief that there is a certain amount of corruption in the way in which honours are given. That is the plain English of it. Do not let us underrate the importance of the charge. It is that subscriptions to party funds are given in order to obtain honours, and are successful in that object. That is the charge, and a very serious charge it is, as I am sure everyone in the House will agree. It is not merely a charge of discreditable practice, as the Prime Minister called it: it is a charge of actual corruption. It means not only the degradation of the honours themselves – and, personally, I think that that is a serious matter – but something much more serious. It means that someone or other, not necessarily the Prime Minister himself, but some of his advisers, are allowing their judgment and sense of official duty to be swayed by the transfer of money for a particular purpose, though that purpose may be unavowed. If that be allowed to continue, and if that impression be not corrected authoritatively, it must mean the increasing degradation of public life. . . .

I am not in the least in a position to know how far the general impression that some such practice does prevail, and has for some time prevailed, is right or not. Nor do I know whether it be true or not that it is getting worse, that it is getting more unashamed, more blatant. But that that impression exists now in the public mind it is simple folly for us in this House to deny. We know it. We hear, everyone of us who keeps his ears open, constant stories – very likely many of them quite untrue – and we observe the immense increase of honours during the last few years, which is not explained by the War. Putting aside all the War honours, you still have an enormous increase, and the increase is not accounted for by honours granted to soldiers and sailors. The great mass are what are called business men and politicians and, though I am by

77

no means prepared to say that neither of these classes should have honours. Yet it is not true that the increase of honours is accounted for by the War. Then, of course, we have the relatively few instances of gross miscarriages in these public functions in the recent peerages of which mention has been made. . . .

Lieut.-Commander Kenworthy:

The hon. and learned Member for Cambridge University [Mr Rawlinson] made the extraordinary statement that it did not matter very much if a gentleman, who was otherwise respectable, desired to pay a large sum of money in order that he might be ennobled. . . . You are not simply giving such a man a handle to his name and giving his children in perpetuity handles to their names. You are enabling him to become a legislator. You do not merely advance his social aspirations but you make him a hereditary legislator, with the power of hindering Measures passed by this House, and of initiating legislation in another place. If there is anything in the power of the House of Lords you make him into a person who for good or ill can alter the destinies of his country, and you do so for nothing more or less than a money payment. I think it scandalous that there should be even the suggestion that such a system is respectable or is to be defended. . . .

Mr Austen Chamberlain:

I am not the heir to an hereditary peerage. If I can control my fate, I shall be known to the end of my life by the title which I have borne from the beginning of it, and it may be that, being thus divorced from the aristocracy, I am not competent fully to share the deep feelings which stir the breast of the hon. and gallant Member. If I cannot share his feelings and cannot altogether understand them, it is hopeless for me to try to convert him, but I think I do understand the feelings of the ordinary Members of this House and of the public outside.

For twenty years or more, at intervals, questions have been raised as to the sale of honours or the grant of honours to unworthy recipients in return for contributions to party funds. I have heard more than one of those Debates. I have sometimes, sitting on that side of the House, thought there was a great deal in the criticisms that were brought forward. I have heard ugly rumours. I know enough not to believe ninety-nine one-hundredths of those rumours. I do not know enough to say that the one-hundredth may not be true, and, if it be true, it is a scandal. It is a scandal which it is in the interest of all of us to prevent. But even if it be not, and if there be no scandal, and the highest at which you can put your charge is that sometimes a mistake has been made. . . .

The great field of honours is not in challenge today. The honours given to the Services – the Army, Navy, the Air Force, the Departments of the Civil Service, the Colonial Service – those are not in question. The whole question is what is known as political honours. Now the backbone of the political list is the House of Commons itself. That, with one exception, to which I shall refer later, is not challenged. The service of the country in a party where we are organised as a party Government, the service of the country in Parliament as members of a party, is recognised as one of the claims to public honour, and I hope that it will continue to remain so. . . .

If my right hon. Friend the Patronage Secretary, or anyone else, tells me that so-and-so has been an active supporter of our party and a generous donor to our funds through his life, and I find him otherwise worthy of the honour which it is suggested he should have, the fact he has been such a generous donor would be to me, and has been to me in the short time during which I have had to deal with these matters, an additional recommendation. [*Interruption.*] I am speaking for myself, and should like to be quite frank with the House. Am I to say that, if a man gives a large contribution to a hospital, that is a claim to an honour; but that if he gives, through a long period of years, generous support to his party, that is no reason why I should consider him for a party honour – and political honours are all party honours? I say it is absurd.

2·10 SOCIAL SETS

From Beatrice Webb, Our Partnership, *1948, pp. 337–9.*

In contrasting two different sets of 'society', Beatrice Webb's account of two dinner parties in 1906 reveals more about her own, probably not unrepresentative, puritanical criticism of aristocratic behaviour than it does about any fundamental and socially significant divisions within these circles.

March 20th. – Two dinners, that well illustrated a subtle distinction of atmosphere – one at the Asquiths, the other at the George
Hamiltons. The former consisted of the Russian Ambassador, the
Desboroughs, Lord Goschen, the Dickson Poynders, Mrs Lowther
(the Speaker's wife), Lord Hugh Cecil, Mrs Lester (Mrs Corn-
wallis West's sister), one or two aristocratic young men, and the
Asquiths' daughter and Raymond. The large garish rooms, the
flunkeys and the superlatively good dinner, gave a sort of 'Second
Empire' setting to the entertainment. Lady Desborough, Margot,
Mrs Lester and Lady Dickson Poynder were all very *décolletée* and
highly-adorned with jewels. The conversation aimed at brilliancy –
Margot's sparkling little disjointed sayings, kindly and indiscreet,
Lady Desborough's somewhat artificial grace, Lady Dickson
Poynder's pretty folly, Mrs Lester's *outré* frankness, lending a sort
of stagyness to the talk; we might have all been characters brought
on to illustrate the ways of modern 'society' – a twentieth-century
Sheridan's play. They were all gushing over G.B.S., and I had to
entertain the ladies after dinner with a discourse on his philosophy
and personality – mostly the latter. We came away feeling half-
flattered that we had been asked, half-contemptuous of ourselves
for having gone. And not pleased with the entourage of a democratic
Minister.

Very different the George Hamiltons. Here the party consisted
of the Neville Lytteltons, Lady Arthur Russell, the Herbert
Jekylls, Sir Francis Mowatt – persons belonging to much the same
set as the Asquith party though of a dowdier hue. But the reception
in the cosy library was homely, and the dinner without pretentious-
ness – the George Hamiltons treating us as if we were part of a
family party – no attempt to shine, just talking about the things
that interested each of us in a quiet simple way. It would have been
almost impossible to show off, so absolutely sincere and quiet was
the tone. And yet the conversation was full of interest and lingered
willingly on each subject. After we ladies had left, Sidney said that
he listened with eager interest to a long interchange of official
experience between Lord George, Mowatt and Lyttelton, as to the
administration of the War Office and the relations between
Cabinet, War Minister and permanent staff – Jekyll and Sidney
listening and occasionally intervening. And, as we drove away, we
felt that we had had a restful evening, learnt something and gained
stimulus from the refinement and public spirit manifest in our

hosts and their guests. The Tory aristocrat and his wife were, in relation to their class, living the simple life; and the Yorkshire manufacturer's son was obviously 'swelling' it, to use the vulgar expression for a vulgar thing.

2·11 LIFE AT THE TOP OF THE TREE OF NOBILITY

From John, Duke of Bedford, Silver-Plated Spoon, *1959, pp. 8–9.*

The style of life here described was of course no longer typical for the twentieth century nobility.

My grandfather lived an extraordinary life. He had an income of well over two hundred thousand pounds a year and lived completely isolated from his contemporaries and the affairs of his times. His only concern was the administration of his estates. He regarded himself as something of an innovator in agriculture and forestry, and wrote one or two books on the subject which I believe are classic examples of how not to run such matters. He regarded it as modern and up-to-date to sell off landed property and buy stocks and shares because the return was greater. Unfortunately he picked such equities as Russian bonds and completely overlooked the possibilities of capital appreciation on land. Otherwise Woburn was run exactly as it had been since the eighteenth century. Even the means of getting there from London belonged to the stage-coach era. He maintained two large houses in Belgrave Square, both kept fully staffed, although I doubt if he was in them twice a year, usually to attend the meetings of the Zoological Society, of which he was the president.

He kept four cars and, I think, eight chauffeurs in town, eating their heads off. They were responsible for the first part of the journey down to the country of any guests. The town car used to take you as far as Hendon, where you had to get out and join the car which had been sent up from Woburn. You never travelled with your suitcase, that was not considered the thing to do. It had to come in another car, so you had a chauffeur and a footman with yourself, and a chauffeur and a footman with the suitcase, with another four to meet you. Eight people involved in moving one person from London to Woburn. This régime went right on until my grandfather died in 1940.

Sometimes, as an alternative, the oldest car, with the oldest chauffeur, would pick you up and deposit you at Euston, where he handed you a first-class ticket. At the other end, another great barouche would be waiting to take you to the house. There you were allotted your own personal footman, who stood behind your chair at meals, while a small army of another fifty or sixty indoor servants kept the archaic household going. My grandfather had refused to install central heating at Woburn except for the corridors, so that there were always seventy or eighty wood fires crackling throughout the Abbey in the winter, even in the bathrooms. . . .

There were still a number of oil lamps around and one man had the sole duty of trimming them and keeping them filled. They had tried to install electricity once in the early years of the century, but a section of the wiring had caught fire and they returned to primitive methods until not very long before I went there for the first time. . . . It seemed to have been installed in a very slap-dash fashion and I asked the estate electrician why it had been done so badly. He explained that my grandfather had never allowed any workmen to be seen in his presence, and when they were putting the wiring up the main staircase they had to post two men, one at the top and one at the bottom, to keep watch. If my grandfather appeared in the distance they all ducked into a cupboard until he had gone past.

3   Landownership

3·1 FRUITS AND FAILINGS OF FEUDALISM

From Thomas Carlyle, Past and Present, *1843, Book 3, ch. 8 and Book 4, ch. 1.*

Despite his opposition to the tenets of *laissez-faire* capitalism and what he regarded as the spurious claims of radicals and Chartists, Carlyle was no uncritical admirer of the performance of land-owners although an enthusiastic defender of the institution of a landed aristocracy.

It is well said 'Land is the right basis of an Aristocracy': whoever possesses the land he, more emphatically than any other, is the Governor, Viceking of the people on the Land. It is in these days, as it was in those days of Henry Plantagenet and Abbot Samson; as it will in all days be. The Land is *Mother* of us all; nourishes, shelters, gladdens lovingly, enriches us all; in how many ways, from our first wakening to our last sleep on her blessed mother-bosom does she, as will blessed mother-arms, enfold us all! . . .

I say you did *not* make the Land of England, and, by the posses-sion of it you *are* bound to furnish guidance and governance to England! That is the law of your position on this God's Earth; an everlasting act of Heaven's Parliament, not repealable in St Stephen's or elsewhere! True government and guidance; not no-government and *laissez-faire*; how much less *mis*-government and Corn-Law! . . .

What looks maddest, miserablest in these mad and miserable Corn-Laws is independent altogether of their effect on 'increase of trade' or any other such effect: it is the continual maddening proof they protrude into these faces of all men, that our Governing Class, called by God and Nature and the inflexible law of fact, either to do something towards government or to die and be abolished – have not yet learned even to sit still and do no mischief! . . .

That Feudal Aristocracy, I say, was no imaginary one. To a respectable degree, its *Jarls*, what we now call Earls, were *Strong-Ones* in fact as well as etymology, its Dukes *Leaders*; its Lords *Law-wards*. They did all the Soldiering and Police of the country, all the Judging, Law-making, even the Church-Extension; whatsoever in the way of Governing, of Guiding and Protecting could be done. It was a Land Aristocracy; it managed the Governing of this English People, and had the reaping of the Soil of England in return. It is, in many senses, the Law of Nature, this same Law of Feudalism; – no right Aristocracy but a Land one! Curious are invited to meditate upon it in these days. Soldiering, Police and Judging, Church-Extension, nay real Government and Guidance, all this was actually *done* by the Holders of the Land in return for their Land. How much of it is now done by them; done by anybody? Good Heavens, '*Laissez-faire*, Do ye nothing, eat your wages and sleep', is everywhere the passionate half-wise cry of this time; and they will not so much as do nothing, but must do mere Corn-Laws! We raise Fifty-two millions, from the general mass of us, to get our Governing done – or, alas, to get ourselves persuaded that it is done: and the 'peculiar burden of the Land' is to pay, not all this, but to pay, as I learn, one twenty-fourth part of all this. Our first Chartist Parliament, or Oliver *Redivivus*, you would say, will know where to lay the new taxes of England! – Or, alas, taxes? If we made the Holders of the Land pay every shilling still of the expense of Governing the Land, what were all that? The Land, by mere hired Governors, cannot be got governed. You cannot hire men to govern the Land: it is by a mission not contracted for in the Stock-Exchange, but felt in their own hearts as coming out of Heaven, that men can govern a Land. The mission of a Land Aristocracy is a *sacred* one, in both the senses of that old

84

word. The footing it stands on, at present, might give rise to
thoughts other than that of Corn-Laws.

3·2 CORN LAWS AND THE BURDEN OF LANDOWNERS

From Lord Milton (Earl Fitzwilliam), First, Second and
Third Addresses to the Landowners of England on the Corn
Laws, *New ed. 1839, pp. 4–5 and 14–15.*

Lord Milton attacks the Corn Laws and the claims of landlords that
their special responsibilities justify the artificial raising of the
price of corn.

The Corn Law is said to be just, because the landowner is liable
to charges, from which other classes of the people are exempt. He
alone is liable, it is said, to highway rates, to county rates, to poor
rates; in short, to all local taxation, and, *therefore*, it is just that
artificial means should be taken in order to raise the value of his
property. In this, as in every other argument, the truth of the
premises must be ascertained, before we admit the soundness of
the conclusion. In the first place, then, is it true, that the landowner alone is liable to all this local taxation? That, in a great
degree, it falls ultimately upon the *real property* of the country, no
doubt can be entertained; but there is a material difference between
its falling upon real property, and its falling upon land. *Land*, in
the sense in which only it can be used, in order to justify the conclusion in favour of the Corn Laws, means, that land only which
is employed in producing corn: but this is by no means the only
species of real property upon which these local charges fall. . . .
But it is said, that the land appropriated to the growth of corn
bears a larger proportion of these charges than the other species of
real property. That this may be the case, in some districts, will not
be disputed, but in others it is quite the reverse. Admitting, however (which I do not), that it is in the main true, it by no means
follows that the corn-growing land is entitled to any special favour.
The mere circumstance of the owners of this description of land
being the most extensive proprietors, is no argument for bestowing
upon us any peculiar protection. It is probably the cause of our
having obtained it; but may it not have been conceded to our

influence rather than to our arguments? Supposing it, however, to be just that compensation should be made to the landowner for the exclusive charges which the community is said to have thrown upon him . . . it will not follow that the compensation ought to be made by raising the prices of corn and of bread. . . . The high price of corn does not fall exclusively upon any peculiarly favoured classes; it falls upon the entire community, and not less upon the landowners and agriculturists than upon the other industrious classes. . . .

By some, however, I am told, that the charges upon the land-owners are heavy; that their estates are loaded with mortgages and family settlements; that they are called upon to maintain a certain state in the country; that, for these purposes, their rents must be kept up: and that, to keep up rents, corn must be dear. I hope that these difficulties of the landowner are exaggerated by imprudent advocates of the Corn Laws: for, depend upon it, no impartial judge can ever think that such arguments justify the imposition of a heavy tax upon the community. That the Corn Laws are a heavy tax, no man can doubt, nor that you yourselves pay a large portion of it. Do not flatter yourselves that you escape from this impost. Consider what are the habits of the landed gentry, from the smallest to the most extensive proprietors, who reside upon their estates, and derive their incomes from the rent of land occupied by others. Let each individual among you enter seriously upon this inquiry. Examine your respective expenditures in the gross, analyse them in detail, and you will find that the price of corn affects their amount most materially. The wages of your day labourers, whether employed upon the farm, or in the garden – the wages of your menial servants – the feeding of your dogs – of your horses – your travelling expenses – the repairs of your buildings, whether for use or recreation – the amount of all these, and other sources of expense, which form the great bulk of your annual outlay, whether upon a large or upon a small scale, is materially affected by the price of provisions. . . . I am far, however, from contending that you derive no advantage from extra prices, and their consequence, extra rents – you do derive an advantage, and an unjust advantage, from them. Its value, however, is not to be measured by the extra rent which you receive; it is only a portion of the extra rent which goes into your pockets, for while the extra rent is augmenting your receipts, the extra prices are augmenting your expenditure. The other classes of the community have no set-off against the injuries inflicted upon them by high prices; to them the loss is unaccompanied by the slightest compensation, so that the result of the modern Corn Laws is to confer only the fraction of a benefit upon one, and *that* the wealthiest class of the nation, and to do unmixed evil to every other class.

3·3 LANDLORD INTEREST

From Richard Cobden, Incorporate your Borough, A Letter to the Inhabitants of Manchester by a Radical Reformer (*1837*) *pp. 1–2*. (*Anonymous pamphlet by Cobden, republished in Wm. E. A. Axon*, Cobden as a Citizen, *1907*.) *See 4·8 for an account of its origin.*

Lord John Russell declared in the House of Commons a few days ago that the *landed interest* has, and ought to have, an ascendancy over the town populations in the parliamentary representation of the country; but he forgot to explain his meaning by the term *landed interest*. Let us try to supply the omission. There are the labourers on the soil, who constitute forty-nine out of fifty of the rural population; what influence has this vast majority ever possessed in the counsels of the empire? Consult the fires of Swing, the history of the Dorchester labourers, and the report of the new poor law commissioners, for an answer! The tenants-at-will form, probably, one in a hundred of the inhabitants of the agricultural districts, and the fifty pound Chandos clause has given to their landlords, I had almost said their *owners*, such a recognised property in their mockery of a franchise, that we no longer shudder when we see them, at a general election, marching by hundreds, like gangs of white slaves, to the hustings, to vote at the command of their tory drivers. Does Lord John mean that the opinions of these helots have any ascendancy in the legislature. No; for his lordship's term, *landed interest*, read the *landlord interest* – the interest of the aristocracy and squirearchy of the country, a body constituting not a fraction of one ten thousandth part of the entire community, as opposed to the just interest of the nation at large! The *landlord* interest, we are told, by its child and champion, the home-secretary, has a right to dominion over the towns, – this is a claim of very ancient standing. We read in history, that more than five hundred years since, the barbarous ancestors of these very same feudal landlords used to make excursions from their strong holds, to plunder, oppress, and ravage . . . the peaceable and industrious inhabitants of the towns; until at length, the Kings of England, . . . gave to the principal towns charters of corporation, or *co-operation*, which enabled their inhabitants to govern themselves, and protect their persons and property from such lordly depredators as chanced to inhabit the neighbouring baronial castles. The battle of our day is still against the aristocracy; and not the young and innocent occupant of the throne. The lords of Clumber, Belvoir, and Woburn, although they can no longer storm your town, and ransack your stores and shops, at the head of their mailed vassals, are as effectually plundering your manufacturers and their artizans; for, by the aid of their parchment votes and tenant-at-will serfs, they are still enabled to levy their infamous bread tax upon your industry. And must you tamely submit to this pillage, or, like your ancestors of old, will you not resist the aristocratic plunderers?

3·4 HEREDITARY LANDOWNERSHIP

From Hansard, *3rd Series, vol. 152, 1137–8, columns 1143–6, 1153–4, Debate of 2nd March 1859.*

Few issues in the discussion of questions related to land ownership allow one to focus on the whole issue of the relationship between landed property and the established social and political system better than the disposal of landed estates in cases of intestacies. While under such circumstances *real* estate was divided among the dependants, the law laid down that land was to pass undivided to the eldest son. Naturally this maxim only follows on the established practice concerning the succession to land. Most estates of any size were settled and passed in entail to the eldest son who held it as tenant for life for the benefit of his eldest son. In seeking to amend the law relating to intestacies the radicals who repeatedly moved this matter in Parliament in effect attacked the system of entail, while the defenders for their part upheld it as the basis of aristocratic power.

The Solicitor General (Sir Hugh Cairns): Hon. Members opposite said that . . . the present law as to descent was a wretched remnant of feudal policy; that it had its origin in fuedal times, and that before the fuedal times it was unknown in this country. His answer to that was, that he did not care what was its origin. He would grant that it had its origin in feudal times; but there could be no objection to it if it could be shown that it was in consonance with the present feeling of the country, accompanied as it was by what we had not under the feudal system, the freest power of disposition of property. No doubt, unaccompanied by that free power of disposition, a law which passed real property to the eldest son was a heavy grievance. But along with this law there had grown up two circumstances which entirely changed its character, this free power of disposition, and the accumulation of a mass of personal property, which was unknown in the feudal times, by which provision could be made, and by which the law made provision, for younger children. The consequence was, that whatever might have been the origin of the law, it had begun by justifying the dispositions made in conformity with it, and these dispositions in turn had engendered habits and produced a state of circumstances which had become in turn the justification of the law. Like everything else in nature, one thing had reacted upon another. The law had produced a certain state of feeling in society, and that state of feeling so produced had become in turn the justification of the law. But looking at it as a question of policy, what were the results which flowed from this law? In the first place, it harmonized with an hereditary monarchy and an hereditary peerage. In the next place, speaking of the principle of the law, not merely as it affected the disposition of the estates of intestates, but as manifested in the habits of the country with regard to entails and settlements, it tended to maintain a class in this country distinct from the aristocracy of mere wealth and the aristocracy produced – and rightly produced – by successful commercial enterprise. The law and the custom together, acting one upon the other, kept a class distinct, in consequence of their connection with the land, from those other classes who were of course in themselves as important elements as the aristocracy of the country. In the next place, this law and custom were favourable to the agriculture of the country. The tendency of this country, with regard both to agriculture and manufactures had been to undertake production on a large scale, and hon. Members opposite would not disagree with the doctrine of Mill, that wherever a people had once undertaken production on a large scale in agriculture, commerce, or manufactures, they would not willingly relinquish its advantages. Again, the law was most important in a social point of view. It kept families together by preserving the headship of families. The certain effect of a division of property such as that recommended was in the second generation to dwarf a family down to the rank of petty squires, and in the next generation to dwarf it to the condition of mere peasants. In the next place, while it preserved to them their social station and position, the law excited younger brothers to ambition and emulation in a manner that no other system in any country was ever known to do before. And, lastly, the benefit of it did not flow merely to the children of a family, but it stimulated the parent of the family also to make provision by frugality, economy, and industry for his younger branches, at the same time that it gave him the certainty of the importance of the family being preserved by the headship of his eldest son. . . .

Mr Robert Lowe : said that . . . there were generally two sets of considerations contemplated by the owners of real estate – namely, those relating to the family title and social position, which no doubt ought to have their due weight, and also those based on the natural affection which a man bore to his own children, and his wish to see them suitably provided for according to their station. . . . The point, however, which he wished to impress upon the House was, that this was in no degree a question of public policy. The State ought not to interfere with the distribution of estates, but should leave it perfectly optional with the owner. The dangers conjured up by the learned Solicitor General were purely chimerical, because it was wholly incredible that we who had enjoyed the power of freely disposing of our property should revert to the barbarous device of divesting the settlor or testator of that power and placing him under the control of the law. The point really was this, where a man, either by accident or design, had not availed himself of his right to make a will, was the law to make a will for him? And if so, what should that will be? In these two questions lay the whole gist of this discussion. His right hon. Friend answered them by saying it should be such a will as would be agreeable to the feelings and consonant with the will of the landed interest. The present state of our law with respect to land was the result of a series of conflicts in which the landed interest had invariably been on the illiberal side, and had as invariably been overborne and conquered by the feeling of the country as well as by the highly technical procedure of the Courts. The feeling of the landed interest ought no more to be decisive on this question than the feeling of the commercial interest ought to be decisive in a commercial question, or that of the legal profession in a legal question. . . .

It was felt on all hands that it was for the benefit of the family and for the advantage of agriculture that the property should be kept together; but it was also felt that provision should be made for the younger children. If the law charged the land for the benefit of the younger children, there would be no cause for complaint; but at present it committed a great injustice by giving all to the eldest son. The simple object of the Bill was to do what every honest and honourable man would do, and for that reason he should give it his support. . . .

Viscount Palmerston : said that . . . he objected to this Bill on every possible ground. The proposition contained in it was at variance with the habits, customs, and feelings of the people of this country, and incompatible with the maintenance of a constitutional monarchy. . . . He held that a constitutional monarchy required the existence of a landed aristocracy – by aristocracy meaning landed gentry, whether titled or untitled. Unless you had such a body, filling the intermediate place between the Crown and the bulk of the people a constitutional monarchy such as that in England could not in practice exist. The moment that body sunk into insignificance you lost the controlling and regulating power which was absolutely essential to the safe working of our representative institutions. We had seen that in other countries where the equal division of land prevailed the landed aristocracy, the landed gentry, had sunk into comparative insignificance, because the importance of the body must be the aggregate importance of the individuals who composed it. If you had a peerage and a gentry reduced to individual poverty it was impossible that they could exercise those functions in the State which were essential to the maintenance of a balance between the different Powers which composed the fabric of our representative constitution. He objected to the Bill, on that ground, and it was no answer to him to say that this measure would still leave a man the option of disposiing of his property as he pleased

by will. If it were true, as he believed it was, that a great constitutional principle was involved in the maintenance of landed
estates, you ought not to leave it to the accidental choice of the
landowner whether or not his property should descend in the
manner most adapted to the maintenance of our existing institutions.

3·5 OWNERSHIP OF LAND AND ITS EFFICIENT USE

From J. S. Mill, Principles of Political Economy, *6th ed.
1865, vol. I, pp. 286–91.*

After the repeal of the Corn Laws had broken some of the
monopolistic powers attached to land and at the same time had
reduced the prerogative of the landed proprietor, attention began
to focus on the economic consequences which followed from the
established system of landownership. The practice of entail,
supported by the special protection engaged by the landed estate
through the law of succession, was attacked as socially and economically undesirable. J. S. Mill went even further in advocating
State interference with the exercise of the rights of landownership
by advocating what could be regarded as nationalization of land.

The most flagrant condemnation of the landed system of the
time came from the situation in Ireland. When the *Principles of
Economy* were written shortly after the Irish Famine, Mill con-
demned the prevailing condition in the strongest terms. In subsequent editions (such as the one from which this extract is taken)
he did not leave out this paragraph, but inserted a footnote
pointing out that it had been written eighteen years before and
much had changed for the better.

In Great Britain, the landed proprietor is not unfrequently an
improver. But it cannot be said that he is generally so. And in the
majority of cases he grants the liberty of cultivation on such terms,
as to prevent improvements from being made by any one else. In
the southern parts of the island, as there are usually no leases,
permanent improvements can scarcely be made except by the
landlord's capital; accordingly the South, compared with the
North of England, and with the Lowlands of Scotland, is still
extremely backward in agricultural improvement. The truth is,
that any very general improvement of land by the landlords, is

hardly compatible with a law or custom of primogeniture. When the land goes wholly to the heir, it generally goes to him severed from the pecuniary resources which would enable him to improve it, the personal property being absorbed by the provision for younger children, and the land itself often heavily burthened for the same purpose. There is therefore but a small proportion of landlords who have the means of making expensive improvements, unless they do it with borrowed money, and by adding to the mortgages with which in most cases the land was already burthened when they received it. But the position of the owner of a deeply mortgaged estate is so precarious; economy is so unwelcome to one whose apparent fortune greatly exceeds his real means, and the vicissitudes of rent and price which only trench upon the margin of his income, are so formidable to one who can call little more than the margin his own, that it is no wonder if few landlords find themselves in a condition to make immediate sacrifices for the sake of future profit. Were they ever so much inclined, those alone can prudently do it, who have seriously studied the principles of scientific agriculture: and great landlords have seldom seriously studied anything. They might at least hold out inducements to the farmers to do what they will not or cannot do themselves; but even in granting leases, it is in England a general complaint that they tie up their tenants by covenants grounded on the practices of an obsolete and exploded agriculture; while most of them, by withholding leases altogether, and giving the farmer no guarantee of possession beyond a single harvest, keep the land on a footing little more favourable to improvement than in the time of our barbarous ancestors.

Landed property in England is thus very far from completely fulfilling the conditions which render its existence economically justifiable. But if insufficiently realized even in England, in Ireland those conditions are not complied with at all. With individual exceptions (some of them very honourable ones), the owners of Irish estates do nothing for the land but drain it of its produce. What has been epigrammatically said in the discussions on 'peculiar burthens' is literally true when applied to them; that the greatest 'burthen on land' is the landlords. Returning nothing to the soil, they consume its whole produce, minus the potatoes strictly necessary to keep the inhabitants from dying of famine;

93

and when they have any purpose of improvement, the preparatory step usually consists in not leaving even this pittance, but turning out the people to beggary if not to starvation.* When landed property has placed itself upon this footing it ceases to be defensible, and the time has come for making some new arrangement of the matter. . . .

Landed property is felt, even by those most tenacious of its rights, to be a different thing from other property; and where the bulk of the community have been disinherited of their share of it, and it has become the exclusive attribute of a small minority, men have generally tried to reconcile it, at least in theory, to their sense of justice, by endeavouring to attach duties to it, and erecting it into a sort of magistracy, either moral or legal. But if the state is at liberty to treat the possessors of land as public functionaries, it is only going one step further to say, that it is at liberty to discard them. The claim of the landowners to the land is altogether subordinate to the general policy of the state. The principle of property gives them no right to the land, but only a right to compensation for whatever portion of their interest in the land it may be the policy of the state to deprive them of. To that, their claim is indefeasible. It is due to landowners, and to owners of any property whatever, recognised as such by the state, that they should not be dispossessed of it without receiving its pecuniary value, or an annual income equal to what they derived from it. This is due on the general principles on which property rests . . . . When the property is of a kind to which peculiar affections attach themselves, the compensation ought to exceed a bare pecuniary equivalent. But, subject to this proviso, the state is at liberty to deal with landed property as the general interests of the community may require, even to the extent, if it so happen, of doing with the whole, what is done with a part whenever a bill is passed for a railroad or a new street. The community has too much at stake in the proper cultivation of the land, and in the conditions annexed to the occupancy of it, to leave these things to the discretion of a class of persons called landlords, when they have shown themselves unfit for the trust. The legislature, which if it pleased might convert the

---

* I must beg the reader to bear in mind that this paragraph was written eighteen years ago. So wonderful are the changes, both moral and economical, taking place in our age, that, without perpetually re-writing a work like the present, it is impossible to keep up with them.

whole body of landlords into fundholders or pensioners, might, *à fortiori*, commute the average receipts of Irish landowners into a fixed rent charge, and raise the tenants into proprietors; supposing always that the full market value of the land was tendered to the landlords, in case they preferred that to accepting the conditions proposed. . . .

To be allowed any exclusive right at all, over a portion of the common inheritance, while there are others who have no portion, is already a privilege. No quantity of movable goods which a person can acquire by his labour, prevents others from acquiring the like by the same means; but from the very nature of the case, whoever owns land, keeps others out of the enjoyment of it. The privilege, or monopoly, is only defensible as a necessary evil; it becomes an injustice when carried to any point to which the compensating good does not follow it.

For instance, the exclusive right to the land for purposes of cultivation does not imply an exclusive right to it for purposes of access; and no such right ought to be recognised, except to the extent necessary to protect the produce against damage, and the owner's privacy against invasion. The pretension of two Dukes to shut up a part of the Highlands, and exclude the rest of mankind from many square miles of mountain scenery to prevent disturbance to wild animals, is an abuse; it exceeds the legitimate bounds of the right of landed property. When land is not intended to be cultivated, no good reason can in general be given for its being private property at all; and if anyone is permitted to call it his, he ought to know that he holds it by sufferance of the community, and on an implied condition that his ownership, since it cannot possibly do them any good, at least shall not deprive them of any, which they could have derived from the land if it had been unappropriated. Even in the case of cultivated land, a man whom, though only one among millions, the law permits to hold thousands of acres as his single share, is not entitled to think that all this is given to him to use and abuse, and deal with as if it concerned nobody but himself. The rents or profits which he can obtain from it are at his sole disposal; but with regard to the land, in everything which he does with it, and in everything which he abstains from doing, he is morally bound, and should whenever the case admits be legally compelled, to make his interest and pleasure consistent with the public good. The species at large still retains, of its original claim to the soil of the planet which it inhabits, as much as is compatible with the purposes for which it has parted with the remainder.

3·6 VIRTUES AND VICES OF LANDLORDISM

From James Caird, English Agriculture in 1850–51, *1852, pp. 24–6, 98, 134–5.*

Caird was not only concerned with agricultural techniques and farmers' efficiency for he also shows how the attitude, policy, sagacity or rapaciousness of the landowner affect agricultural production and with it the well-being of the farming population – as these four examples from different counties show.

The first estate of great magnitude through which we pass [in Oxfordshire] is that of the Duke of Marlborough at Blenheim. From various causes very many of the farms on this estate are being surrendered to the Duke, who now holds under his immediate management somewhat more than 5000 acres of his own land. When his Grace succeeded to the property about ten years ago, the rents were very low, the land being generally underlet. From low rents, with probably indolent farming, the change appears to have been too sudden, and in consequence of an addition of a third being placed on the rental without the concomitant outlays to which landlords must generally submit for the accommodation of larger stock and the manufacture of heavier crops, many of the farmers left the estate, and those who remained, in very numerous cases, permitted their land to fall into a bad state of cultivation. Hard pushed by the times, with higher rents and lower prices, the little capital that remained has been rapidly diminishing; the Duke declines to make any abatement, and as soon as a farm is so completely reduced as to be untenable, it reverts to the landlord. The country exhibits a poverty-stricken and neglected look, and there is no confidence of a friendly or even feudal character between landlord and tenant. This is much to be regretted, as the farms are many of them very desirable in point of extent and quality, varying from 600 to 700 and 900 acres, and well adapted for green crop and stock farming. . . .

Great part of the land which forms the subject of this letter is let on yearly tenure. Farming is not, on the whole, carried on with any degree of spirit; and of this the farmers are themselves quite conscious. 'We are not farming', one of them said to us: 'we know that we are not farming; we are only taking out of the land what we can get from it at the least cost, as we don't know how long we may remain in possession, and have no security for what we might be disposed to invest in improved cultivation.' . . .

The mansion, which was formerly the seat of Lord Rivers, is of moderate size, and in rather a low situation, but the park which surrounds it is extensive and well wooded. The stream which flows through the grounds and the extent of woodland scenery make it very picturesque. But the stubborn nature of the soil renders this estate, as an agricultural property, expensive to improve. For many years his Grace [the Duke of Wellington] has laid out on its improvement nearly the whole amount of its rental. The same liberal expenditure on a kindly soil would have been tenfold more productive, but the true spirit of a benevolent landlord is the more strikingly displayed on a field where there can be so little return for it. It is delightful to his countrymen, among all classes of whom his Grace is, and ever will be, distinguished, as emphatically 'The Duke', to find that in the more private capacity of a landlord his duties are performed with the same wisdom, attention, and unswerving faithfulness, which have rendered his public character so exalted. . . .

In a county where this heavy soil predominates, it must be evident that great exertions are necessary to render its cultivation profitable. The landlords of Essex generally, however, do not cooperate with their tenants in carrying out permanent improvements. With few exceptions, they have shown complete indifference to agricultural enterprise, neither laying out capital themselves, nor offering such security as would induce their tenants to do so. They impose restrictive and ill-considered covenants even on their most intelligent tenants, and preserve their hedgerow timber with the utmost rigour. The 'root ditches', by which the farmer in some parts of the county cuts off the connection between the hedgerows and his fields, to prevent them from robbing his corn crops of their nutriment, are not allowed to be made on certain estates. An explanation of all this suicidal and unaccountable mismanagement, may be found in the fact, that the landed property in the county is incumbered with mortgage debts and other liabilities to the extent of half its value, while the proprietors are never-theless extremely tenacious of the influence which their position gives them over their tenants, and are afraid to entrust them with such security of tenure as might diminish that influence. These mortgages and embarrassments naturally throw the landlords into the hands of solicitors, who, having themselves no practical know-ledge of the subject, send down land valuers from London to fix the amount of rent to be charged. But that intelligent supervision, which the personal knowledge of either the proprietor or a duly qualified resident agent should give, is in such cases wholly wanting; and a tenantry who are encouraged neither by sympathy nor example, and who are positively obstructed in their voluntary efforts for improvement, soon lose the spirit of enterprise by which alone the difficulties of clay-land cultivation can be overcome. . . .

The Duke [of Bedford] then selects his tenant from the various applicants, and offers the farm to him at the rent fixed by the agent. It is generally accepted at once, and by a picked man. All the tenants have the option of, and are encouraged, to take leases subject to fluctuation in the price of corn. One half of the tenantry accepted leases of various duration – twelve, sixteen, and some twenty years. Those who prefer a fixed rent have shorter leases – seven or eight years, and then a readjustment of rent, according to prices. The rental of the estate at present is rather more than in 1834 and 1835, but a very large outlay has been made in improve-ments to maintain it. In some cases these improvements are equivalent to a reduction of 12 to 15 per cent. There is no system of general temporary abatements. If a complaint is made, the case is at once considered on its own merits, and, if requisite, the rent is readjusted. At the end of every lease a readjustment takes place. . . . Game is not preserved, and hedgerow timber injurious to the tenant is at once felled and removed.

A system of husbandry is prescribed to the tenantry, from which they are not permitted to deviate except by consent of the agent. On light land that system is the four-course; on strong land the same, with the substitution of beans in lieu of a portion of the clover, and such extent of dead fallow as may be necessary. On new land, much of which has been broken up in consequence of the Tithe Commutation Act, two white crops are allowed at the commencement. . . .

The comfortable accommodation and welfare of the labourers,

is a consideration with the Duke of Bedford not less important than equitable arrangements with his tenantry. Cottages are built in numbers sufficient to suit the wants of the different farms, with a due proportion for the mechanics also necessary. The cottages are situated near the farms on which their occupants are to be engaged. They are held directly from the Duke, from week to week so that both the labourer and the farmer are kept in some degree of check. Thus an ill-conducted labourer can be promptly dismissed from the estate, while a trifling jealousy or pique on the part of the farmer is not necessarily acquiesced in by the landlord. All the cottages have two rooms on the ground floor, and two or three sleeping apartments up stairs. They are fitted with kitchen range, and copper, – and one fireplace up stairs, – outbuildings for wood, ashes, and other conveniences, – and an oven common to each block of cottages.

3·7 THE ENGLISH LANDOWNERS IN IRELAND

From an Irish newspaper in 1865 reprinted by W. Steuart Trench in his Realities of Irish Life, *2nd ed. 1879, pp. 368–73.*

English absentee-landownership in Ireland showed the economic power of landlordism at its purest, and at the same time it provoked the most violent reaction in the form of rent boycotts and incendiarism. Trench was the agent of the Marquis of Bath in Ireland.

VISIT OF THE MARQUIS OF BATH TO HIS FARNEY ESTATE, IRELAND

'*Carrickmacross, Tuesday, May 16, 1865.*

'Today was what might aptly be termed a special carnival in the quaint old town of Carrickmacross. It being generally understood that this was the first visit of the Marquis of Bath to his estates in Ireland, nothing was spared on the part of the inhabitants and his tenantry of the surrounding country to render everything worthy of the occasion, and from the active preparations, which for some time past have been going on, it was evident that a true Irish welcome was in store for his lordship. Indeed to do justice to all parties concerned, the reception was one that cannot be forgotten by the noble stranger, for it was at once unmistakably cordial and sincere. From an early hour the town presented an appearance such as it rarely has occasion to do. The triumphal arches, with appropriate devices, the floating banners and gay streamers were looked upon by the old people with wondrous eyes, for it was not every day that such sights broke in upon their quietude. All joined, however, in the rejoicing, when it was known that their landlord, who had already endeared himself to them by his kind and benevolent actions, was about to pay his first visit to Ireland. . . .

'At four o'clock precisely, his lordship alighted at the Inniskeen railway station, and was received by W. Steuart Trench, Esq., and several other influential gentlemen. Having proceeded to the 'Broken Bridge' in a carriage and four handsome greys, the Marquis was met by his tenantry, who greeted him with loud cheers, and immediately formed into procession, marching into the town in great order. The scene was considerably enlivened by the performance of the musical band. The entrance into the town was one which was characterised by those marks of welcome which a loving people never fail to bestow on the deserving. At this time the streets were thronged to a great extent, so much so that in some parts there was scarcely room to pass. His lordship having adjourned for some time to Essex Castle, proceeded to the spacious Market Hall, where it was intended the address should be presented. The place was adorned with flags and festoons, and everything appeared appropriate to the occasion. At the head of the hall a throne was erected, and superb carpets were strewn on the floor. Shortly after six o'clock the noble Marquis entered, and immediately a large number of the people availed themselves of the space in the body of the room, where a hearty cheer had been kept up for a long time. . . .

'Thomas McEvoy Gartlan, Esq., then read the following address:

' "TO THE MOST HONOURABLE THE MARQUIS OF BATH.

' "We, the tenants of your lordship's estate in the Barony of Farney, Ireland, beg leave to assure you of the deep pleasure and gratification we feel at seeing you amongst us, and we offer you a cordial and respectful welcome.

' "The connection that we and our ancestors have had as tenants with your lordship and your noble house has been of long standing, and we trust it may continue uninterrupted, and with satisfaction and confidence on the part of both landlord and tenant.

' "We venture to believe that a personal knowledge of the character and condition of your tenantry and your estate may induce you to repeat your visit, and the fact of your lordship being allied to a family high amongst our Irish nobility tends to strengthen this hope.

' "Whilst surveying the fruits of your own liberality in the improvements which have been carried out by your agent, Mr Trench, with that energy and intelligence for which he is so eminent, we hope your lordship will also see cause to appreciate the improvements which have been effected, remotely as well as recently, both by our predecessors and ourselves, and we trust that in the present cultivation of the soil your lordship may recognise indications of industry and perseverance.

' "We have experienced from your lordship and your ancestors much kindly consideration, not only in the relations which subsist between us as landlord and tenants, but also in the ready response by which any claims for contribution to local purposes, charitable or otherwise, have been met; and thus, as well as in the liberal expenditure which you have directed to be made in the judicious improvement of your estate, your lordship, though absent, has not been unmindful that 'property has its duties as well as its rights'.

' "We sincerely hope that the cordial feelings of mutual kindness and confidence which now exist between your lordship and your tenantry may long continue to prevail; and again welcoming you to Farney, and tendering every kind wish for the welfare and happiness of yourself and your noble family.

' "We have the honour to be, my lord, your lordship's faithful friends and tenants.

' "Signed on behalf of the tenantry,
"THOMAS McE. GARTLAN
' *"Chairman of Public Meeting"*.

'His lordship replied as follows:–

' "Gentlemen, – I thank you for the kind welcome with which you have met me on this my first appearance amongst you.

' "I thank you for the respect with which you are pleased to speak of the memory of those who have gone before me.

' "I sincerely hope that the happy relations which at present subsist between me and my tenants may long continue on as satisfactory a footing as they now are; no effort on my part shall, I assure you, be wanting so to maintain them, and to deserve that good will and kind feeling with which you are now pleased to receive me. I regret that important engagements will render my stay here so short. I hope, however, before long to renew my visit and make that intimate acquaintance with the country and its inhabitants, which both so well deserve. . . .

' "I am glad that your testimony justifies the entire confidence which I have and do place in Mr Trench, whose character and abilities are too well known to need any praise of mine. I feel that during my necessary absence he has been a faithful representative of my wishes and intentions. In the management of affairs here, while protecting the interests of my property, he has been the advocate of just and liberal dealing with those who reside upon it, and has, I assure you, been ever most willing to bear testimony to all that the estate owes, to the past as well as present enterprise and industry of the tenants.

' "Again thanking you for the cordiality of your welcome, I trust that our mutual relations may long subsist on the friendly and pleasing footing I now find them."

'Mr Trench then introduced several of the tenantry to his lordship, who warmly shook hands with them, and expressed himself highly pleased with the reception which had been accorded to him.

'His lordship, accompanied by Mr Trench, then withdrew amid loud expressions of welcome.

'Shortly after nine o'clock the whole town was brilliantly illuminated. A series of fireworks were exhibited opposite the Court-house, and about half-past nine the town of Carrickmacross could be compared to nothing but a glare of dazzling splendour.

'When all had subsided the people retired with that order and decorum which had characterised the proceedings all through, proud in themselves at the reception which they had given to a worthy and benevolent landlord.'

3·8 OWNING LAND AND FARMING LAND
From The Economist, *24th October, 1857.*

The article published by *The Economist* under the above heading provides a fitting corrective to the picture of the improving and experimenting landowner which has so frequently been drawn.

It was with truth said during some anti-corn law debate, 'that a landowner is no more a farmer than a shipowner is a sailor'. Yet we constantly see men in virtue of ownership of land claiming to be regarded as leaders and instructors at agricultural meetings; while in other cases landowners are rated because they do not grace with their presence the local agricultural meetings which occur in the vicinity of their estates. In all this there is much confusion and error. A landowner drawing his income from his estate may, and occasionally does, take a practical interest in farming, but he is far more frequently like a man walking with his eyes open who sees not, or sees only through the mists of his own prejudices. He is devoted to game or field sports; or he is absent from his property three parts of the year, and leaves all details of management to his steward. He has far less knowledge of all that concerns farming and farmers, than the shipowner has of navigation and sailors. His interest depends far less on his own watchfulness.

Yet we find the great object of the managers of agricultural meetings is to obtain, if they can, some landowners of note to preside and talk at their dinners, and where they succeed, it is commonly to the exclusion of everything of interest to the practical farmer. But, in truth, save where they have some political object to promote or influence to uphold, the larger landholders seldom appear at the local agricultural associations. . . . But so far as husbandry is concerned, they might all and each of them just as well have said their say at a missionary meeting or a race or hunt dinner, or the soirée of a mechanics' institute. Their purpose and their talk were alike political. And such in fact is nearly ever the case where the landowners – the *Dii Majores* we mean – attend agricultural meetings. They simply hinder such meetings from being agricultural meetings at all. . . . When, as now, agriculture has been removed from the domain of politics, the landowners, as such, are for the most part out of place, they are out of their element, at agricultural meetings. All the questions now affecting

husbandry in this country are economical, and into such landowners do not enter kindly. . . .

Again, we find landowners blamed for absenting themselves
from local agricultural societies, and that even where they afford
support by subscriptions. Thus, at the Durham Society's meeting
. . . the absence of the great landed proprietors and gentry of the
county formed the subject of an indignant article by the *County
Advertiser*. It is said:–

'They have contributed liberally to its funds. Their names are
on its subscription lists. They are understood to approve, and to
"wish well", &c.; but as for attending its meetings – taking any
personal interest in its actual well-doing – showing any personal
respect for its conductors – that is quite another matter; that they
will not, and do not. Their money is given – their countenance,
their personal influence is utterly withheld. Whoever else may
think proper to dine and chat with farmer Hodge and farmer Hob-
nail, they will not. . . . How, and why, is this? Are the interests of
agriculture of no vital importance to agricultural proprietors? Is it
enough for them, and for all the purposes of their aid and countenance, to contribute an annual guinea, and say, "God speed the
plough"? Hitherto, for some reason, it has not pleased God that
the plough should speed so well in Durham as in the adjacent
counties. It has not pleased him that, with the exception of one
class of cattle breeding, our agriculture should take other than a
comparatively low standing. Will the landed proprietors elevate it –
will they improve matters – by shirking the only possible instrument of improvement, the only possible stimulus to improvement?
We fancy not. We may say, with perfect seriousness, that things go
ill with the agricultural world when its natural heads and chiefs
will not meet even to dine together once in twelve months – will
not give their personal and social countenance to what is intimately
connected with their own personal fortunes and social standing.'

Now all this is quite beside the real question at issue, namely,
how landlords can best promote the interests of agriculture? . . .
Let the stewards of great landowners attend the dinners, and they
may perhaps hear some wholesome matter from the farmers, but
their masters will be far more comfortable and useful elsewhere.
The business of a landowner – the management of land as property
in the best manner – is something quite distinct from farming. It
consists in rendering the land attractive to the best class of farmers,

the men of skill and capital, by means of permanent outlays combined with conditions of letting which are consistent with profitable farming. It is not by attending agricultural meetings and
talking about farming or anything else that the landowners will
learn to know something more of their own business than they are
commonly acquainted with.

3·9 LANDOWNERSHIP AND ENTREPRENEURSHIP

From James Caird, The Landed Interest and the Supply of
Food, *1878, pp. 102–4.*

In his concern to improve the nation's food supply Caird compares
the landowner with the businessman and finds him frequently
wanting in both managerial skill and commercial sense.

This knowledge of business is a matter of great moment to those
who employ so vast a capital as the English landowners, a capital
far beyond the entire value of our railways, mines, ironworks,
canals, and gasworks put together. Men of the highest capacity
with special training and qualifications, are employed in the
management of these. Constant watchfulness of the progress of
invention, by which large results may be obtained on a given
expenditure, is absolutely necessary to procure a profit in the
general competition. The landowners of large estates entrust the
management of their property to agents, more or less qualified,
many very capable, but often hampered by the pressing need of
their employer for the largest return of rental at the least cost. The
land-owner himself too seldom takes such an active and intelligent
interest in the details of management as would convince him of
the need to keep his farms in a similar state of high working order.
It is not with him really a question of business. Let us take, by
way of comparison, a manufacturer, merchant, or shipowner,
employing each a capital equal to that of a landowner who has a
rental of £5,000 a year. What would be thought of the prospects
of a woollen manufacturer who, without the slightest preparation
or special knowledge, embarked £100,000 in that business? Or of
a man who took over a mercantile concern of the same extent,
without having ever before written or read a business letter? Or of
a young military officer giving up his commission to take the

direction and responsibility of a great shipowning house? And yet this is in effect what is done every day by the majority of English landowners. They complain that the business so undertaken 'is not sufficiently lucrative to offer much attraction to capital'. And people are surprised that within the narrow limits of the British Isles, with a teeming, wealthy, meat-consuming people, so large a proportion of the cultivated land is still permitted to remain only partially productive.

3·10 PREDICAMENTS OF HEREDITARY LANDOWNERS

From S. G. Osborne, Letters to the Editor of The Times, *2 vols. 1890, vol. 2, 214–17. (Letter of 15th May, 1865.)*

The Reverend Sidney Godolphin Osborne had long championed the cause of the agricultural workers; his account of the problems facing the landowning class, from which he himself had sprung, though critical, does not lack sympathy.

I can understand a landed proprietor arguing after this fashion. I want to save every farthing I can to buy land to add to my estate, to put by portions for my daughters, to redeem the mortgages on the estates I bought last, to add the new wing to my house, to throw more small farms together, and have new homesteads for them. I therefore won't build a cottage so long as my tenants can get labourers from any other quarter. Or, I want space without population: villages are nuisances, the children pull the hedges, the labourers make paths and poach, there is always somebody begging for something, where there is a village; then there are fevers and things of that sort. Why should I create dwellings, when I want to avoid having dwellers? I offer wages and get the men for the day, they go home elsewhere at night. Because this is hard on these, am I to sacrifice my own view, and plant families about the place, to my own annoyance? This style of argument would, I fear, be credited, however little creditable; true, the great owning interest would rise as one man to repudiate it; but I fear the denial might only raise a smile, it would not carry conviction.

Again and again in my thirty years' experience of rural matters, have I heard agents to estates confess – that the demand made upon them to meet 'charges' which must be paid; the private expenditure of the owners, and the necessary repairs, left little if any margin for the expense of keeping up the property labour 'plant'; that the increased luxury in which owners live, the craving they have to enlarge their landed estates, does for ever act to preclude expenditure in cottage building, and make it sound policy to decrease cottages, to save rates, and avoid repairs. . . .

We have no right to expect landowners to be better than other men, but they have a status and many privileges which seem to demand they should not be worse. They are set on a hill, and a very high one; if they are looked up to they should repay the inspection their high position would seem to court – be examples of the use, not the abuse of wealth and the power it affords. It is my creed estate management will improve; wherever landed property falls into new hands we see it does so. Ancestral prejudices are venerable, but they have had their day. . . .

It is but fair to admit that the case of many a landowner is one calling for compassion. He suffers from the folly of those who have preceded him. He is over-housed and over-domesticed. His park and his gardens are the admiration of visitors, a source of cost to himself, ill-repaid by any pleasure or profit he derives from them. Additions have been made to the estate at a cost never yet repaid; there is an incessant cry for repairs, the land bought remains, the buildings are falling down. He has political influence to sustain at no little pecuniary cost. His position as an owner calls for a luxury of life the property owned is not equal to if it is to do its plain duty to itself. To retrench is to lose caste, to go on with the present expenditure can only be done by putting pressure where there can be no revolt. The labourers he is free to deal with as he will; there is a limit to tenant endurance. He, with other men, has paterfamiliar cares and taxation, but his are heavier than those of most men. The son and daughter question never sleeps with him. The payments to and for sons, present and prospective, admit of no alleviation; position has to be kept up; the successor must be educated, launched on the world, and married, with a view to proper qualification for the succession. Younger sons are expensive. Mothers require great outlay for many years on the fair wares of which they seek a fitting disposal. Every post brings appeals from estate claimants on the liberality it should show to the good objects of its several parishes.

3·11 ANCIENT FEUDALISM AND MODERN GAME PRESERVATION
From The Economist, *16 September 1865, p. 1118.*

> Nothing showed the seigneurial spirit of the owner of landed
> estate more than game rights. With the development of '*battue*
> shooting' the link between game preservation and sport became
> increasingly tenuous.

The spirit of feudalism is manifest in every part of our law of real
property, especially in that part which applies to landlords and
tenants, the great practical manifestation of that spirit is to be
found in the game system. It is the game to which landowners
seem to cling with unreasoning tenacity. It is the reservation of
game rights to the landlord, – by contract in England and by
force of law in the absence of special contract in Scotland, – which
more than anything else prevents the adoption of sound and
rational leases, and the application of true commercial principles
to contracts for the occupation of farms. And it is for the sake of
game that our landowners lose many opportunities for improvement of their property and their incomes. Why is this? The
apologists of game-preserving say it is for the sake of sport, that
British landowners are keen sportsmen, and cannot be blamed for
availing themselves of the opportunity of securing their sports
which the ownership of land affords. But this is not the truth, or
at all events, the whole truth; and in the majority of cases it is the
reverse of the truth. For it is the fact, that though game-preserving
has largely increased during the last forty or fifty years, sport in
connection with game has declined. Indeed, sport is inconsistent
with modern game-preserving. The essence of sport consists in a
certain degree of uncertainty in finding the game, in watching and
controlling the dogs, who are the sportsman's assistants, and in the
robust exercise which is one of the chief rewards of the sportsman.
But none of these things are incident to the *battue* and the game
preserve. The preserve must not be disturbed more than a few
days in the season, or the pheasants and perchance the hares
would wander into other preserves. Dogs are simply in the way of
battue shooting, where a little army of beaters drive the game across
the range of the effeminate shooters' guns; while the exercise
consists only in standing at certain points to which the game is

driven. Sometimes, in damp weather a board is provided on which the *robust* shooter stands, lest his feet should get damp!! In fact, game-preserving is more a matter of ostentation than sport. . . .

Now the influence of public opinion seems to be acting upon the landowners. We have had occasion to notice the action of the farmers, especially of the Scotch farmers, during the late elections, in reference to game. There can be no doubt that the evil of game-preserving has attained such a height, both in England and in Scotland, that it must be abated. It is utterly inconsistent not merely with the advancement of agriculture, but with the maintenance of husbandry at its actual standard, and both English and Scotch landowners will, in deference to public opinion or from a more rational view of their own interests, ere long find it necessary to abandon the German system of game preservation.

Mr J. Badenach Nicolson, of Glenbervie House, Kincardineshire, a Scotch landed proprietor, has in a seignorial sort of way given limited permission to his tenants to shoot hares and rabbits. The notice is so curious, and breathes so much of the feudal spirit in its tone and provisions, that (concession though it be) it illustrates so forcibly our remarks, that we give it entire:–

To the Tenants on Glenbervie, Mondynes, &c.

Most, if not all, of your leases bind you to protect the *game* upon your farms; but there is no express stipulation in any of your leases prohibiting the killing of rabbits. It is, however, the fact that most, if not all of you have abstained from killing rabbits as fully as if you had been expressly prohibited by your leases from doing so.

It is not Mrs Nicolson's intention to abandon the rights which the common law and her covenants with you give her over the wild animals to be found on the land in your occupation. But it is her wish to exercise these rights in the way least burdensome to you. With that view she proposes as follows:–

1. That each tenant shall be (himself) entitled to shoot rabbits at any time of the year, and on any part of his farm, arable or pasture.

2. That each tenant shall be entitled (himself) to shoot hares on the *arable* land of his farm, between 12th August and 1st March.

3. That wherever a tenant does not himself shoot, he shall be entitled to name one person to do so in his stead, such person being his own near relative, or in regular employment on the farm.

4. That Mrs Nicolson will, by her gamekeeper and otherwise aid her tenants in keeping down the hares and rabbits on their farms within such bounds as to prevent any one having just ground of complaint.

5. That this arrangement shall continue in force from 12th August, 1865, to 12th August, 1866.

3·12 'BAD' SQUIRES

From William Stubbs, Village Politics, *1878, pp. 153–8.*

William Stubbs, clergyman and historian, wrote this little tract at a time when the first stirrings of agricultural unionism made themselves felt.

THE LANDLORD

It would be possible, I am aware, to draw a picture of a vicious, selfish landlord, living in absolute idleness and luxury, callous to every social obligation which his property imposes. That there are such men, I fear, cannot be denied. . . .

But the 'bad squires', I am willing to allow, are the exceptions and not the rule. It is not so much, as it appears to me, in wilful viciousness or wastefulness of living that our typical English squire is apt to fail. It is rather in his ignorance, entirely vicious in its action, I grant, of what modern industrial society requires of him, that he is wanting. He is still too often clinging in the nine-teenth century to conceptions of landed property and its social duties which are more worthy of the twelfth. The straggling relics of feudal manners still hang about him. His principles of govern-ment are those of 'the beneficent-paternal-despotism' character. His theory of the true relations of rich and poor is that of protection on the one side, obedience on the other. Condescending bene-ficence and affectionate patronage on his part are to be met with grateful deference and loyal submission on the part of his depen-dants. It is not in the quantity of his sympathy, but in its quality, that he fails. He would do many excellent things for his labourers, it is true; he would build them cottages, he would educate their children, he would clothe the needy, he would feed the hungry, – but all these he does not do in the most excellent way. *The mercy of the squire's gift he will not forgo. It is the justice of the labourer's right that he cannot admit.*

I have no desire to depreciate altogether the graciousness of the feudal ideal. It has much about it, I do not deny, which is very seductive. Gratitude and devotion, obedience, docility, deferential awe, meekness, personal subjection, – all these are doubtless very excellent qualities in their place. But their place is not in the minds of the labouring class in an industrial age. Personal energy and self-help, independence, enterprise, vigour, thrift, – these are rather the qualities and the virtues upon which for the future we should wish popular well-being and well-doing to depend. The working men of our towns have long since come out of leading-strings. If their rural brethren are not yet quite so far advanced on the path of popular progress and freedom, they are certainly no longer children over whom paternal rights can with safety be asserted. More and more every day is it becoming evident, that if advice or sympathy or assistance is to be offered to them it must come, not as from the patron, but as from the friend. . . .

The old feudal order is giving place to the new economic one. The very basis and ground-work of this labour struggle of the last few years is that the epoch of charity in the rural districts is closed, and the industrial age has begun. It is useless, I say, to resist this change. The sensible course, as it appears to me, for a just landlord, is to accept that change as inevitable, and to use such moderating influence as he may possess to make the transition from the old to the new conditions as easy and gentle as possible.

3·13 THE NEW DOMESDAY

From J. Bateman, The Great Landowners of Britain and Ireland, *4th ed. 1883, pp. 144–5, 298–9, 495–8.*

The 'Returns of Landowners, 1873' published in three large folio volumes (Parliamentary Papers 1874, LXXII and 1876, LXXX) attempted to give a county by county analysis of the ownership of non-urban land. On the basis of these returns John Bateman attempted to construct an anatomy of landownership and especially a register of the large landowners, that is, those with estates of three thousand acres or more rented at three thousand pounds per annum upwards who owned forty-five per cent of all agricultural land between them, discounting waste land and land in the possession of public bodies. Some extracts from the register and tables from the appendices will serve to illustrate Bateman's findings.

MURRAY-DUNLOP, Mrs, of Corsock, Dalbeattie, N.B.

		acres	gross annual value
s. 1851, m. 1844.	Kirkcudbright	12,774	5,213

DUNMORE, Earl of, Dunmore, Stirling, N.B., &c.

		acres	gross annual value
Coll. Eton.	Inverness	74,000	2,339
Club. Guards, Carlton, Turf.	Stirling	4,620	8,072
b. 1841, s. 1845, m. 1866.		78,620	10,411

Served in Scots Fusilier Guards and as Lord in Waiting.
Without shooting rents and exclusive of 4,000l. for minerals.

DUNNE, The Misses (three), of Brittas, Conaslie, Q. Co., &c.

		acres	gross annual value
b. 187–, 187–, 187–, s. 1878.	Queen's Co.	9,215	2,833
	Roscommon	1,544	777
	Co. Dublin	583	725
		11,342	4,335

DUNRAVEN, Earl of, K.P., Adare Manor, Limerick, &c.

		acres	gross annual value
Coll. Ch. Ch. Oxon.	Glamorgan	23,751	23,974
Club. White's, Guards,	Gloucester	537	471
Windham, Garrick.	Limerick	14,298	10,814
b. 1841, s. 1871, m. 1869.	Co. Kerry	1,005	123
	Co. Clare	164	96
Served in 1st Life Guards.		39,755	35,478

The Gloucester property and land in Glamorgan, rented at 40l., are retd. as belonging to the Dowager Lady Dunraven (Lady Hylton).

DUNSANDLE and CLANCONAL, Lord, Dunsandle, Galway.

		acres	gross annual value
Club. Carlton, Kildare St.	Co. Galway	33,543	11,860
b. 1810, s. 1847, m. 1864.	Tipperary	3,514	5,333
Served in 11th Light Dragoons.			
		37,057	17,193

DUNSANY, Lord, Dunsany Castle, Navan.

Club. Carlton, Travellers',	Co. Meath	4,379	7,219
United Service.	Kilkenny	2,320	855
b. 1808, s. 1852, m. 1846.	Co. Cavan	31	26
Served in Royal Navy	Radnor	1,670	1,580
Vice-Admiral ret.)			
		8,400	9,680

DU PRÉ, Caledon George, of Wilton Park, Beaconsfield.

Coll. Eton, Ch. Ch. Ox.	Bucks.	6,876	10,500
Club. Carl., Cons., Trav.,			
b. 1803, s. 1870, m. 1833.			
Served in 1st Life Guards.	Sat for Bucks.		

DURHAM, Earl of, Lambton Castle, Durham.

Coll. Eton.	Durham	14,664	63,929
	Northumberland	15,807	7,742
b. 1855, s. 1879.			
Served in Coldstream Guards.		30,471	71,671

DUTTON, Hon. John Thomas, of Hinton House, Alresford.

Coll. Har., Ch. Ch. Ox.	Hants	5,124	6,970
b. 1810, s. 1862, m. 1836.			

All woods not included.

DUTTON, Hon. Ralph Heneage, of Timsbury Manor, Romsey.

Coll. Trinity, Cambridge.	Hants	3,470	4,436
Club. Athenaeum, Carlton.	Somerset	1,280	1,597
b. 1821, s. 1864, m. 1848.			
Sat for S. Hants and for Cirencester.		4,750	6,033

MANSFIELD, Earl of, K.T., Scone Palace, Perth, N.B., &c.

		acres	gross annual value
Coll. Westminster.	Perth	31,197	23,052
Club. Carlton, Travellers'.	Dumfries	14,342	13,389
b. 1806, s. 1840, m. 1829.	Clackmannan	1,705	1,751
Served as Lord High Com.	Fife	795	638
to the Kirk of Scotland,	Middlesex	539	730
and as a Lord of the	Derby	250	268
Treasury.	Cheshire	224	3,110
Sat for Aldboro', Wood-	Cumberland	22	30
stock, Norwich, and for			
Perthshire.		49,074	42,968

Exclusive of coals rented at 1,886l.

MANSFIELD, George Patrick Lattin, of Morristown Lattin, Naas, Co. Kildare.

		acres	value
Coll. Oscott.	Co. Kildare	4,542	3,709
Club. Kildare St., Dublin,	Waterford	1,097	708
St. George's.			
b. 1820, s. 1842, m. 1843.		5,639	4,417

MANVERS, Earl, Thoresby Park, Ollerton, &c.

		acres	value
Coll. Eton, Ch. Ch.	Notts	26,771	36,788
Oxon.	Lincoln	5,010	6,020
Club. Carl., Beac., Sal.	Derby	3,729	5,067
b. 1825, s. 1860, m. 1852.	Wilts	1,500	2,400
Sat for South Notts.	York, W.R.	1,026	1,374
		38,036	51,649

The Wilts figures are only approximate – the value does not include mines or tithe.

MAR and KELLIE, Earl of, Alloa Park, Alloa, N.B., &c.

		acres	value
Coll. Radley, Brase. Oxon.	Clackmannan	6,163	8,256
Club. Carlton, Jun. Carlton,	Fife	149	325
New Edinburgh.			
b. 1839, s. 1872 and 1875.		6,312	8,581
m. 1863.			

Exclusive of 5,320l. for mines, feu duties, &c.

MARJORIBANKS, Sir John, Bart., of Lees, Coldstream, N.B.

		acres	gross annual value
Coll. Eton, Ch. Ch. Oxon.	Berwick	3,332	6,063
Club. Carlton, Fine Arts.	Northumberland	820	850
b. 1830, s. 1834, m. 1858.			
		4,152	6,913

MARJORIBANKS, The Lady, Ladykirk, Berwick, N.B.

		acres	gross annual value
s. 1873, m. 1834.	Berwick	6,832	11,754

MARKER, Richard, of Combe, Honiton.

		acres	gross annual value
Coll. Harrow, Ch. Ch. Oxon.	Devon	6,527	6,833
Club. St. James's.	Dorset	804	644
b. 1835, s. 1865, m. 1865.	Somerset	128	270
		7,459	7,747

Including 380*l.* retd. in his mother's name.

MARLAY, Charles Brinsley, of Belvedere, Mullingar, Co. Westmeath, &c.

		acres	gross annual value
Coll. Eton, Trin. Cam.	Westmeath	9,059	5,766
Club. Trav., White's, Carl.	Louth	3,067	3,126
b. 1831, s. 1847.	Co. Cavan	1,668	929
	Limerick	453	428
	King's Co.	38	33
		14,285	10,282

APPENDICES

1. – *A Table showing the Distribution of the Area of the United Kingdom among the Great Landowners themselves, divided into Six Classes.*

Class 1	No. of persons holding 100,000 acres and upwards		44
,, 2	No. of persons holding between 50,000 and 100,000 acres		71
,, 3	No. of persons holding between 20,000 and 50,000 acres		299
,, 4	No. of persons holding between 10,000 and 20,000 acres		487
,, 5	No. of persons holding between 6,000 and 10,000 acres		617
,, 6	No. of persons holding between 3,000 and 6,000 acres		982
			2,500

This table excludes holders of large areas the rental of which does not reach 3,000*l*. . . . This and the following tables do not take in the Metropolitan area, the Isle of Man, or the Channel Islands, or the estate of the Hon. C. W. White.

Holders of between 2,000 and 3,000 acres, or of between 2,000*l*. and 3,000*l*. rental from estates of over 3,000 acres 1,320

This table, as well as Table 2, was compiled in 1879; the alterations which have since taken place in the distribution of English land would not materially alter it, or them. Some men have increased their wealth, or, in the expressive North country phrase, 'kept a-scrattin' of it together', while divers eminent firms of auctioneers have been kept busy dispensing the dirty acres of those more unfortunate or more lavish. In this the 'merrie month of May' chaos reigns in Ireland; in half that distracted kingdom the peasantry are now virtually owners of the soil, – paid for though it may have been, and in many cases was, with Saxon cash, the fruit of Saxon toil and industry. . . .

2. – *A Table showing the Landed Incomes of such of Her Majesty's Subjects as possess 3,000 acres rented at 3,000l. per annum and upwards, divided into Six Classes.*

Class 1	Landed incomes of 100,000*l*. and upwards		15
,, 2	Landed incomes of between 50,000*l*. and 100,000*l*. . . .		51
,, 3	Landed incomes of between 20,000*l*. and 50,000*l*.		259
,, 4	Landed incomes of between 10,000*l*. and 20,000*l*.		541
,, 5	Landed incomes of between 6,000*l*. and 10,000*l*.		702
,, 6	Landed incomes of between 3,000*l*. and 6,000*l*.		932

2,500

Holders of 2,000*l*. rental and below 3,000*l*. or under 3,000 acres 1,320

3·14 'GOOD' LANDLORDS

From The Daily News, *25 September and 4 October 1891, reprinted in* Life in Our Villages, *1891, pp. 106–15; quoted from M. A. Havinden, Estates Villages, Reading, 1966.*

This account of the Berkshire villages of Arcington and Lockinge, the property of Lord Wantage, makes clear the 'benevolent despotism' of the landowner whose estates comprise one or more villages and who largely controls and administers the estates' population. Lord Wantage's reply, from which an extract is also quoted, justifies his activities while refuting the charge of authoritarianism which the article makes.

One of the most interesting and instructive scenes of rural life in England may be found in the villages of Lockinge and Ardington ... I went over yesterday because two or three years back I understood that the owner of this vast estate was going to crown and complete the remarkable little social system he has created here, by admitting his people to a share in the profits of his farming, and I wished to learn a little about the result of it. In previous articles I have already dwelt upon the undisputed advantages of farming on a large scale with sufficient capital. Some at least of these advantages were obvious enough before I had gone far on to the estate. On scores of other farms I had seen thousands of acres of over-ripe corn still exposed to the caprices of this cold and rainy autumn. At Lockinge all was gathered in and stacked safe and sound in splendid-looking ricks; much of the land was already under heavy manuring, and not a little of it was ploughed up. Abundant capital, the finest appliances, and a full staff of men had enabled Lord Wantage to take advantage of every hour of fine weather. I understood that magnificent crops had been gathered in in fine condition, and the owner of the estate and his agent, Major Carter, both military men, were able to betake themselves to the German Manoeuvres, while small farmers all around were still struggling with their corn and growling at the weather. . . .

The estate is beautifully timbered; the cottages with their ornamental eaves and pointed gables, their fanciful chimney-stacks and pretty porches overgrown with ivy and roses, their grassy slopes and lawns and shrubs and flower-beds, all present innumerable points of view with which the artist would be enraptured. Every villager has, or may have, his allotment. There is an admirable reading room and a public house in charge of a salaried manager who has no interest whatever in pushing the sale of drink, but who is especially required to provide soup in winter, and tea and coffee and other non-intoxicants at all times. There is a first-rate cooperative store, with commodious premises, at which the people can get all the necessaries of life, clothes, grocery, bread, meat, and provisions, on profit-sharing terms. The bakery is a beautiful little place, with patent ovens and the newest machinery. In addition to all this, over a hundred villagers are employed in municipal workshops, so to speak – shops fitted with all kinds of the latest machinery and the best appliances – saw-mills, carpenters' shops, blacksmiths' shops, painters' shops, wheel-wrights' shops – all for the building and repairing and general maintenance of the property on the estate. There are two churches and an excellent school. In short, it is a little self-contained world in which nobody is idle, nobody is in absolute want, in which there is no squalor or hunger, while in the midst of it all is the great house of Lockinge, the beautiful home of Lord and Lady Wantage, always ready to play the part of benevolent friends to all who need their help, and who, indeed, by all accounts, seem sincerely desirous of promoting the happiness and well-being of their people. . . .

Having said so much in favour of this delightful Berkshire colony, it seems ungracious to turn round and declare that the whole thing is radically rotten and bad, and that the whole system of things here is another illustration of that 'model' village life which is merely another name for social and political death. Lord Wantage is not to be attacked. He stands high in the esteem of all his neighbours and friends – unless maybe some of the tradesmen in the little town of Wantage, who are naturally angry with co-operative supply stores – and he has most laudably and consistently carried his Conservative principles into action. Materially, the result on the face of it is delightful and as a means of keeping the control and management of the people by the aristocracy nothing could possibly be better. But for all the purposes of political life and social progress and human development it is utterly bad. Lord Wantage has done for the people, in the true spirit of benevolent Toryism, what the people ought to be able to do for themselves – not individually, of course, but collectively and unitedly, and by their own sturdy independent and manly effort. I don't know what Lord Wantage's personal wish may be with regard to the voting power of his own people but I am sure that those people themselves have no idea whatever that they are free electors. 'Any politicians here?' I asked an old man as I walked up the road with him through Lockinge. 'What's them?' said the man with a puzzled air. 'Politicians', I bawled, thinking the old man was a little deaf or very stupid – 'Politicians – you know what politicians are'. 'Be-em animals they goes out to shoot?' said the old fellow. Then I saw the waggish twinkle of his eyes that told me plainly enough he was only making a fool of me. He knew very well what politicians were, but he wasn't going to talk about such matters at Lockinge, and I couldn't induce him to. All around I heard Ardington and this village spoken of as a little political dead sea, in which no public opinion ever was known to manifest itself. Nobody would say that Lord Wantage was a man to exercise any improper influence on his people; but he is a strong Tory, has been a member of the Tory Government, his agents are Tories, and he owns all the land and houses, and can give or take away employment. I could not find anybody who knew of a political meeting having been held in these places. I heard it rumoured that there was one man who dared to avow himself a Liberal, but I couldn't find him. 'O yes, Sir', said a woman in the place, 'they all votes Lord Wantage's way, of course. It wouldn't do for 'em to go again 'im'. I am assured that the admirable little public house in Ardington is to a great extent a failure, because the men find that they are not free to talk there, and that whatever they say is liable to be carried by the birds to the agent's or bailiff's ears. The people are managed and governed and controlled without the least voice in their public and collective affairs, and, though they undoubtedly have strong opinions on certain matters, they dare not give expression to them. For instance, the people have allotments for growing their own vegetables, but they must not keep a pig. They have flower gardens in front of their cottages; if they don't keep them in order the bailiff will be down upon them. A labourer doesn't quite like his cottage; there is no possibility of shifting without the bailiff's consent and arrangement. 'They daren't blow their noses over at Ardington without the bailiff's leave,' said a labourer in the neighbourhood. The people control nothing, have no part whatever in anything like public life, nor any voice in matters directly affecting their own welfare. . . .

It has been said in your columns that it is easy to draw pleasant pictures of the condition of the agricultural worker under the care of a beneficent landlord. But why assume that such a condition can only be purchased at the expense of freedom to think and act for himself? The fact that we live in democratic days is no reason for disparaging and discouraging the legitimate influence landlords may exercise over their neighbours and tenants by helpful supervision and by friendly interest in their affairs which ought not, and which do not, interfere with the freedom of speech and liberty of action which are the right of all alike, of labourers as well as landlords. I am, Sir, your obedient servant,

Wantage'

3·15 THE CAUSES OF SALES OF ESTATES

From the Report of the Departmental Committee on Tenant Farmers and Sales of Estates. *Parliamentary Papers 1912/13, XLVII, p. 5.*

The Committee was set up by a Liberal Government opposed to landlordism and was concerned with improving the lot of the tenant farmer; its remarks on the position of the landowners started with a distinct bias against them.

6. The Committee are satisfied that there are an abnormal number of estates being broken up and sold at the present time. The Committee were informed that agricultural land to the value of one and a half million pounds was disposed of during 1910, whilst in 1911 the value of the agricultural land sold exceeded two million pounds. Moreover, there seems every indication that the tendency to break up the large agricultural estates is likely to continue.

7. In the opinion of the majority of the witnesses who appeared before the Committee, the increase in the number of agricultural estates, which have recently been offered for sale, is partly due to a feeling of apprehension among landowners as to the probable tendency of legislation and taxation in regard to land. Whether this feeling of apprehension is well founded or not, it undoubtedly does exist. It would appear that one of the primary causes of the want of confidence on the part of landlords, and their desire to sell the whole or portions of their agricultural estates, is the accumulation of and the fear of the effect of recent legislation, although no evidence was adduced that purely agricultural land has actually been injuriously affected by existing legislation, except by the death duties which are also applicable to personalty. From some of the evidence the Committee gather that any assurance with respect to future legislation would go a considerable way towards restoring confidence to landowners, thus resulting in the continuance of the system of land tenure, which, in the opinion of such witnesses, has worked admirably from the point of view of the tenant farmers of the country.

8. The Committee are disposed, however, to think that there may be other reasons which have been important factors in bringing a larger number of estates into the market. The evidence of some

of the witnesses goes to prove that, in certain parts of the country, land is at present let at rents below its present economic value. With a certain amount of increased agricultural prosperity and the consequent demand for agricultural land for occupation purposes, landlords might be disposed to increase rents, but many find it preferable to sell. Another reason may be found in the fact that many agricultural estates are mortgaged more or less heavily, and that, at present prices, a sale will often enable the vendor to pay off the mortgages and to retain an income in excess of what he has been receiving as owner of the land, and in other cases mortgagees are realising their securities.

9. The ownership of land entails heavy responsibilities, and, heretofore, landowners have, in many cases, been content with a comparatively small return on their capital, partly in consideration of the social position and amenities conferred by such ownership. Many owners, finding they are now in a position to sell to advantage, are relieving themselves of these responsibilities, and it is probably a combination of these reasons which have resulted in the increase in the number of estates which have been and are being offered for sale.

3·16 DEATH IN BATTLE AND DEATH DUTIES

From C. F. G. Masterman, England after the War, *1922, pp. 31–5.*

In the useless slaughter of the Guards on the Somme, or of the Rifle Brigade in Hooge Wood, half the great families of England, heirs of large estates and wealth, perished without a cry. These boys, who had been brought up with a prospect before them of every good material thing that life can give, died without complaint, often through the bungling of Generals, in a foreign land. And the British aristocracy perished, as they perished in the Wars of the Roses, or in fighting for their King in the great Civil War, or as the Southern aristocracy in America, in courage and high effort, and an epic of heroic sacrifice, which will be remembered so long as England endures.

There is taking place the greatest change which has ever occurred in the history of the land of England since the days of the

Norman Conquest: with the possible exception of the gigantic robberies of the Reformation. It is being effected, not by direct confiscation, but by enormous taxation, which is destroying the whole Feudal system as it extended practically but little changed from 1066 to 1914. Until now the land-owning class has always been able to absorb the intruders which came in with great wealth to obtain the prestige and amenities which belonged to ownership of great estates. Thus, in the eighteenth century, England saw the 'nabobs', who had plundered India, purchase or build great country houses, with acres which gave them possession of the tenants, the labourers, and of many seats in Parliament. Later came the wealth of the Sugar Islands. And then the big manufacturers and traders commenced to see how they could obtain enjoyment, bought titles, and renovated bankrupt estates, and passed from allegiance to Nonconformity into the broad bosom of the Church of England. . . . In return for all the money spent on improvements and sport and non-economic rents (for practically all the estates in Southern England were supported by incomes derived from outside), all that villages and farmers were asked to do was to vote for the nominee of their owners at infrequent elections, local or national; and most of them were very content to make the exchange, counting an infrequent vote as but of little importance in comparison with social comfort and liberal repairs, and the remission of rent in hard times. The system might have continued until the last aged labourer had been borne to his rest, and no one was left to till and dig and harvest the produce. But, with the most patriotic support to the Government in the great challenge of 1914, the Feudal system vanished in blood and fire, and the landed classes were consumed.

For it is impossible to imagine, in the vast changes now taking place, that much which is left of the old landed system will be able to assimilate the new owners. . . . I note that in one year one firm of auctioneers declare that they have disposed of the area of an English county. I note that sales are being announced every day in the newspapers, of an average of perhaps half a dozen of greater or lesser historic country houses, and of estates running into many thousands of acres. And wherever I have visited, up and down Southern England, I have come upon visible evidence of this transformation. The smaller squires went first, almost unnoticed, and with only occasional bitter complaint at passing from the homes of their ancestors to the suburbs or dingy flats of London or the villas of the salubrious watering-places. Then came the outraged cry of the owners of large historic estates, proclaiming that with the burden of income-tax and super-tax, and the fall in the value of securities, and the rise in the price of all estate necessities, they also would be compelled to relinquish the gigantic castles and houses which had been the pride of the countryside for hundreds of years. Their property perished in battle, no less than their children. They are not yet conscious of what has happened. They believe, many of them, that by borrowings and economies for a few years, better times will come with a return to something like 'normal' conditions. But there are no 'normal' conditions possible for them, for at least their generation, if not for ever. Their method of life has vanished as completely as that of the French Nobility after the march of the Revolution. Some new families may be founded by some rich men. But the greater number of these houses will become as the Châteaux and Castles of the Loire or the Indre; Chambord, a monstrous dead skeleton all cold and empty where once feasted and revelled beautiful women and gallant men. . . . Already the discussion has ceased to be academic. What use can the places be put to if no one can live in them: schools, centres for aerodromes, or convalescent homes for ex-soldiers or tuberculous children? Some of the smaller and less unwieldy are already turning into a kind of boarding-house, holding several families. . . .

There may be those who can rise to some sense of satisfaction, even at a transformation which has ejected them from the homes of their ancestors. After all, they have given property while others have given lives for the saving of England in a dark hour. They may feel pride in the thought that such houses may be used for beneficent purposes by the community long after they are dead, and neither destroyed nor put to some mean purpose. This is what they have 'given' in the 'Great War' – given, while other men have received increased wealth and emoluments by sharp contracts for munitions with a Government Department lax in cutting prices so long as the goods could be delivered speedily. The old generation passes with its children: the best of these children dead, the very type of its method of life, maintained for so long, vanished for ever.

3·17 THE ETHOS OF THE ESTATE AND ITS FUTURE

From The Times, *19 May 1920.*

> The war and the immediate post-war period was accompanied by the large-scale sale of landed property. A correspondent in *The Times*, in an article titled 'Changing Hands; A Note of Resignation', hoped that in the change of ownership the spirit of the place and the traditions of the Country House could still be preserved.

We all know it now. Not only from the advertisements, not only from various attractive little descriptive paragraphs, not only from the numerous notice-boards with which the countryside is disfigured, but from personal experience amongst our friends, if not actually of our own: 'England is changing hands'.

So far only the practical side of the matter seems to have attracted public attention; how much will such and such an estate sell for? Will a profiteer buy it? Will it be turned into a school or institution? Has the mansion house electric light and modern drainage? The world has apparently forgotten Mrs Hemans:–

> The stately homes of England,
> How beautiful they stand,
> Amidst their tall ancestral trees
> O'er all the pleasant land.

Some six years ago a shudder ran through the land at the thought of the possible defilement of those homes by alien hands; today the burden is not so heavy; the sacrifice is not indeed made into alien hands, but to fellow-countrymen more prosperous. True, money has been received in return, but that money is already earmarked.

For the most part the sacrifices are made in silence. 'The privileged classes', to use the old name, take it all for granted. It had to be. Only the background of their lives is gone. The historical associations need not be enumerated; they are all in the beautiful illustrated book to be had on application to the land agent. What will not be found there are the intangible things; the loving care the estate has received from each successive owner; how each in turn grew to know every nook and corner of his vast possession, from his earliest days when as a nursery child he played with the acorns under the trees, or later made adventurous expeditions on lake or river, or in adolescence shot over every corner, knowing the haunts of the wildfowl and the hare, or from the old-world stables (a feature of the place, *vide* the book) rode forth to the meet, his duty to the place ever before his mind. His very nurse would hold up to him as awful warnings the young ne'er-do-wells who had wasted their substance; the keeper as he taught him to handle his gun would encourage him to feel that this estate could, if properly managed, rear more pheasants and have a greater variety of game than any other of its size. The old coachman who had taught him to ride would prate of the various hunters bred on the place and of the racing stable where he had served as a lad, and so, as in Rudyard Kipling's 'Habitation Enforced', he would find himself hemmed round with safeguards as to the traditional way of living on his estate; and, most powerful influence of all, the example of his grey-haired father, eager for every detail of the day's run or sharing in the excitement of the 'hot corner' of the shoot, the pillar of the Bench, the unofficial adjuster of many a local grievance; and the gentle busy mother, knowing every detail of her establishment which she reigned over with her excellent housekeeper as viceroy, at home in every cottage on the place, unofficial dispenser of medicines and appealed to in every big trouble. The girls, bright-faced, busy young women, would have their classes for the village maidens, and be an ever present help when the question of their outfit for service loomed in the distance.

Now, such is the minor consequent tragedy of all we have gone through, all this busy intricate life must be swept away – 'England is changing hands'.

The sons perhaps are lying in far-away graves; the daughters, secretly mourning some one dearer than a brother, have taken up some definite work away from home, seeking thus to still their aching hearts, and the old people, knowing there is no son or near relative left to keep up the old traditions, or so crippled by necessary taxation that they know 'the boy' will never be able to carry on when they are gone, take the irrevocable step; the obliging agent appears, deferential, sympathetic, yet businesslike.

But it must not be assumed that those who have bought the birthrights will wilfully misuse them. What nobler use, for instance, could the old places serve than a school or institution, as the setting of the youth and energy of the future? Environment means much in education. Surely some old servitors will linger about to tell how it was in the old days?

And the newcomers must not be disappointed; at first it will be hard for them to realize how much personal work is needed to make a large or even a moderate-sized country house run smoothly, The mere engagement of a first-rate housekeeper and butler entrusted with the selection of the underservants, and a free hand as to wages, will not fulfil their new responsibilities. If they are eager (partly from a sense of patronage, partly from a desire to help others) to make efforts towards personal benevolence, they must not be surprised if at first they meet with a cold reception. With the demesne they have not purchased the humbler dwellers on it. Only let them beware of committing the unpardonable crime of not appreciating the wonderful treasure they have acquired. Let them really live in the old house for the greater part of the year, fit up the old nurseries (with all modern improvements if they will), but see to it that they are duly occupied by a troop of healthy happy children, not for the benefit of one or two poor little pampered mortals requiring the local practitioner's presence once a week as a matter of course.

There lies the clue to England's well-being in the future. Let the next generation blend the new ideals and aspirations with the old experience and traditions – then, though England will have changed hands, the old spirit will remain.

3·18 TAXATION AND THE BURDEN ON LANDOWNERSHIP

From the Central Landowners Association's Quarterly Circular, *February 1922, pp. 4–7.*

In a letter to the Chancellor of the Exchequer the Association, which counted the majority of landowners as members, protested at the heavy burden of tax and estate duties in which they saw not only the ruin of individual landowners but also a threat to the landowning class and to the institution of landownership as such.

Out of his net income the landowner has to face the upkeep of his house and grounds, abatements of rents, compensation paid to outgoing tenants, provision towards payment of Death Duties, outlay on improvements, and, in the majority of cases, jointures, family charges, interest at increased rates on mortgages, and donations and subscriptions incidental to ownership. All these items are necessary and unavoidable outgoings, with the result that heavy taxation is paid upon incomes which are frequently minus quantities.

In 1909, returns were obtained from 241 agricultural Estates, which showed that the average expenditure over the preceding five years on repairs and reinstatements necessary to maintain rents, amounted to 23·93 per cent of the gross rental. In 1919, which was an abnormal year, owing to scarcity of materials, and the difficulty of obtaining labour, the average expenditure on the accounts examined was 25·29 per cent, and in 1920, 35·85 per cent. As the post-war cost is $2\frac{1}{2}$ to 3 times the pre-war rate for such works of maintenance, these comparisons clearly indicate that agricultural Estates are not being maintained on the pre-war standard, the owners being unable to incur the expenditure. Depreciation of capital represented by buildings and other works is, therefore, proceeding at an abnormal rate. The capital represented by land and its equipment is immense, amounting to two-thirds of the total invested in the agricultural industry, and the depreciation of such a great national asset must inevitably affect the financial stability of the Country.

At no time was the investment of capital in agriculture more necessary than the present, the need for an increased production of home-grown foodstuffs having been so clearly demonstrated since the outbreak of War. But capital will not be attracted unless there is prospect of a fair return. . . .

It should be noted that the amount of interest which a landowner can charge on new works and improvements, more particularly where the expenditure is forced upon him to meet changes in agricultural practice, is limited by the letting value of the holding in the open market, and that, consequently, under existing conditions, such work cannot be undertaken.

Individual landowners in large numbers have, much against their inclination, been forced to sell their homes as the only alternative to insolvency, and it has been estimated by a competent authority that 700,000 acres of agricultural land have been disposed of annually for some time past. But, from the national standpoint, the real problem is left untouched, as the sales only mean transfer of ownership. Many of the new occupying-owners have been forced to borrow for the purpose of purchase, and their first experience of ownership under such heavy burdens is to find themselves without the necessary funds to work their land properly or to make any expenditure upon capital improvements.

The agricultural landowner without any outside resources is no longer able to maintain his position under the present overwhelming burden of taxation, and the existing scale of Death Duties. Many country houses which formerly supported a number of workers are being closed, with a consequent increase in unemployment, reduction in rateable values, and loss of local trade. The impression is spreading far and wide that agricultural property is a ruinous possession. The value of agricultural land is falling, and the fall has been accelerated by the provisions of the Agriculture Act, 1920, which gave the tenant additional security at the cost of the landlord. This depreciation, resulting in certain loss to the Exchequer, cannot be avoided so long as the present crushing and unequal burdens remain upon the land. . . .

We do not ask for any special favour for landowners. We recognise that we must share equally with others the burden of the Country's expenditure; but we are charged with the duty of presenting the case of the landowning class, which has done great service to the Country and has never failed it in an emergency. This class is now in imminent danger of complete destruction, and it is respectfully submitted that the burden of taxation upon agricultural land is unfair and confiscatory, and calls for immediate redress.

4 Interests, influence and elections

4·1 PERSONAL INFLUENCE

The documentation on the extent of political venality, proprietary boroughs, bribery, and undue influence is enormous. The evidence is not only of swaying voters by gifts of money or promises of favours but also of direct intimidation. Our records are of course the outcome of electoral contests; up to 1867 we find that in most elections the majority of the seats were uncontested, and even at the beginning of this century up to one quarter of MPs were returned unopposed. The power of individuals and of families was, therefore, often implicit rather than obvious for the electorate. Such contests as those described in the first extract were rather rare; the 'influence' to which Mr Justice Pickford refers on the whole approvingly in his trial of an election petition in 1910 was a rather late flowering of the species. The extracts published below cover almost a century. They are taken from the following sources:

4·1·1 T. H. B. Oldfield: *The Representative History of Great Britain and Ireland*, 4 vols. 1816, iv, p. 280.

4·1·2 *Hansard*, 3rd Series, V, 221–2 [1831] re the proposed disfranchisement of the borough of Minehead which included Dunter, the property of Mr Luttrell.

4·1·3 *Revolutions without bloodshed, or Reformation preferable to revolt* (1794). Reprinted in G. D. H. COLE and A. W. FILSON, *British Working Class Movements, Selected documents*, 1789–1875, 1951, p. 52.

4.1.4 *Parliamentary Papers*, 1868-9, VIII, Select Committee on Municipal Elections, Minutes of Evidence, p. 244.

4.1.5 *Parliamentary Papers*, 1910, LXXIII. Minutes of Proceedings on the Trial of the Parliamentary Election Petition for the Eastern Division of the County of Dorset, p.2 (from the Judgment of Mr Justice Lawrance).

4·1·1 *NORTHAMPTON TOWN CORPORATION*

It was incorporated by charter of King James I., *anno* 16—, and consists of a mayor, two bailiffs, a recorder, and 48 common-councilmen, out of whom the mayor is chosen, who is ever after reputed an alderman.

RIGHT OF ELECTION

April 26, 1665 – in the Inhabitant Householders not receiving alms.

Number of voters – 1,300.

Returning officer – the Mayor.

Patron – Marquis of Northampton, one member.

POLITICAL CHARACTER

This town presents us with the most violent contest for aristocratic pre-eminence that has taken place for the last century.

It happened at the general election in 1768, when the present Sir George Osborne, bart., was supported by his uncle, the late Earl of Halifax; Sir George Bridges Rodney, afterwards Lord Rodney, by the late Earl of Northampton, father of the present marquis; and the Hon. Thomas Howe, brother of the admiral, afterwards Earl Howe, supported by the late Earl Spencer. Sir George Osborne and Sir George Bridges Rodney were returned; but upon a petition to the House of Commons, the Hon. Thomas Howe and Sir G. B. Rodney were declared duly elected; and Sir George Osborne of course lost his seat.

The effects of this struggle were of such a tendency to the parties embarked in it, as to cause the estates of the Earl of Halifax to be sold soon after his death for the benefit of his creditors; the Earl of Northampton to live out of his native country; and the fortune of Earl Spencer to be considerably hurt. The enormous expenses with which this paroxym for power was accompanied, have since permitted the independent party to exercise their right to the election of one representative. . . .

4·1·2 DEBATE ON REFORM 1831

Mr *Luttrell* rose to express his heartfelt grief at seeing the rights of his constituents torn from them so unconstitutionally and so unjustly as they would be by this Bill. He considered also, that the rights given to him by his station in connection with the borough, were about to be violently and unjustifiably taken from him. The Representation of the borough had been in his family from generation to generation, and he considered it as his birthright. He denied the power of that House to deprive him of rights which he derived from the Constitution. If it could be so, then it also had the power of passing a law to take from him his castle. . . .

4·1·3 PAMPHLET OF 1794

Such are the changes which might take place were that reform of Parliament to be accomplished which the Duke of Richmond and Mr Pitt *once* recommended, and which those patriots who have been exiled from their ungrateful country, or are languishing in *Bastiles*, without power of obtaining a trial, have so constantly and intrepidly laboured to effect. Consider, Fellow-Citizens, whether these changes be desirable – if they be, then ask yourselves *if they* are to be expected from a House of Parliament whose journals bear the assertion, THAT THE SEATS IN THAT HOUSE ARE BOUGHT AND SOLD LIKE STANDINGS FOR CATTLE IN A FAIR – from an Assembly which, instead of being composed, as its name imports it should be, of the real representatives of the COMMONS of this kingdom, is disgraced by a band of men sent there by an ESTABLISHED System of Private PATRONAGE:– 306 out of 513 of its members being appointed by the TREASURY and 162 individual PEERS and rich BOROUGH MONGERS.

TRAITORS! TRAITORS! TRAITORS!

4·1·4 SELECT COMMITTEE ON MUNICIPAL ELECTIONS, 1868–69

6212. And are the great majority of the landowners Conservatives? – Nearly all Conservatives.

6213. Was there much coercion used at the last election by the landowners? – Very much indeed.

6214. In what way was it applied? – In every possible way that we can imagine; the shopkeepers having their custom withdrawn, officers removed from offices, and notices to quit to tenants, and congregations even turned out of the rooms in which they had been worshipping.

6215. Are you in a position to give any examples? – Yes.

6216. Will you first give examples, not of tenants receiving notices to quit, but other cases of coercion? – In some cases tradesmen have lost their customers.

6217. Has that been to any considerable extent? – To a very great extent. It is understood that Conservatives have coalesced together to withdraw their custom from every Liberal voter.

6218. And have those threats been carried into effect? – They have.

6219. Have any persons who had offices been dispossessed of them? – Yes; and they have had their salaries reduced.

6220. What kind of offices? – Assistant overseers, for instance.

6221. And you attribute that entirely to political causes? – Yes, altogether.

6222. Have any Dissenting congregations been turned out of the room in which they used to worship? – Yes, in two cases.

6223. Now will you turn your attention to notices to quit, which you say were sent to tenants; how many of those notices were served in the county of Cardigan? – It is understood that about 200 have been served.

6224. Have you had any special means of knowing that those notices have been served? – Yes; I have visited several parts of the county.

6225. Have you seen any of the notices? – Yes. I have seen many of them.

6226. Did not you make it your special business to ascertain those facts? – I did.

6227. You went all over the county, did you not, in order to make yourself personally conversant with the facts? – I went over nearly the whole of the county.

6228. Have those notices been served by nearly all the Conservative landlords? – By very nearly all.

6229. Is it generally supposed that they have acted in concert? – Yes, it is believed so.

6230. Were the notices served before the election or afterwards? – Afterwards; on the rent-day, the 25th of March; the election having taken place in November.

6231. How many of those notices were to tenant farmers? – I have found out about 30 or 35.

6232. Did those men all vote for the Liberal candidate? – They did, or they remained neutral.

6233. Can you give the Committee any examples without mentioning names, so far in detail that the Committee may understand the specific cases? – I have here a letter written by a landlord, dated the 4th of September 1868: 'Dear Sir, I have enclosed you your half-year's receipt for rent due the 25th March 1868, for which I am thankful to you. As there will be an election for Cardiganshire before Christmas I hope we shall vote the same side. We have been friends now for many years, and I hope we shall continue so'. Another letter followed from the same person to the same tenant.

6234. Had he received any letter in the interval from the tenant in answer to the first? – No.

6235. What is the date of the second letter? – This is dated in November last year, also previous to the election. 'Dear Sir, I have received a letter from Cardigan informing me that you are wavering in your opinion which side you will give your vote at the coming election. My opinion is that every man who is living on the property of the Church is bound to support it, otherwise he is a traitor to it; and, as you and Mr So-and-So and myself have now been friends for so many years I hope we shall continue so, and go to the poll and vote together, as I intend to be at the election'.

6236. Did the man vote? – Yes, against his landlord's wish, and he had notice to quit afterwards.

4·1·5 JUDGMENT ON ELECTION PETITION, 1910

Mr Justice Lawrance: In order to thoroughly appreciate this case which is, I need hardly say, of very great importance, I think perhaps the best thing that I can do, in the very few remarks I am going to make, will be, in the first place, in a very few words, to see what was the position of the parties on both sides at the time and before this election took place.

The history of the case, very shortly, is that up to the year 1904 the political position of the Wimborne family was that they were supporters of the Conservative cause. In 1904 they changed their opinions. Up to 1904 I rather gathered from a remark inadvertently dropped by Lady Wimborne, that she had something to do with an association, of which one heard in years gone by, called the Primrose League, she spoke of it as a Habitation. In 1904, of course, there was a change. Up to that date whatever proper influence might be brought to bear, and it would be a poor thing for the country if those possessing wealth, position, and so forth, should not exercise some influence upon those who are, I was going to say under them, but in these days one ought not even to say that, but subject to their influence, in those days, up to 1904, I suppose whatever influence could be exercised properly and fairly with regard to the neighbours and tenants of the Wimborne Estate, would be exercised in favour of the Conservative cause; but after 1904 the same influence would be exercised with regard to the opposite party.

4·2 A COUNT OF THE CONSTITUENCIES

From B. Pool (ed.), The Croker Papers, 1808–57, 1967, pp. 103–4.

Croker was a leading Tory journalist and in his capacity as the confidential adviser of the party's leaders, he was the nearest to a 'party manager' the Conservative Party could produce at the time. He is corresponding with Canning.

Croker to Canning   *April 3rd, 1827*

... I think it right to send you a memorandum which will show you, in one view, how impossible it is to do anything satisfactory towards a Government in this country without the help of the aristocracy. I know that you must be well aware of this, yet the following summary may not be useless to you, though I know that it is imperfect.

[*Enclosure*] Number of members returned to the House of Commons by the influence of some of the Peers:–

Tories – Lord Lonsdale 9, Lord Hertford 8, Duke of Rutland 6, Duke of Newcastle 5, Lord Yarbro' (for W. Holmes) 5, Lord Powis 4, Lord Falmouth 4, Lord Anglesey 4, Lord Aylesbury 4, Lord Radnor 3, Duke of Northumberland 4, Duke of Buccleuch 4, Marquis of Stalford 3, Duke of Bucks (2) 3, Lord Mount-Edgcumbe 4 – 70; besides at least twelve or fourteen who have each two seats, say 26 – 96.

Whigs – Lord Fitzwilliam 8, Lord Darlington 7, Duke of Devon 7, Duke of Norfolk 6, Lord Grosvenor 6, Duke of Bedford 4, Lord Carrington 4 – 42; with about half a dozen who have each a couple of seats, 12 – 54. . . .

Croker to Canning   [*Same date.*]

I really did not mean to attach any importance to the list of the aristocratical members, nor do I surmise that they have, at this moment, any peculiar influence with the King. . . . All I meant to do was to show how powerful the aristocracy is, and how necessary it is to have a fair proportion on the side of a Government. You will observe that I included the Whigs as well as the Tories. . . . I arrive at this conclusion . . . that the *old Tory* and the *steady Whig* aristocracies have at least 150 members in the House of Commons, not by influence or connection, but by direct nomination, and that no Government which did not divide them could stand for any length of time. I think the peers, &c., who are not either old Tories or old Whigs may have about a dozen members. . . .

Canning to Croker   *April 4th, 1827*

Your list is good for nothing without commentary. Add therefore, if you can, to these names the *price* that Government pays for their support, in Army, Navy, Church, and Law, Excise and Customs etc. And then calculate what number of unconnected votes the same price distributed amongst others would buy in the market if the Crown were free.

I send you a memorandum* which, I think, will surprise you.

---

* The memorandum showed that of 116 members returned by the Tory aristocracy 18 held political office, and of those 18 'no less than 12 are persons on whom the patrons confer that favour at the request of the Government'. Croker appears as one of the two office-holders in the eight seats for which Lord Hertford was patron.

The aristocracy, powerful as it is, does not enjoy any great share of political *office* in the House of Commons. So that, in fact, a Government has less to give them, than at first thoughts one would have supposed. . . .

4·3 *A LOCAL POLITICAL FAMILY*

From J. W. Lowther, Viscount Ullswater, A Speaker's Commentaries, 2 vols, 1925, I, pp. 10–14.

Lowther himself was MP for Penrith from 1886 to 1921. Many of his ancestors had sat for Westmorland constituencies. His family owned extensive areas of the county.

To turn now to an earlier generation of my family. My grandfather was Colonel Henry C. Lowther. . . . As a young man he had served in the Peninsular War and was in retreat to Corunna under Sir John Moore. . . . He first entered Parliament in 1812 as member for Westmorland. There he sat as a silent member, for fifty-five years, and became the 'Father of the House'. . . . His chief characteristics were extreme neatness, great punctuality and good manners. . . . He also suffered from . . . extreme diffidence in public speaking . . . when he was compelled by circumstances, to say a few words at a public banquet, his speech was limited to the one sentence 'least said, soonest mended'. . . .

The eldest of that generation was William, 2nd Earl of Lonsdale. . . . Though never a protagonist in the politics of the nineteenth century, he was always a firm supporter of Disraeli, was Postmaster General 1841–1845 and President of the Council in 1852. He was Lord Lieutenant of Cumberland and Westmorland, and took leading part in all the political life of those counties. He was a great art collector, buying much French furniture and many old Masters. . . .

The sisters of these two brothers were Lady Elizabeth, Lady Mary, Lady Anne and Lady Caroline Lowther.

Lady Mary married Lord Frederick Cavendish Bentick, youngest son of Henry, 3rd Duke of Portland, for many years M.P. for Whitehaven. . . . She held a considerable position in London Society, and had been offered, but had declined, the position of governess to King Edward VII when a boy.

Lady Anne married Sir John Beckett, a successful barrister, and at one time Attorney General. . . .

Lady Caroline was the most remarkable of the four sisters. She married in 1815 Lord William Powlett who became Duke of Cleveland in January 1864. Her reign as Duchess was short for he died in September 1864, but as Caroline, Duchess of Cleveland, she was a well-known figure in London Society for a great many years.

4·4 THE UNREFORMED HOUSE OF COMMONS

Table from John Wade (ed.), The Black Book, *1835, p. 626.*

Analysis of the House of Commons elected in 1830

Relations of peers	256
Placemen and pensioners	217
Officers in the army ..	89
Officers in the navy	24
Lawyers	54
East India interests	62
West India interests	35
Bankers	33
Agricultural interests	356
Miscellaneous	51

Many of the members belonged to several classes or interests, and have been enumerated in each, which swells the nominal number of individuals. It is apparent that the vast majority were connected with the Peerage, the Army, Navy, Courts of Law, Public Offices, and Colonies; and, in lieu of representing the People, only represented those interests over which it is the constitutional object of a real House of Commons to exercise a watchful and efficient control.

4·5 POLITICIANS AND THEIR REWARD

From Hansard, *3rd Series, vol. XXXVI (1837) columns 855–7, House of Commons.*

The traditional view that after the Reform Act of 1832 politics lost its connections with material rewards is slowly being revised.

The railway lobby is one of the most obvious expressions of the interplay between politics and business. Many of the railway MPs were members of the new entrepreneurial middle class but land-owners can be found among the ranks of railway directors.

[*Railways – Jobbing by Members*]

Mr Warburton, in conformity with the notice he had given on the preceding evening, rose to present two petitions to which he had adverted yesterday. The first was from the owners of land in Kent, and related to the Deptford and Dover Railway. There were three names appended to the petition, one of which he knew to be that of a most respectable individual. The amount of the capital of this projected company was 3,000,000*l*. There were various minor allegations contained in the petition, to which it would be un-necessary for him particularly to advert. . . .

The real complaint was contained in a short clause of the pe-tition, which he would read. He had stated, that the capital of the company was said to be 3,000,000*l*. Now, the House was aware, that by the standing orders, it was necessary to lay before the House a list of the subscribers to such undertakings, whose joint subscriptions amounted at least to fifty per cent of the estimated capital. . . . Now, what the petition alleged was, that those persons had no real interest in the undertaking, that they were, in fact, mere men of straw, whose names had been obtained previous to the list being delivered in, in order to make up the fifty per cent required by the orders of that House, before any progress could have been made with the Bill which was introduced. . . . There were other allegations in the petition, which showed that the affair had but too much the character of a bubble company; for it was stated that there were other persons of gambling habits, and no property, who appeared on the list as subscribers to the extent of 300,000*l*., in addition to the 224,900*l*. already alluded to. . . . He had mentioned yesterday that those petitions involved the names of some hon. Members of that House, in the transactions to which they referred; not that any direct charge was brought forward, but only that there appeared on the list of the provisional committee the names of certain Members of that House. The names men-tioned were those of Sir Andrew Leith Hay, and Mr Hesketh Fleetwood. There was no charge against those Gentlemen beyond that of culpable negligence in allowing their names to be connected with a body, the character of which they had not sufficiently ascertained. He entreated the House to consider the consequences of hon. Members of that House allowing their names to appear on the list of directors of Companies, the respectability of which they had not sufficiently investigated. These were the gaudy flies which hid the barb by which the public were hooked and caught. He, therefore, entreated the House to grant him a Committee to investigate the whole matter, that hon. Members and the public might know the consequences which followed from allowing their names to be connected with such speculations. There were, he regretted to say, Gentlemen in that House, who did allow their names to be connected, with too much ease and unwariness, with companies like the present.

4·6 RULING CLASS AND RADICAL LEADERSHIP

From William Lovett, The Life and Struggles of William Lovett, *1876, pp. 91–2.*

Out of the body which Lovett describes grew the London Working Men's Association (see next head note).

A short time however before this an attempt was made towards the formation of 'A Society for Promoting a Cheap and Honest Press', but little was done beyond the publication of an excellent address on the subject, written by Dr J. R. Black, an American, who had previously taken an active part in the collection of Cleave's and Hetherington's fines. We found, however, that we had collected together a goodly number of active and influential working men, persons who had principally done the work of our late committee; and the question arose among us, whether we could form and maintain a union formed exclusively of this class and of such men. We were the more induced to try the experiment as the working classes had not hitherto evinced that discrimination and independent spirit in the management of their political affairs which we were desirous to see. A lord, a M.P., or an esquire was a leading requisite to secure a full attendance and attention from them on all public occasions, as well as among those who called themselves their betters. They were always looking up *to leadership* of one description or another; were being swayed to and fro in opinion and action by the *idol* of their choice, and were rent and divided when some popular breath had blown that *idol* from its pedestal. In fact the masses, in their political organisations, were taught to look up to '*great men*' (or to men *professing greatness*) rather than to great principles. We wished therefore to establish a political school of self-instruction among them, in which they should accustom themselves to examine great *social and political principles*, and by their publicity and free discussion help to form a sound and healthful public opinion throughout the country.

4·7 TOWARDS A COUNTER ÉLITE

From The Rotten House of Commons, *An Address by the London Working Men's Association* (*1835*) *pp. 2–8*.

Working class radical dissatisfaction with the effects of the reforms of 1832 and the political system in general emerges clearly from this document. The London Working Men's Association was founded in 1836, its members including many leading Chartists and Radicals.

TO THE WORKING CLASSES OF THE UNITED KINGDOM

Fellow Countrymen

The Members of the Working Men's Association believing that a great and doubtful crisis is at hand, and that its result for evil or for good will principally depend on the mutual understanding among our own class, deem it to be their duty to address you on this important occasion. And in addressing you they are desirous of honestly and fearlessly avowing their sentiments regarding the great principle of right and justice, however in practice it may affect the selfish projects of any party in the state. We would willingly cast the mantle of oblivion over our past history – we would even endeavour to erase from our memories the atrocities, the persecutions, and the injustice, that for ages have been perpetrated against our class, if a disposition was even now evinced, on the part of our rulers, to commence the reign of JUSTICE and HUMANITY....

But, fellow countrymen, judging from the marshalling of forces and threats of defiance, we fear a similar disposition is not found among the various factions, whose continual strife for power and plunder is the curse of our country; their aim is to perpetuate the reign of wrong, and to consolidate their power at the expense of justice. . . .

Under a just system of government there would be but one party, *that of the people*; whose representatives would be actuated by one great motive, *that of making all the resources of our country tend to promote the happiness of all its inhabitants.*

Far different, however, are the views of those who now govern England, nay, (with few exceptions) of those of their constituents who give them the power to govern. Each seems actuated by an exclusive interest; and exclusive privileges seem, in their estimation, the wisest legislative measures.

Will it, think you, fellow countrymen, promote our happiness – will it give us more comforts, more leisure, less toil, and less of the wretchedness to which we are subjected, if *the power and empire of the wealthy be established on the wreck of title and privilege?*

Yet to this end we believe, is the tendency of the present contest now waging between the two great parties both in and out of parliament – between the agricultural and privileged classes on the one hand, and the monied and commercial classes on the other. If the past struggles and contentions we have had with the latter to keep up our wages – our paltry means of subsistence; – if the infamous acts they have passed since they have obtained a portion of political power form any criterion of their disposition to do *us* justice, little have we to expect from any accession to that power, any more than from the former tyrants we have had to contend against.

There are persons among the monied class, who, to deceive their fellow men, have put on the cloak of reform; but they mean not that reform shall so extend as to deprive them or their party of their corrupt advantages. Many boast of freedom, while they help to enslave us; and preach *justice*, while they assist the oppressor to practise wrongs and to perpetuate the greatest injustice towards the working millions. . . .

These persons, under various pretences, and with a show of liberality, daily enlist in their ranks some portion of our deluded countrymen; and by opposing them to each other, accomplish their objects of deceiving and fleecing the whole. So long as we continue to be duped by some new political chimera, which they have ever at hand to amuse us, – so long as we continue to seek political salvation through the instrumentality of others, instead of our own exertions, so long will *party* be triumphant, will corrupt legislation prevail, will private peculators and public plunderers flourish, and so long must we continue to be the mere supplicating cringing vassals of a proud, arrogant, speech-making few; whose interest it is to keep us the mere toiling charity-ridden set we are, the unhappy dupes of the idle and the designing.

Fellow countrymen, have you ever enquired how far a just and economical system of government, a code of wise and just laws, and the abolition of all the useless appendages of state would affect the interests of the present 658 members of the House of Commons? If you have not, begin now to enquire, and you will soon lose any vain hopes you may entertain from that house as at present constituted. Nay, if you pursue your enquiries in like manner respecting the present constituents of that house, to see how far their interests are identified with yours, how far just legislation and efficient reform would deprive them of their power to grind and oppress you, you would be equally hopeless of benefits from that quarter. To satisfy yourselves in this respect, propose for your own judgment and reflection the following questions:–

Is the FUNDHOLDER, whose interest it is to preserve the debt and burthens of the country, and who revels in extravagance on the cheap productions of labour, a fit representative for us?

Is the LANDHOLDER, whose interest leads him to keep up his rents by unjust and exclusive laws, a fit representative for working men?

Are the whole host of MONEYMAKERS, SPECULATORS, and USURERS, who live on the corruption of the system, fit representatives for the sons of labour?

Are the immense numbers of LORDS, EARLS, MARQUESSES, KNIGHTS, BARONETS, HONOURABLES, and RIGHT HONOURABLES, who have seats in that house, fit to represent our interests? many of whom have the prospect before them of being the *hereditary legislators* of the other house, or are the craving expectants of place or emolument, who shine in the gilded circle of a court, or flutter among the gaieties of the ballroom, who court the passing smile of royalty, whine at the ministers of the day, and when the interests of the people are at stake, are found the revelling debauchées of fashion, or the duelling wranglers of a gambling house.

Are the multitude of MILITARY and NAVAL OFFICERS in the present House of Commons, whose interest it is to support that system which secures them their pay, and whose only utility is to direct one portion of our brethren to keep the other in subjection, fit to represent our grievances?

Have we fit representatives in the multitude of BARRISTERS, ATTORNEYS, SOLICITORS, and all those whose interests depend on the dissensions and corruptions of the people; persons whose prosperity, depending on the obscurity and intricacy of the laws. . . .

Is the MANUFACTURER or CAPITALIST, whose exclusive monopoly of the combined powers of wood, iron, and steam, enables him to cause the destitution of thousands, and who has an interest in forcing labour down to the *minimum* reward, fit to represent the interests of working men?

Is the MASTER, whose interest it is to purchase labour at the cheapest rate, a fit representative for the WORKMAN, whose interest it is to get the most he can for his labour?

Yet such is the description of persons composing that house, and such the interests represented, to whom we, session after session, address our *humble petitions*, and whom we in our ignorant simplicity imagine will generously sacrifice their hopes and interests, by beginning the great work of political and social reformation.

Working men, enquire if this be not true, and then if you feel with us, stand apart from all projects, and refuse to be the tools of any party, who will not, as a *first and essential measure*, give to the working classes EQUAL POLITICAL AND SOCIAL RIGHTS; so that they may send their own representatives from the ranks of labour into that house to deliberate and determine among *all those other interests*, that the interests of the labouring classes, of those who are the foundation of the social edifice, shall not be daily sacrificed to glut the extravagances and luxuries of the few. If you feel with us, then you will proclaim it in the workshop, preach it in your societies, publish it from town to village, from county to county, and from nation to nation, that there is no hope for the sons of toil, till those who feel with them, who sympathise with them, and whose interests are identified with theirs, have an *equal right* to determine what laws shall be enacted or plans adopted for justly governing this country.

To this end, fellow workmen, are wanted, a FREE PRESS, UNIVERSAL SUFFRAGE, the Protection of the BALLOT, ANNUAL PARLIAMENTS, EQUAL REPRESENTATION, and no PROPERTY QUALIFICATION for members.

4·8 SQUIRE RULE OR LOCAL DEMOCRACY

From R. Cobden, Incorporate Your Borough! *183–, pp. 4–9.*

The Municipal Corporation Act of 1835 laid the foundations for a democratic form of local government in place of the rule of the Lord of the Manor and of the Justices of the Peace recruited largely from the landowning class. The adoption of the Act required petition to the Crown by a majority of rate-payers. In the fight for this Richard Cobden published anonymously the pamphlet *Incorporate Your Borough! A letter to the inhabitants of Manchester*, extolling the citizens to take action. He describes his own experience as a juror for the 'election' of the leading officers of the town. It is apparently very rare – Morley did not list it in the bibliography of Cobden's writings given in his *Life of Richard Cobden* – and the extract given below is taken from the facsimile reprint in Wm. E. A. Axon, *Cobden as a Citizen*, 1907.

By a provision of the municipal corporation reform act, the Privy Council has the power to incorporate any town whose inhabitants petition for the privilege. Birmingham lately held a great public meeting, in its noble town hall, for that purpose, at which its popular members, Messrs Attwood and Scholefield, and all the Radical leaders attended, when resolutions were unanimously and enthusiastically passed in favour of an immediate application to the Privy Council for an incorporation of that borough. Fellow-townsmen! follow the example of the men of Birmingham, who are always foremost in the path of reform, – INCORPORATE YOUR BOROUGH. The mode of securing the advantages of democratic self-government for your town is easy and simple. Let a public meeting be called, and resolutions be passed in favour of the object desired; then appoint a committee, to prepare a petition to Her Majesty in council. . . .

Recollect that the massacre of the 16th of Aug., 1819, could not have occurred, if Manchester had then been incorporated according to the provisions of the present municipal reform act; – and why? Because the united magistrates of Lancashire and Cheshire, who then entered the town, to hold their bench at the Star Inn, take the command of the police, and order the soldiers to cut down and trample upon unarmed crowds, would, in such a case, have no more jurisdiction over Manchester than Constantinople. No! – INCORPORATE YOUR BOROUGH! and thenceforth, neither Mr Hulton, of Hulton, nor any Tory squire or parson, will ever come into your town at the head of a dozen magisterial bumpkins, first to let loose a troop of fox hunters, disguised as yeomanry cavalry, to try the metal of their swords upon helpless women and children, and afterwards to return public thanks to the officers and men for their extreme forbearance on the occasion! No; for by one of the provisions of the corporation reform act, no person can be appointed to the office of justice of the peace in any of the boroughs holding quarter sessions, unless he live within the limits prescribed for the residences of the burgesses. In this clause alone, I find a sufficient reason, if there were not an hundred others, for applying for an act of incorporation, and thus to place for ever the population of our town and neighbourhood beyond the control of a booby squirearchy, who abhor us not more for our love of political freedom, than for those active and intellectual pursuits which contrast so strongly with that mental stupor in which they exist – I had almost said – vegetate.

I have endeavoured to give you a faint outline of the new municipal reform act, under the provisions of which it is in your power to place your borough; but let me now glance for a moment, for the sake of contrast, at the kind of government which this place at present suffers under. The chief municipal officer is the borough-reeve, appointed at the court-leet of the lord of the Manor; the two constables being chosen at the same time and manner, for the heads of the police; and the three are universally recognised as the highest authorities of the town; and responsible for the peace, lives, and properties, of this populous, wealthy, and somewhat excitable community. Now, how will my readers, who are not in the secret, be surprised when they are told of the manner in which these important functionaries are appointed to the government of the second town in the British empire! It cannot be better explained than by describing the proceedings at the last court-leet of the Lord of the Manor, when it was my amusing fate to be summoned as one of the jurors. . . .

At the appointed hour, ascending by a flight of steps in Brown-Street, leading up to several other apartments, and to a dancing master's academy amongst the rest, I reached the door of the manor court-room, which is large, and altogether destitute of furniture, whose row of tall, old-fashioned windows, would, but for the crust of smoke and dirt that covered them, have afforded a cheerful light. The atmosphere of the room was heavy and stale; it had probably been confined ever since the last public meeting of the tee-totallers was held there, a month before. . . . The jurors were . . . penned within a small enclosure at the farthest extremity of the room; the representative of the Lord of the Manor took his seat in a small desk springing from the wall; his legal agent sat below; the oaths were administered to the jurymen; and the assessor, having in about three minutes and a half delivered his charge, adjourned the court till the afternoon. Whilst these preliminaries were going on, I looked over the enclosure which, I supposed, was designed to separate the crowd of spectators from the jurors, and I counted, besides the police constables, exactly *seven individuals*, and they, one by one, walked listlessly away, leaving the jurors only in the deserted and murky chamber; and we now proceeded to make choice of three persons to fill the offices of boroughreeve and constables of Manchester, – a task in which we were greatly quickened by the piercing cold vapour with which the apartment was filled. Having dispatched messengers to the individuals nominated, summoning them to appear in the afternoon, to be sworn into office, we separated. At the appointed hour, the court and jurors again assembled, when the gentleman who had been nominated to the office of boroughreeve attended, and claimed to be exempted on the ground of ill health, and previous services. The jurors protested that there was not another person remaining in the township liable, and at the same time eligible, to fill this high office. . . . Our choice next fell upon an individual absent from Manchester, and the court was adjourned for two days, that he might have time to appear. On reassembling at the appointed time, he presented himself to protest against the nomination; but he yielded reluctantly, and the honour was at last gently forced upon him. The two individuals chosen constables were also unwillingly compelled to take the oaths of office. The cryer soon afterwards formally adjourned the court to the *Mosley Arms Hotel, for dinner*, at which all present laughed heartily; and thus, very appropriately, terminated the *farce of a mock election of officers to govern the affairs of the town of Manchester.*

Neither the boroughreeve nor the constables whom I joined in electing, were known to me, privately or publicly. I had not the least knowledge of them, personally or by repute; and other jurors were alike in the dark upon the subject of their qualifications. The jury summoned to appoint those officers are selected by the legal agent of the Lord of the Manor; they attend unwillingly; the constables serve their offices unwillingly; the boroughreeve submits to his appointment unwillingly; the public is indifferent to the whole proceeding, not one in ten thousand of the population of Manchester attending to witness it; probably not one person in fifty of the inhabitants of the borough knows even the names of the boroughreeve and constables at this moment; and not one individual in two hundred is acquainted with them personally. Yet, to them is entrusted the guardianship of the peace of the town; and, in case of emergency, on them should we be compelled to depend for conduct to command the confidence of a population of 100,000 persons, of whom not five in 100 ever heard of their names. . . .

The difficulty in appointing individuals residing within the township, who alone are liable to serve the offices of boroughreeve and constables, arises from the circumstance of almost all the merchants, manufacturers, and wholesale dealers having removed their residences into the out-townships, where they are beyond the jurisdiction of the Lord of the Manor's court-leet. There is another circumstance, however, which, whilst it explains partly the difficulty, will also throw a light upon the aristocratic spirit which clings more or less to everything having a feudal origin. It is, of course, very well known that hundreds of respectable and wealthy *shopkeepers* reside within the township of Manchester; but it is not equally notorious that it has always been a maxim, at the election of municipal officers, that no retailer was eligible to fill the office of boroughreeve or constable! And so anxious have the Tory manufacturers and wholesale dealers been to apportion amongst their own order, dignities, however humble, that even the menial offices in the gift of Sir Oswald Mosley's feudal court have been distributed in the same aristocratic spirit. A late parliamentary candidate for the borough of Salford held the high office of ale taster; and the Manchester Directory for 1833 records that our richest banker, an individual whose princely fortune would entitle him to a dukedom in any other country in Europe, held the responsible post of *muzzler of mastiff dogs and bitches*! The tone which has so long prevailed in the government of the town has naturally enough pervaded all our public institutions, and even entered into the private arrangements of social life. It is well understood, for example, that if the shop-keeper's family be not formally interdicted from entering our public assemblies, they would not be consulting their own interest or enjoyment by attending them, and the retailer would find it, probably, almost as difficult to gain admission to our clubs and our concert, as he might to obtain the privilege of *entré* to the Queen's court. The *wholesale* dealer in fustians or fents, whose *bundles* occupy a garret or cellar, from which they only issue in the gross, may, however vulgar, in mind or ill-bred in manners, gain admission without difficulty to places of privileged resort, from which the retail mercer or jeweller, with perhaps ten times the wealth, and whose vocation demands some refinement of manners and cultivation of mind, would feel himself excluded. What wonder, with these facts in view, if we sometimes meet with Tory-radicals or operative Conservatives! What wonder if the sincere democrat, finding a counterfeit aristocracy everywhere current, should grow bewildered at the sight of the spurious imitations, and to escape deception, prefer such as bear the genuine stamp of nobility! ...

But another of the difficulties in the way of finding proper persons to fill the offices of boroughreeve and constables remains to be noticed. There has been a tacit, if not an avowed, exclusion of Dissenters from these appointments. No person has yet been allowed to fill the post of boroughreeve, who would not attend at the Collegiate Church every Sunday, and thus afford his official sanction to the high Church and high Tory doctrines which are said to be promulgated from its pulpit. One of the merits of the new corporation charter, and not its least, is that it recognises no distribution of sects; and if, to use the language of one of the speakers at the late meeting to petition for the incorporation of Birmingham, 'the Dissenters should avail themselves of this and every other fragment of power to counterpoise the influence brought into play against them', then I need not doubt of the active cooperation of that most influential body in Manchester, when I say to them more especially – INCORPORATE YOUR BOR-OUGH.

4·9 THE TERRITORIAL CLASS IN PARLIAMENT

From Bernard Cracroft, 'The Analysis of the House of Commons, or indirect Representation' in Essays on Reform, *1867, pp. 156–65 and 327–9.*

The original paper was written in the course of the controversy over electoral reform which preceded the Second Reform Act and in support of an extension of the franchise. Its author, a Cambridge Fellow, was primarily concerned with the consequences for the character of politics which flowed from the fact that Members of Parliament were not the delegates of their constituencies, that their influence derived from factors other than the votes of the constituents who elected them and that there was little danger in a substantial increase in the electorate swamping the House of Commons and substantially altering the character of the representation. In the context of a discussion on the character of a ruling class this paper is equally interesting for the light which the analysis throws on the restricted social basis of politics in the Victorian era. For this reason I am reproducing some of the tables which Cracroft appended to his paper and which were reproduced as an appendix of the *Essays on Reform.*

Like everything else, the House of Commons may be analysed in a variety of ways. It may, for instance, be analysed into Liberals and Conservatives, into Protectionists and Freetraders, into Churchmen and Dissenters, into Reformers and Anti-reformers. But these familiar distinctions are subordinate to more general views of the House of Commons in its representative character.

Taking a wider circle, perhaps the most general division which arises on a first glance at the subject, is of the Commons indoors . . . and the Commons out-of-doors; and this again implies a classification of constituencies without. This division, rough and idle as it might appear, has one recommendation. It touches immediately the whole question of direct and indirect representation. And the distinction between direct and indirect representation is the key to the whole question of Reform.

In an assembly of delegates an analysis of the delegates themselves would be unnecessary, ... but, in the English House of Commons, a Member not being a delegate, but a representative whose freedom is only limited by certain considerations, we have to take into account both the Member himself within the House, and such influence as his constituency may or might be able to exercise upon him from without. ... The present essay is chiefly concerned with the Members themselves – with the Commons indoors rather than with the Commons out-of-doors; and the end proposed is to show what manner of House it is, take it all in all, which is elected under the present elective system; and, being elected, what are the broad representative results of their election.

To take a salient but not by any means a solitary example. The insurance offices have no direct representation in Parliament at all. They do not figure in the Reform Bill. ... At the polling-booth their voting power is nothing. But in the House itself, partly owing to the high character and great intelligence of their conductors, partly owing to their prodigious wealth, and partly owing to the enormous interests with which they blend, they are most heavily represented. Between fifty and sixty Members of Parliament are directors of insurance companies; and when Mr Sheridan, the recognised leader of this influential phalanx, rises in his place to plead for the remission of the Fire Duty, or expound any other grievance connected with those offices, his statements are listened to, quite independently of himself, with an attention and a care conceded to one who speaks not only with knowledge and authority, but with a certain well-understood if undefined power at his back. ... Let us take one more preliminary example, though of a different kind. The aristocracy and the landowners are overwhelmingly represented not only in the House of Lords, but in the House of Commons. A stranger might ask how and by what means. The answer would be, certainly not in virtue of their own voting power at the polling-booth. That is *nil*. Certainly not by virtue of any legal enactment in their favour. The Constitution recognises Crown, Lords, and Commons; but the Lords alone have their seats secured to them in the House of Lords by the Constitution. There is no law compelling the constituencies to return any particular class of men to the House of Commons. The property qualification has been abolished. How, then, do members get there; and when there, how is their representation of those who sent them there to be measured and defined? The answer in the case of the aristocracy is evident. They get there not by direct but by indirect influence – by the power, in short, of their prodigious antecedent advantages, by their irredeemable start in the race for power. When there, they represent, *directly* their constituencies, *indirectly* themselves; yet, from the very nature of things, in such a manner that the indirect representation throws, and must necessarily throw, the direct representation into the shade. It is in the nature of things that a man's self should be nearer to him than his constituency. There is a homely saying, that a man's skin sits closer to him than his shirt. And, without any imputation on their good faith, so it is with Members of Parliament. Single individuals are no doubt capable of preferring the interests of others to their own. Single Members of Parliament, with personal interests of their own, may prefer public to private considerations. But, in the case of classes dealing with class interests, it is the law of their being that they should consider themselves paramount and necessary to the public welfare. . . .

Such a tendency is not peculiar to landowners. It happens, however, that, in this country, a concurrence of causes has given greater solidarity to their order, and greater solidity to their power, than to any other class in the community. Not only have they the natural tendency of all orders and classes in all countries and times, when they can, to represent themselves, but it might almost be said that in this country they cannot help representing themselves. So vast is their traditional power, so broadly does it sit over the land, so deep and ancient are its roots, so multiplied and ramified everywhere are its tendrils, and creepers, and feelers, that the danger is never lest they should have too little, but always lest they should have too much power, and so, even involuntarily, choke down the possibilities of new life from below. . . . They have a common freemasonry of blood, a common education, common pursuits, common ideas, a common dialect, a common religion, and – what more than any other thing binds men together – a common prestige, a prestige growled at occasionally, but on the whole conceded, and even, it must be owned, secretly liked by the country at large. All these elements, obvious in themselves, but difficult to measure and gauge, go to make up that truly and with-out exaggeration tremendous consent of power, often latent, often disguised, never absent, which constitutes the indirect representa-tion of the aristocracy in the House of Commons. . . .

These instances of indirect representation are only two out of the vast number which belong to the time-honoured anomalies of our system, but it is enough if at first starting they enable the reader fully to realize the importance in any discussion on Reform of keeping in view the distinction between voting power at the polling-booth, and representative power inside the House. . . . If the argument so well known in the present day as the 'swamping argument' could have any application at all to English affairs, those who rely upon it should consider this fact. All the constituencies are swamped already, as it is! Numbers already prevail there. Land, wealth, intelligence, are already outvoted at the polling-booth. Yet so little are they outvoted in the House of Commons, that they sit there alone, and the only question really at stake is, whether, under such a constitution as ours is, numbers as such can ever be heard there at all.

This brings me to the first branch of the analysis in view: – direct representation, and its broadest division, population and land. How is population, merely as population, in the bald arithmetical sense of mere numbers, represented in the House? How is land represented? At first sight, and on a superficial view, the answer appears decisive and unqualified. Numbers are, it might be said, overwhelmingly represented there. Land not at all, or scarcely in any decent ratio. Looking at the United Kingdom as a whole, and dividing it broadly into boroughs and counties, we find that a population of eighteen million souls in the counties have only 256 Members in the House of Commons, whereas a population of eleven millions in boroughs have 396 Members. . . .

I dwell upon this, because it is one of those salient facts peculi-arly likely to impress the imagination of a practical people, and peculiarly adapted to shut out the light of any more recondite arguments, however conclusive, on the other side. Doctor Johnson, stamping his foot on the ground to shake down the Berkeleyan cobwebs, was not more confident of the strength of his position than the practical Tory, who sets his foot on this great fact and proclaims that land is grossly unrepresented. Yet 'this great fact' is wholly delusive. It is honeycombed by a thousand underground channels. True it is, that in the apparent result the boroughs have 396 Members, the counties 256.* But let us see how this gross result is 'redressed' in minute detail.

And first, of these 396 borough Members a couple of hundred Members, at least, belong to what is called technically the territorial class. The House may be roughly divided into landowners, with their relatives (including of course the aristocracy there), and mercantile Members. Those Members who belong to neither class are so few, that they may for the present purpose be neglected. . . . But with the utmost diligence, and the help of the 'Joint Stock Companies' Directory', and every other source of information I could obtain, I cannot discover that the mercantile, manufacturing, and shipping interests, including also owners of collieries, have more than 122 Members in the House. Of these four or five sit for counties. Then there are in the House 78 bankers or bank directors, but many of these are either landowners themselves or connected with peers or landowners. . . . On the whole, the list of Members who are merchants or bankers, or both, and nothing else, may fairly be taken at considerably under 150. And this leaves out of view the possibility and probability of their also being landowners, though not known as such to the public. Deducting these from the 396 borough Members, there remain 246 borough Members, who are almost to a man landowners, or connected with landowning interests. If we add 246 to 256 we get 502 as the ascertained number of the territorialists in the House of Commons. The number is probably much larger; but, as a curious confirmation of a result for which, without a personal knowledge of each individual in the House, it would be impossible to vouch, the number of Public School men and University men given in Dod is, as far as I could count them,† 429, and, as the list of the remaining 229 comprises some sixty or seventy names belonging to the aristocratic element, additional light is thrown upon the calculation. . . .

In other words, land, which at first sight appears to have only 256 Members in the House, has, in reality and for practical uses too, some 500 Members, and more, who get there by hook or by

* _The six University Members are left out. They add to the indirect representation of the landed interest._

† _They may be more. They are not less._

crook, men of the same ideas and feelings and bias – men who, in spite of every superficial political difference of opinion, belong, so to speak, to one vast cousinhood. And this is one aspect under which we begin to see how the representation of mere numbers, so powerful on paper, is in practice neutralized. . . .

In dealing with the landed interest, as compared with the mercantile, it has been found necessary to argue in some degree hypothetically. It is almost impossible without personal inquiry to find out, within a large debatable margin, who is, and who is not, possessed of a landed estate. But in the matter of the aristocratic interest inside the House of Commons, Dod's 'Parliamentary Guide' furnishes the materials for a very adequate analysis. According then to Dod, in the Parliament of August, 1865, there were returned 71 baronets, 11 elder sons of baronets, 19 younger sons of baronets, and 8 grandsons of baronets; a total for the baronetage alone of 110. There were also 37 peers, or elder sons of peers; a total of 116 Members of Parliament for the peerage, and for the peerage and baronetage together a total of 226. Besides these there are one hundred Commoners sitting in Parliament who are connected with the peerage by marriage or descent. The aristocratic class, or element, in the House of Commons has therefore a grand total of, at least, 326 Members. . . .

These men are not mere separate units, like insurance office directors; they are not a mere Venetian set of a few families, but, to repeat an expression already used, one vast cousinhood. It was lately said of Lord Granville, that he represents the 'cousins in Parliament'. If he does, he may be congratulated on his political power, for 'the cousins' mean simply three-fourths of the House of Commons, and the connexion of those three-fourths not only with one another, but with the House of Lords. . . .

Some time ago an ex-governor of the Bank of England in the House of Commons told one of the profoundest political writers of the day, that he himself was related to thirty other Members of Parliament, all sitting with him at that time. And this view gives us an insight into the extraordinary political *solidarity* of the upper classes. The parliamentary frame is kneaded together almost out of one class; it has the strength of a giant and the compactness of a dwarf. For in this respect one Parliament is very much like another.

Again – and this consideration deserves the utmost attention –

there is in this country a distinct parliamentary class, which numbers at the outside some three or four thousand names. The total number of candidates since 1832 is hardly over four thousand; and if you look down the list of polls since 1832 in Acland's 'Imperial Poll Book', the same names recur again and again, not only as successful Members, but as unsuccessful candidates. Each constituency seems to be laid siege to by a given number of men, who appear to remain round it in expectancy, year after year, for five, ten, twenty years. This class belongs to the upper ten thousand, and spends its life in following the tide of public opinion in the constituencies, and taking advantage of every new turn in the tide. The Reform Bill made vast changes in the legislation of the House of Commons, but, as Lord Russell then prophesied, it has left class ascendancy quite untouched. Perhaps the number of new men is increased by two or three score. Perhaps the men who are now returned to Parliament are on the average older men, sedater politicians, greater worshippers of the respectabilities. . . . But on the whole the centre of gravity of political power is just where it was before the Reform Bill – far above the belt, nor is it likely that any extension of the suffrage or any redistribution of power will place it elsewhere. Under any Reform Bill, the same classes who wield political power now will continue to wield it. The real difference will be that as the constituencies change, so will those who study their favour, and they will take problems, social and political, into consideration which they hitherto ignored. . . .

APPENDICES

*Aristocratic Element in the House of Commons**

Conservatives	175
Liberals	151
Total Aristocratic	326

Analysis:–

Baronets	71
Elder Sons of Baronets	11
Younger Sons of Baronets	19
Grandsons of Baronets	8
Baronetage . . . . Total	—— 109

Elder Sons of Peers	37	
Younger Sons of Peers	64	
Grandsons of Peers	15	
Peerage . . . . Total	——	116
Commoners connected by Marriage or Descent	100	
Aristocratic . . . . Total	——	326

Another view:–
Alliances

(1) Between Baronet and Baronet . .	23	
(2) Between Baronet and Peer . . .	53	
(3) Between Peer and Peer	79	
Alliances. . . . . Total	——	155

Another view:–

Members representing One Peerage by Marriage or Descent	117	
Members representing Two Peerages by Marriage or Descent	67	
Members representing Three Peerages by Marriage or Descent	18	
Army and Navy	271	
Officers exclusive of Guardsmen		54
Guardsmen		58
Militia		48
Yeomanry		56
Volunteers		44
Naval		11

* *This table is compiled exclusively from Dod's 'New Parliament'; it does not include those squires and owners of landed property whose connexion with the Peerage does not appear there.* [*Cracroft's footnote*].

Universities, Schools, Professions, Business, etc.

Public Schools and Universities:–		
Oxford	136	
Christchurch		76
Balliol		9
&c.		&c.
Cambridge	110	
Trinity		88
St. John's		12
&c.		&c.
London University	7	
Dublin	27	
Edinburgh	9	
Glasgow	3	
Public Schools:–		
Eton	105	
Harrow	52	
Rugby	23	
Westminster	17	
Winchester	9	
Charterhouse	7	
Shrewsbury	5	
Sandhurst	5	
Woolwich	4	
Honour Men	45	
First Class Men	19	
Double Firsts	3	
Double Seconds	8	
Other Classes	4	
Passmen	the rest.	
Authors	78	
Lawyers	100	
Queen's Councillors		24
Magistrates	175	
Deputy Lieutenants	235	
High Sheriffs	28	
Railway Directors	179	
Insurance Office Directors	53	
Bankers	78	
Brewers	12	
Dissenters	84	

Clubs, Trade, Dissent

Clubs:–

Conservative Clubs.	249
Liberal Clubs	221
Travellers'	88
University Clubs	82
Athnaeum	48
Army and Navy Clubs	52
Guards'	19
Boodle's	45
White's	42

Trade:–

Ship Owners	7
East India Merchants	4
Iron Masters	10
Cotton Merchants and Calico Printers	7
Worsted and Carpet Manufacturers	5
Silk Manufacturers	2
Miscellaneous	87
Total	122

Dissent:–

Independents	13	
Baptists	1	
Wesleyan	1	
Unitarians	12	
English Presbyterians	1	
United Presbyterians	3	
Free Churchmen	2	(Supposed)
Quakers	4	
Jews	5	
English Roman Catholics	2	
Irish Roman Catholics	40	(Supposed)
General Total	84	

4·10 'INEVITABLE PARLIAMENT MEN'

Sir Lewis Namier coined this phrase when analysing the mid-eighteenth century House of Commons. He applied it to men who from an early age had felt themselves destined for a political career or who accepted in the most natural fashion the opportunity to enter Parliament when it occurred. Such men could still be found in large numbers in the nineteenth century and on a decreasing scale even in the present one. The memoir literature of politicians gives insight into such careers and into the milieu and attitude of mind which made them feasible. Six extracts from the vast volume of biographies of Victorian and Edwardian politicians are given in this section.

4·10·1. *From B. Mallet,* Thomas George, Earl of Northbrook, A Memoir, *1908, pp. 26–7.*

Sir Francis Baring, Banker and Politician, wrote as follows to his son, the future Viceroy of India and Liberal politician, at the end of the latter's stay at Oxford in 1846.

'Have you ever asked yourself the question', he wrote, 'what you intend to do with yourself in life? One portion of the question is answered for you. . . . Your position is fixed – that of an English country gentleman; and it will be your business in life to do your duty in that state of life to which it has pleased God to call you. . . . Have the English country gentlemen, then, any business? To my mind no one more. All men are not fitted for the performance of all these duties, but it is in the discharge of some that men of property in this country do their duty to their God, benefit their country, and contribute to their own happiness. For happiness any labour is better than idleness, but labour in the line of duty is the sweetest. . . . It is for you a little to think over what your inclination and talents lead you to in the different branches of your own condition of life. You may look to public life if your feelings turn that way, or you may lead a quieter life and still be a very useful and good man. As to public life I would say a word. I have never tried either directly or through your tutors to rouse your ambition or to turn your mind to such a course; my own course and conversation no doubt indirectly may have had that effect; but it has been my endeavour to leave you as much free to act according to your inclination as was possible under the circumstances. I don't wish to tempt you or to drive you into the career . . . I shall be as satis-fied if you are a *worthy* country squire as if you were a leading Whig speaker. I don't wish to frighten you from it. It has its ups and downs, its cares and pleasures, like other lines of life. If, indeed, power or office or some wretched peerage is the object of a public man, of all men perhaps he is the most miserable; but if his opinions are approved by his conscience and his course is honest he will find that labour in the line of duty has its blessings whether he be in office or not. . . . I do not wish to control you in this, nor indeed has it ever been my course to strain too hard the tie of parental authority, but I trust you will do something to fit yourself for the duties of your after-life, and make up your mind to perform these duties when they fall upon you.'

4.10.2. *From C. Whibley*, Lord John Manners and His Friends, *2 vols. 1925, I, pp. 85–6, 92–5.*

Lord John Manners was a younger son of the Duke of Rutland; he entered Parliament when he was twenty-three.

No sooner did Lord John enter Mr Hodgson's chambers than he divided his time, as many others have done before and since, between Lincoln's Inn and the West End. During the day he drew conveyances, read Blackstone . . . and studied the law of Mortmain, which in later life he did his best ineffectually to abolish. In the evening he went 'flying about to parties', as he told Granby, 'simply because I have not the moral courage to say "no"'. His desire, doubtless, chimed with his lack of moral courage. He got the best of life wherever he went. He fell in love and out of it with a speed and frequency great even for a young man in his first season. He danced, he dined, he went to race-meetings with all the zest of youth. Once when his father won the Leicester Cup they brought it back triumphantly in the carriage with them. Nor were he and George Smythe and Baillie-Cochrane, his most frequent companions, always as sedate as became aspiring legislators. They gave joyous, even noisy, dinners at Greenwich and Richmond. . . .

Smythe was the first to find a seat. In January 1841 he went down to Canterbury in opposition to Wilson, a somewhat truculent Whig. His contest was distinguished by a loyal speech which he made in defence of the Queen, then by no means a favourite of the Tories, and by a thoroughly characteristic attempt to force his opponent to a duel. . . . When the day of the poll came, Smythe found himself gallantly supported by his friends. Lord John's account of the first election at which he assisted reveals a state of things which would seem strange indeed today, and proves that they took the fight in a proper spirit of gaiety.

'On Saturday, this day week', wrote Lord John on 6th February, 'posted with Loftus, Cochrane, and Captain Ryder Burton to Canterbury. Found dear Smythe in good spirits and health. On Monday was the nomination; we marched to the place first; 'twas dreadful weather, snowing and cold, and we were kept some time. . . . We had the show of hands, and afterwards marched round the town in anticipated triumph. . . . In the evening we joined the Committee, who allotted us various duties. . . . I got to bed before 2 – up the next morning by half-past 7: poll began at 8. At first we were rather nervous, but soon all was right: at midday the High Street was crowded, and fears of a row obtained; some chaps blackguarded Cochrane for a row during last night, and one wanted to fight him. Whenever Smythe appeared he was positively mobbed, so popular had he made himself: at last 4 o'clock struck, and the account made his majority 163: much larger than his most sanguine friend ever hoped for. . . .

Lord John's own turn was not long in coming. In June 1841, Lord Melbourne's Ministry, having been beaten by 36 votes on its budget . . . it succumbed at last to a vote of no confidence, and a General Election followed immediately. Lord John was at first in some perplexity about a seat. Cambridgeshire was dismissed from his mind as too costly; . . . Grantham, which he himself would have preferred, was forbidden by his father, who saw a constant embarrassment in its proximity to Belvoir, and Lord John began to fear that he 'would be shelved'. In the end Manners-Sutton of Kelham came to the rescue with the offer of Newark, and thither Lord John went on 16th June to begin his canvass.

4.10.3. From Lady G. Cecil, Life of Robert, 4th Marquis of Salisbury, *2 vols. 1921, I, pp. 36–7.*

Lord Robert Cecil, as he then was, wrote this letter in 1853 on the eve of his return from New Zealand where he had gone to regain his health. In the same year he was elected for Stamford where the

> Cecil family had considerable influence; he was then twenty-four
> years old. At the time of writing Lord Robert was, of course,
> not yet heir to the title.

'Now I have got my health the question is what am I to do with
it? I have been thinking a good deal over a conversation on that
weighty question which we had one night in the summer drawing-
room, but without coming to any satisfactory result. As Peel used
to say, there are three courses open – assuming of course, as you
then said, that in choosing some plan of life, the prospect of the
greatest usefulness ought to be the only guiding principle of
selection. (1) The House of Commons is undoubtedly the sphere
in which a man can be most useful: but my chances of getting into
it are, practically, none. (2) Orders is the profession which I should
place next to it in usefulness: but from my uncertain health and
my inaptitude for gaining personal influence I am as little fitted
for it as any man I ever met. (3) There is the profession of which
you once thought – the bar. My own opinion on the subject is unchanged. It seems to me to unite the evils of the other two. It is
more destructive of health than any other profession, and among
the hundreds who yearly flock into it, I am about as likely to attain
eminence in it as I am to get into Parliament. Moreover it requires
no prophetic eye to see that even now it is passing away. People
have tasted the sweets of cheap law in the County Courts and they
will not long spare Chancery or Westminster Hall. . . . Further; a
clergyman or a statesman or a doctor, are as such, useful men.
Their professions do good. But the barrister is at best but a tolerated evil. He derives his living from the fact that the law is unintelligible: and in proportion as modern legislation succeeds in
making it accessible and simple, he will disappear. . . . The bar
therefore not only does no good, but is a public nuisance – though
perhaps for the present inevitable. I conclude therefore that, for
me, at the present day, legal eminence is not attainable, and if it
were would scarcely be worth having. I am speaking solely in
reference to usefulness. The money question I set aside: for I will
live on my fortune, whatever that may be: and if I can not do it in
England, why I must do it out here. But as I have few luxurious
tastes, I do not think I shall have much difficulty. To return: this
is not a satisfactory view of my prospects: but the fact is that for
gentlemen without money there are very few openings of useful-

ness. It may, perhaps will, end in my doing nothing in particular, and trying to eke out my means by writing for newspapers. But even that seems to me preferable to the bar. It is, after all, only a question of duty: for all modes of life are equally uninviting. . . .

4.10.4. From B. Holland, Life of the Duke of Devonshire, *2 vols, 1911, I, pp. 55, 79–83.*

A letter from Lord Palmerston to the then Marquis of Harting-ton's father about the acceptance of office by Hartington (in 1863) and extracts from the correspondence between Gladstone and Hartington in 1870 when the Prime Minister offered Hartington the Irish Secretaryship. After much persuasion Hartington finally accepted the post.

Before Lord Hartington reached England, Lord Palmerston had addressed the following letter (7th February 1863) to the Duke of Devonshire:–

'Mr Whitbread, the Lay Lord of the Admiralty, is obliged on account of his health to resign his appointment, and I wish to know from you whether we might look to Lord Hartington as a successor to Mr Whitbread in that office.

'The office is one of a good deal of labour, but of labour of a highly interesting kind, being connected as it is with the management of the naval service of the country. Lord Hartington has shown much ability whenever he has taken part in the debates of the House, and I feel very strongly that it is of great importance to the country, and is highly conducive to the working of our Constitution, that young men in high aristocratical positions should take part in the administration of public affairs, and should not leave the working of our political machine to classes whose pursuits and interests are of a different kind. . . .'

Lord Hartington, already, as the son of a great Irish landlord, knew something of Ireland. His knowledge was now to be increased by official experience. Some Cabinet changes took place in December 1870. Mr Chichester Fortescue (afterwards Lord Carlingford), then Irish Chief Secretary, was moved to the Board of Trade. The Prime Minister wrote on 23rd December to Lord Hartington –

'to place his office at your disposal, and indeed something more, namely to press it on your acceptance. In your position, as well as with your capacity, I make bold, as the saying is, to ask of you to step from a less forward into a more forward rank. . . .

The Irish Secretaryship has been for some time a most important office. It is likely to continue so; nay, there are contingencies in which it may become greatly more important than it is.

'You will not I hope feel even inclined to refuse this fence. But if you are so inclined I hope that you will not do so without seeing me that I may explain myself more fully. . . .'

No post in the public service within the United Kingdom does, indeed, give so good a training in the art of statesmanship. The work touches all branches of administration in a great and turbulent province, and at the same time exercises the mind in parliamentary tactics. But Hartington was not ambitious, and his cousin was right in his anticipation of the difficulty in getting him to take this fence. Mr Gladstone's veiled suggestion that the post might be a step towards future leadership was the reverse of an inducement. The following letters show the strength of the resistance which he opposed to the scheme for his advancement:–

> *Chatsworth, Chesterfield*
> *24th December 1870*

My dear Mr Gladstone, – I cannot but feel much flattered by your selection of me for the important post of Irish Secretary. Some reports which had reached me before I received your letter had caused me to consider what I would do in the event of such an offer being made to me, and I had resolved that I would decline it. Nothing but the kind and urgent expressions contained in your letter and in one which I have received from Granville could have inclined me even to hesitate in giving this reply.

My objections are of various kinds.

The difficulties of the Irish Education system, even if legislation upon it be postponed for another year, seem to me to be almost insuperable if it is a necessary condition that the support of the Irish members should be retained.

The management of that body is a fact for which I do not feel any aptitude or inclination.

But I am afraid that I must confess that the considerations which weigh most of all with me are of a more private and personal character. I cannot reconcile myself to giving up almost the whole year to official duties. I imagine that the Irish Secretary ought to be in Dublin during the greater part of the year when Parliament is not sitting. This to me, with all my friends and pursuits in England, would be almost banishment for the time. I presume that it is mainly this obligation which has induced Fortescue to leave the office; but to me as a bachelor the necessity of constant residence in Ireland would be still more irksome. . . .

HARTINGTON.

Devonshire House,
28th December 1870.

My dear Mr Gladstone, – Your second letter only reached me this morning, as I had left Chatsworth. I have also received your telegram sent after you had written. Since writing to you on Saturday, I have thought much on the subject of your offer; and have done my best to overcome the reluctance which I told you that I felt about accepting it.

I am sorry to say that I have not been successful. The more I think of it, the more I feel that it is not a place which would in any way suit me, and that therefore in accepting it, I could not do justice either to myself or my colleagues.

I need not trouble you by repeating and enlarging my list of objections. Singly they would appear to you to be trifling, and collectively I doubt not they would still seem to you quite insufficient. But to my own mind they appear so strong that even if I allowed myself to be persuaded into acceptance against my will, it would be with such reluctance that I feel certain that an office undertaken in such a spirit could only lead to failure.

I am quite aware that in declining this offer I am doing that which may greatly damage my own political prospects. This, however, cannot be of any great importance to any one except myself. I fear, however, that it may be inconvenient to you and to the Government. For this I am very sorry, and I cannot conclude this letter without saying (knowing that you will not misunderstand the spirit in which I say it), that if now or at any future time my present office would facilitate any combination which you may choose to make, it is so far as I am concerned entirely at your disposal. I feel that I have no right to retain an office which is almost a sinecure, when I refuse a place of real work. . . .

HARTINGTON

In the end, the insistence of the First Minister induced his reluctant subordinate to accept the duty, and Lord Hartington entered upon the work which occupied him until his resignation of the Government rather more than three years later.

4.10.5. From Marquis of Crewe, Lord Rosebery, *2 vols. 1931, I, p. 39.*

The occasion of this letter was an enquiry which Rosebery's mother, the Duchess of Cleveland, had received from a neighbouring landowner. (The Duchess was the daughter of the fourth Earl of Stanhope who married Lord Henry Vane, brother and heir to the second Duke of Cleveland, after the death of Rosebery's father.) Rosebery was twenty in 1867.

October 27th, 1867.

My dearest Mother,

Many thanks for your long letter.

I was very much interested about Darlington. But there are so many things to be considered, that it seems impossible: though there is nothing I should like half so well as to represent Darlington.

The first objection is, that though I have no politics, and have never professed any, I am not at all prepared to come forward as a Conservative. Besides the Conservative party has practically ceased to exist, and I think we shall see an entire transmutation of parties before 1869. Anyhow, it is not the time for a young man to commit himself in any way on either side. The next is that my grandfather would probably object, and very naturally, to devote any money which he may fairly destine for his younger children to getting me a seat in Parliament for what might possibly be a very short time. And I should neither feel justified in asking him for money nor my Committee for a subscription. I think the last at any rate an insuperable obstacle; so I shall cease to think of anything of the sort, and if Mr Surtees ever alludes to it again, please tell him that it is out of the question.

4.10.6. From Walter Long (Viscount Long), Memories, *1923, pp. 67–73, 76–7.*

The Long family had owned estates in Wiltshire for several hundred years and had lived at Wraxall since the fourteenth

century. Three Longs in succession had represented Wiltshire
constituencies. Walter Long took over the estates at the age of
twenty-one on the death of his father: he entered Parliament
three years later. This he describes in his memoirs written in the
early nineteen-twenties after illness had forced him out of politics.

I was asked to stand for Marlborough in 1878. Under the old
system, this was a close borough for the great House of Bruce at
Savernake, who were staunch supporters of the Liberal Party. The
Conservatives had maintained their organization and had insisted
upon fighting the seat. They felt that they had been overlaid by the
great influence of the Bruce family and were anxious for a representative of another old Wilts family to champion their cause. I was
not very willing to accede to their request, as I had no great desire
to enter into conflict with the local magnate at Savernake, who
possessed the strong regard of everybody in the county. But I
appreciated the fact that the Conservatives of the borough had kept
the 'flag flying' under very depressing circumstances and I was
persuaded to accept the invitation.

Before giving my final decision, I consulted one or two of our
political leaders in the Northern Division of the County and asked
their advice. The view they expressed offers an interesting commentary upon the political conditions which existed in those days.
They told me that they thought the experience would be useful,
but they added: 'We are doubtful whether Sir George Jenkinson'
(a Gloucestershire squire and one of the Members for N. Wilts)
'will stand again; if he resigns we propose to bring you forward.'

There was no suggestion that they should first consult the
electors of their way of thinking by bringing my name before a
representative committee, as would be the case today. They said
quite definitely that they intended to run me as their candidate!
Consequently I informed the Marlborough Association I would
stand provided that there was no vacancy for the county. If this
did occur, I said, they must hold me free from my obligation to
them. Looking back after all the years which have intervened, with
the experience gained in subsequent elections, I marvel at the
quiet certainty of the local leaders, and my own audacity in assuming that I should be adopted as candidate. . . .

I was not destined after all to take part in an election at Marlborough. Sir George Jenkinson retired from North Wilts, and I

was called upon to stand for that division. The procedure was quite simple. One of the leaders wrote that in consequence of Sir George's retirement, due to ill-health, a meeting would be held at Chippenham, the chief town in the division. He would be glad if I would attend as it was their intention to select me as the candidate, I went in due course and was told to wait in an adjoining room. About half a dozen county gentlemen were present. I was not kept waiting more than a quarter of an hour, when they asked me to join them. I was informed that I had been selected as the Conservative candidate. I had no one to advise me, but as we had been for many generations associated with the county I accepted the invitation. I hope it was with becoming modesty, though I do not think that it was with any misgivings as to the result.

In those days there were two Members for each of the two divisions into which the county was divided. Mr Sotheron Estcourt, who came from the other end of the division – in fact he actually lived in Gloucestershire, though he owned considerable property in North Wilts – had been the other sitting Member. He decided to offer himself for re-election, so we became joint candidates. . . .

For some days after Mr Estcourt and I had been adopted it seemed that we were to be unopposed. Indeed, some of the Liberal leaders had said that as we were both members of families which had been connected with the representation of the county for some considerable time, and as we held what they described as moderate views, it was not their intention to contest the seat.

As I have said, I had accepted nomination without considering what the election might entail upon the candidate, and I remember very well the shock we received when we were informed that a strong Liberal candidate was to be brought out. . . .

As soon as it was known that we were to have a contest our agents set to work to retain every public-house they could get for our committee rooms, and to order post-horses and carriages from all the inn-keepers, some of whom had not a horse or a conveyance to their name. This was the recognized method of the day, and was dictated by two considerations. First, engaging the inns made it impossible for the other side to do so, and therefore agents did all in their power to be first in the field. Secondly, for every horse or conveyance ordered, the inn-keepers were allowed to charge for an equivalent number of rosettes and streamers of the party colours. So the privilege was a real one, eagerly sought after, and it was astonishing to find the high prices which were charged for those particular articles.

4·11 POLITICS AND THE POWER OF THE PURSE

From The Economist, *16 April 1864.*

The article quoted was occasioned by a speech of J. S. Mill in which he argued that political bribery was on the increase. Following this, the paper examined the new class of MPs, men of vast and recent wealth.

The men who have made these fortunes are generally active-minded, pushing persons, ambitious either for themselves, or more frequently for their sons, and the quickest road for an ambitious man with any brains at all is Parliamentary life. What other road indeed is open say to the lucky speculator in cotton? There is no Court favour to gain, and high repute in literature, or the sciences, or the army, comes only to the qualified. It is not that the social status of a member of Parliament is so high – for it is not – but that the possibilities it opens are so very great. English society is aristocratic with reservations, and one of the reservations is this: if a really wealthy man, and we mean by that anybody with more than ten thousand a year clear, displays political ability, all barriers disappear, and the greatest in the land *admit* one who as they think may be greater still. Nobody who may be a Minister of State is allowed to feel any lack of social distinction. This exemption is what men who have achieved wealth really crave for, and year by year the wealthy candidates who present themselves to the boroughs seem to increase. They have rarely much connection, never any hereditary influence, and their object, therefore, is to use the weapon which they possess, the command of ready cash. Sometimes they bribe and bribe heavily, buying not the score or two score of men who once held the balance of power, but an entire majority, every man of whom has received some favour at their hands. This, however, is not the most frequent form of corruption. A far more common one is the direct purchase of the borough under cover of public-spirited benefactions. The agent in a small represented town tells the leading citizens quietly that his 'man' is really interested in the place; that he regrets to see the

Town Hall in such a state, and will rebuild it; that he thinks such a waste ought to be drained, and he will drain it; that he will deepen the streamlet, or found a good school, or 'restore' the Cathedral, or even – we have known the cases we quote – revive the fading glories of the races. The good burgesses believe the promises, which are seldom broken, and the new man with a full purse is duly returned with very little opposition. So general is this system becoming, that the middle boroughs are beginning to be represented by three classes of persons, – old Tories, supported by all the people who are beyond inducements, and who can in quiet times sometimes 'influence' a majority, – men who will utter the Radical Shibboleths, and who excite thereby some enthusiasm, and successful notabilities who can afford to spend great sums. . . .

The career of politics, instead of being thrown open to the nation, is confined to a very limited class, the Premier has to choose among five thousand men instead of half a million. The rich men are not a bad class. On the contrary, men go into business now who in 1800 would have disdained trade, and we have 'double firsts' lending money to princes, and 'honour men' speculating in shipping, or trying to make fortunes out of some new manure. But the class of eligibles becomes limited, and if matters advance in the same direction a little longer, England will be governed by Peers' sons and men with 20,000*l* a year.

4·12 THE CONSEQUENCE OF THE 'OPENING OF THE FLOODGATES'

From Frederic Harrison, 'Parliament after Reform', Fort-nightly, April 1868 and reprinted in his Order and Reform, *1875 (pp. 177–08 of the latter).*

The changes in the electoral system brought about by the Second Reform Act, although profound, affected the character of Parliament only slowly. Frederic Harrison, one of the Act's most ardent advocates, had no illusion on that score.

In fact, the change which has been made is one which, from its nature, cannot be immediately tested. It is not that a great revolution has been effected, but that great possibilities of revolution have. Until the fountains of the great deep are opened, all will remain very much as before. Power and wealth will control elections; the rich governing class will furnish nineteen-twentieths of the members. The corrupt boroughs, the bribery system, the nominee system, the jobbing system will perish hard and slowly. Rank will exert its time-honoured spell, petty interests will divide constituencies as of old, and Beer will be king time and again. The Millennium that the Radical hails, the Chaos that the Tory dreads, are alike the creation of delusion or of panic. The whole thing is in embryo as yet. The workmen are capable of great transforming ideas, it is true; but the ideas are not forthcoming – they have yet to be framed, or at least to be promulgated. They have a great sense of adhesion to their chiefs; but great revolutionary chiefs are in their cradles, or at school. The workmen have a native instinct for vigorous action. But the social force of Conservatism is at present quite paramount. Hence, with ideas still incoherent and unset, without immediate leaders of any genius, and a dense phalanx of material opposition before them, the new electors are certainly not likely to sweep the board; and to all appearance we may say that nothing is changed, but that there are a million of new electors, more or less – nothing, that is to say, on the surface.

Has nothing, then, been done? and have the rhetoric and the vigils of so many sessions been in vain? Yes! an immense work has been done. By transposing the legal balance of power from the wages-paying to the wages-earning class, a great *moral* change has been effected. The new power will slowly consolidate and feel its strength, and will be long in doing so. But in the meantime the barriers and outworks which fenced about the arcana of State are gone. The veil of the temple (reared by the Whigs in '88) has been rent asunder, and priests, acolytes, and worshippers are mingled together in a mass. The elaborate system of checks and counter-checks by which the great and good men who have governed us for two centuries kept public opinion at bay is all gone, at any rate in strictness of law. Formerly, what a jungle of public meetings, of deputations, of parliamentary resolutions, of press eloquence, of battling in committees, and lobbying of members did it need to pass a single acknowledged reform into law! Now, as by law is ordained, the people have only really to wish a thing done, and to mean to have it done, and it will be done. They are not likely to attempt it, but the process is infinitely simplified if they did. The old British Constitution, as invented by the saviours of society at that great and glorious era, resembled nothing in the world so much as the famous automaton chessman. In that ingenious toy the amazed spectator was shown a multitude of wheels, cranks, and pulleys; saw the clockwork elaborately wound up, and heard it move with a strange and rumbling sound. The pieces, we know, were all the time really worked by a concealed player behind, who viewed the board through the sleeve of the figure, behind which sleeve he no doubt occasionally laughed at his dupes. Mr Disraeli now, who loves a surprise, has simply opened the doors, discarded the clockwork, and shown us the man. The wheels and the pulleys are not needed now; we shall hear no more that strange and rumbling sound; we see our man, and we sit down to play a simple game of chess – king, bishop, knight, and pawn – and no legerdemain for the future.

To sum up then the various features of this great change, we may say that they are indirect, not direct; future, not immediate; latent, not on the surface. In a word, it is a *moral* change; a new power, a new tone, new possibilities exist. The old class of men, or men very like them, for the present will continue to sit in the House, but under very different conditions, and with an altered sense of responsibility. When the legal supremacy in the State is vested in an order of men in whom, at least, is latent motive power so vast – men craving for something to be done, capable of blazing up some day if they find nothing done – perhaps something will be done. The victorious soldiers of Caesar are no longer on the Rhine or the Rhone, separated by half a continent from a majestic senate at home. They have not burst in upon the State, but they stand beside the Rubicon, whilst our conscript fathers anxiously deliberate in the Capitol. O, conscript fathers, be wise in time, for there is little to keep them from crossing that historic stream!

4·13 THE POLITICAL CULTURE OF THE ARISTOCRACY

From Mathew Arnold, 'The Popular Education of France' (1861) in his Complete Works, *vol. 2, 1962, pp. 4–6.*

In the introduction to his survey on French education, significantly called 'Democracy' Arnold discusses the relationship between 'Education', or 'culture', and the political system. His analysis is as equally important for the sympathetic account of the strength and rationale of the old system as for the recognition of the new forces which were bound to supersede it.

In England, democracy has been slow in developing itself, having met with much to withstand it, not only in the worth of the aristocracy, but also in the fine qualities of the common people. The aristocracy has been more in sympathy with the common people than perhaps any other aristocracy. . . . Above all, it has in general meant to act with justice, according to its own notions of justice. Therefore the feeling of admiring deference to such a class was more deep-rooted in the people of this country, more cordial, and more persistent, than in any people of the Continent. . . . Democracy is a force in which the concert of a great number of men makes up for the weakness of each man taken by himself; democracy accepts a certain relative rise in their condition, obtainable by this concert for a great number, as something desirable in itself, because though this is undoubtedly far below grandeur, it is yet a good deal above insignificance. A very strong, self-reliant people neither easily learns to act in concert, nor easily brings itself to regard any middling-good, any good short of the best, as an object ardently to be coveted and striven for. It keeps its eye on the grand prizes, and these are to be won only by distancing competitors, by getting before one's comrades, by succeeding all by one's self; and so long as a people works thus individually, it does not work democratically. The English people has all the qualities which dispose a people to work individually; may it never lose them! . . . But the English people is no longer so entirely ruled by them as not to show visible beginnings of democratic action; it becomes more and more sensible to the irresistible seduction of democratic ideas, promising to each individual of the multitude increased self-respect and expansion with the increased importance and authority of the multitude to which he belongs, with the diminished preponderance of the aristocratic class above him.

While the habit and disposition of deference are thus dying out among the lower classes of the English nation, it seems to me indisputable that the advantages which command deference, that eminent superiority in high feeling, dignity, and culture, tend to diminish among the highest class. I shall not be suspected of any inclination to underrate the aristocracy of this country. . . . But I cannot read the history of the flowering time of the English aristocracy, the eighteenth century, and then look at this aristocracy in our own century, without feeling that there has been a change. I am not now thinking of private and domestic virtues, of morality, of decorum. ... I am thinking of those public and conspicuous virtues by which the multitude is captivated and led, – lofty spirit, commanding character, exquisite culture. It is true that the advance of all classes in culture and refinement may make the culture of one class, which, isolated, appeared remarkable, appear so no longer; but exquisite culture and great dignity are always something rare and striking, and it is the distinction of the English aristocracy, in the eighteenth century, that not only was their culture something rare by comparison with the rawness of the masses, it was something rare and admirable in itself. . . .

Probably democracy has something to answer for in this falling off of her rival. To feel itself raised on high, venerated, followed, no doubt stimulates a fine nature to keep itself worthy to be followed, venerated, raised on high, hence that lofty maxim, *noblesse oblige*. To feel its culture something precious and singular, makes such a nature zealous to retain and extend it. . . . The removal of the stimulus a little relaxes their energy. It is not so much that they sink to be somewhat less than themselves, as that they cease to be somewhat more than themselves. But, however this may be, whencesoever the change may proceed, I cannot doubt that in the aristocratic virtue, in the intrinsic commanding force of the English upper class, there is a diminution. Relics of a great generation are still, perhaps, to be seen amongst them, surviving exemplars of noble manners and consummate culture; but they disappear one after the other, and no one of their kind takes their place. At the very moment when democracy becomes less and less disposed to follow and to admire, aristocracy becomes less and less qualified to command and to captivate. . . .

The dissolution of the old political parties which have governed this country since the Revolution of 1688 has long been remarked. It was repeatedly declared to be happening long before it actually took place, while the vital energy of these parties still subsisted in full vigour, and was threatened only by some temporary obstruction. It has been eagerly deprecated long after it had actually begun to take place, when it was in full progress, and inevitable. These parties [Arnold is referring here to the parties which had emerged after 1688]; differing in so much else, were yet alike in this, that they were both, in a certain broad sense, *aristocratical* parties. They were combinations of persons considerable, either by great family and estate, or by Court favour, or lastly, by eminent abilities and popularity; this last body, however, attaining participation in public affairs only through a conjunction with one or other of the former. These connections, though they contained men of very various degrees of birth and property, were still wholly leavened with the feelings and habits of the upper class of the nation. They had the bond of a common culture; and, however their political opinions and acts might differ, what they said and did had the stamp and style imparted by this culture, and by a common and elevated social condition.

Aristocratical bodies have no taste for a very imposing executive, or for a very active and penetrating domestic administration. They have a sense of equality among themselves, and of constituting in themselves what is greatest and most dignified in the realm, which makes their pride revolt against the over-shadowing greatness and dignity of a commanding executive. They have a temper of independence, and a habit of uncontrolled action, which makes them impatient of encountering, in the management of the interior concerns of the country, the machinery and regulations of a superior and peremptory power. The different parties amongst them, as they successively get possession of the government, respect this jealous disposition in their opponents, because they share it themselves. It is a disposition proper to them as great personages, not as ministers; and as they are great personages for their whole life, while they may probably be ministers but for a very short time, the instinct of their social condition avails more with them than the instinct of their official function. To administer as little as possible, to make its weight felt in foreign affairs rather than in domestic, to see in ministerial station rather the means of power and dignity than a means of searching and useful administrative activity, is the natural tendency of an aristocratic executive. It is a tendency which is creditable to the good sense of aristocracies, honourable to their moderation, and at the same time fortunate for their country, of whose internal development they are not fitted to have the full direction. . . .

That elevation of character, that noble way of thinking and behaving, which is an eminent gift of nature to some individuals, is also often generated in whole classes of men . . . by the possession of power, by the importance and responsibility of high station, by habitual dealing with great things, by being placed above the necessity of constantly struggling for little things. And it is the source of great virtues. It may go along with a not very quick or open intelligence; but it cannot well go along with a conduct vulgar and ignoble. A governing class imbued with it may not be capable of intelligently leading the masses of a people to the highest pitch of welfare for them; but it sets them an invaluable example of qualities without which no really high welfare can exist. This has been done for their nation by the best aristocracies. The Roman aristocracy did it; the English aristocracy has done it. . . . They made, the one of the Roman, the other of the English people, in spite of all the shortcomings of each, great peoples, peoples *in the grand style.* And this they did, while wielding the people according to their own notions, and in the direction which seemed good to them; not as servants and instruments of the people, but as its commanders and heads; solicitous for the good of their country, indeed, but taking for granted that of that good they themselves were the supreme judges, and were to fix the conditions.

4·14 HIGH-BORN POLITICIANS AND LOW-BORN POPULACE

From M. Ostrogorski, Democracy and the Organization of Political Parties, *2 vols., 1902, I, pp. 342–5.*

In this massive volume, Ostrogorski, a Russian scholar who lived in Paris, has given us the fullest account of the British party system at the end of the last century. In this description of the activities of the Primrose League, which was founded by Lord Randolph Churchill and his colleagues to bring Toryism to the masses, the author shows the League's subtle role in politically socializing the 'lower orders'.

The League throws its doors wide open to persons of every social condition, down to the humblest, – to small shopkeepers, to artisans, to day-labourers, to washerwomen, to maid-servants, – and once brought together the members of the upper and well-to-do classes overwhelm them with civilities in order to prove to them in an impressive way that the high-born and the wealthy 'are the friends of the poor people'; so that the flame of cupidity kindled in the popular breast by the Radical agitators would die out of itself. The League just supplies the common ground of meeting and provides the opportunities for it. With this object it has elaborated a whole liturgy for the communion of classes by means of fêtes. The Associations have their *social meetings* as well, but it is the League which is the great contriver of them and which has well-nigh identified its existence with them and raised them to the level of a political force, almost of an *instrumentum regni*. Every Habitation organizes as often as possible festive gatherings, rising from simple 'teas' to 'high-class entertainments' and 'fêtes'. The 'teas' which are the most modest of the meetings, are also the most common. Then come the concerts, the dances, the balls. The 'fêtes', which combine all these amusements, are often adorned with small dramatic representations, – *tableaux vivants*, ventriloquism, conjuring, 'Italian marionettes', clowning, etc. . . .

In the monotonous existence of the lower middle class and the populace they supply, down to the modest 'teas', a distraction enhanced by a good many charms, of which the intercourse of the sexes is not the least. They afford young people a legitimate opportunity of meeting each other and of completing in the sphere of sentiment the role of 'knights' and of 'dames' which has been assigned to them for the defence of society. The union of sexes is thus added to 'the union of classes'. It has procured the League a great number of adhesions, perhaps as many as the 'union of classes', which offers not only to young folk but to those of all ages one of the sentimental satisfactions most highly appreciated in England: the delightful pleasure of coming into contact with people of higher social rank.

By paying a subscription of a shilling or sixpence, one becomes the colleague of titled or simply rich personages, one obtains access to their drawing-rooms and parks, which they place at the disposal of the League for its meetings, and there the humblest can rub up against the great ones of the earth. If you only have a competency, leisure, and intelligence, you can even be made a sharer in the labours of the League and enter its 'inner circle'. You take charge of a district in the capacity of 'warden' or 'sub-warden', to conduct the political census, and this gives you an opportunity of reporting and exchanging remarks on the results with the personages who are at the head of the Habitation. With a little more distinction or wealth, a woman of the lower middle-class can take her place, in the committees of which there is no lack in the Habitations, by the side of titled ladies, perhaps marchionesses or even duchesses, and, seated in their grand drawing-room, discuss the affairs of the Habitation on an equal footing. If this does not fall in her way, perhaps she will be vouch-safed the honour, at the innumerable fêtes of the League, of helping the great ladies to make the tea and cut the sandwiches. Her husband or her brother, the 'knight' who spends his life in selling mustard or candles, will receive his cup of tea from the very hands of a 'dame' who is a great lady. . . . Every local delegate is admitted to the receptions given by the exalted ladies of the Grand Council on the occasion of the annual meeting, and the honours are done to him by live duchesses and Ministers or ex-Ministers. True, his share has not amounted to very much, there were several thousand people thronging the gorgeous reception-rooms, but still he carries away a few shakes of the hand and a gracious smile or two.

4·15 POLITICIANS AT THE END OF THE CENTURY

From The New House of Commons, July 1895. *1895.*

While the representation of the boroughs became increasingly the preserve of the business and professional classes, the counties still returned many members of the 'leading families'. The representation of Northumberland and of Nottinghamshire shows very clearly the division of the counties into industrial (e.g. mining) and predominantly agricultural areas. (C=Conservative, R=Radical below).

NORTHUMBERLAND (4).

Wansbeck. 12,234.

FENWICK, CHARLES (R.), of Bebside, Northumberland, s. of John and Jane Fenwick, both parents being in humble circumstances, his father working in the same mine as himself, b. 1850, was for a short time in a colliery school, and commenced work 'on the bank' at nine years of age, and worked at the Bebside Colliery up to the time of his first election to Parliament in 1885. Has been a member of the Commissions on Secondary Education and on Explosions in Royal Mines; is on the executive of the Miners' Association and a member of the Joint Committee; was one of the miners' representatives at the annual meeting of the Trades Union Congress at Aberdeen, and was Parliamentary Secretary to the Trades Union Congress from 1890 to

1894. M. Jane, second d. of Mr Henry Gardner, for many years of Old Cramlington, Northumberland, a miner. M.P. for Wansbeck div. of Northumberland from 1885. 5,629 votes.

Tyneside. 14,932

PEASE, JOSEPH ALBERT (R.), of Snow-hall, Gainford, Darlington, and 44, Grosvenor-gardens, S.W., young, s. of Sir Joseph Whitwell Pease, M.P., first bart., by Mary, d. of the late Mr Alfred Fox, of Falmouth, b. 1860, and educated at Grove-house, Tottenham, and Trinity College, Cambridge (B.A. 1881, M.A. 1884). Is a J.P. and D.L. for Durham, a J.P. for the North Riding of Yorkshire, County Councillor for the Crook division of the county of Durham, was Mayor of Darlington 1889, is a director of Pease and Partners, and of the owners of the Middlesbrough estate, and was assistant private secretary to Mr John Morley 1893-5. M., 1886, Ethel, only d. of Lieut.-General Sir Henry Havelock-Allan, V.C., M.P. Tyneside div. of Northumberland from 1892. 6,066 votes.

Hexham. 10,316

BEAUMONT, WENTWORTH CANNING BLACKETT (R.), of Bywell-hall, Stocksfield-on-Tyne, eld. s. of Mr Wentworth Blackett Beaumont, of Bretton-hall, Wakefield, and 144, Piccadilly, W., who represented Northumberland for 40 years, by his first wife, Lady Margaret Anne, fourth d. of the first Marquis of Clanricarde, b. 1860, and educated at Eton and Trinity College, Cambridge (B.A. 1884, M.A. 1888). Is a J.P. for the West Riding of Yorkshire and Northumberland, was formerly a captain in the 3rd Battalion Royal Welsh Fusiliers (Militia), and has been a lieutenant in the Yorkshire Hussars Yeomanry from 1886. M., 1889, Lady Alexandrian, d. of the fifth Marquis of Londonderry. 4,438 votes.

Berwick-on-Tweed. 9.277

GREY, SIR EDWARD, Bart. (R.), of Falloden, Chathill, Northumberland, and 30, Grosvenor-road, S.W., eld. s. of the late Lieut.-Colonel George Henry Grey, Equerry to H.R.H. the Prince of Wales, by Harriet Jane, young. d. of Lieut.-Colonel Charles Pearson, and grands. of the Right Hon. Sir George Grey, G.C.B., b. 1862, and educated at Winchester and Balliol College, Oxford. Is a J.P. for Northumberland, and was for a short time private secretary to Sir E. Baring (now Lord Cromer), and afterwards assistant private secretary (unpaid) to Mr Childers, when Chancellor of the Exchequer. Was Under-Secretary for Foreign Affairs from August, 1892, to June, 1894. M., 1885 Frances

Dorothy, eld. d. of Major Shallcross Fitz Herbert Widdrington, of Newton-hall, Northumberland. M.P. for Berwick-on-Tweed division from 1885. 4,378 votes.

NOTTINGHAMSHIRE (4).

Bassetlaw. 9,990.

MILNER, SIR FREDERICK GEORGE, Bart. (C.), of 22 Pont-street, S.W., second but eld. surviving s. of the late Sir Wm. M. Edward Milner, M.P. for York 1848–57, by Lady Anne Georgiana, third d. of Mr. Frederick Lumley, of Tickhill-castle, and sister to the ninth Earl of Scarborough, b. 1849, and educated at Eton and Christ Church, Oxford. M., 1880, Adeline Gertrude, d. of the late Mr William Beckett (Denison), M.P. of Meanwood-park, Yorkshire, by the Hon. Helen, third d. of William, second Lord Feversham. M.P. York, Nov., 1883–85, unsuccessful candidate York and Sowerby division of York-shire 1885, and for Radcliffe-cum Farnworth div. of Lancashire, 1886. M.P. for Bassetlaw div. of Notts from Dec., 1890. 4,874 votes.

Newark. 10,485

FINCH-HATTON, Hon. HAROLD HENEAGE (C.), of 11a, Pall-mall-east, S.W., fourth and young. s. of George William, tenth Earl of Winchelsea and Nottingham, by his third wife, Fanny Margaretta, eld. d. of Mr Edward Royd Rice, of Dane-court, Kent, b. 1856, and edu-cated at Eton and Balliol College, Oxford. Was for nine years engaged in cattle farming in North Queensland, and is a director of two com-panies. Was one of the founders and is treasurer of the Imperial Federation League. Unsuccessful candidate East Nottingham 1885, 1886, and 1892. Unopposed.

Rushcliffe. 12,808

ELLIS, JOHN EDWARD (R.), of Wrea Head, Scalby, Scarborough, and No. 40, Pont-street, S.W., eld. s. of the late Mr Edward Shipley Ellis, J.P., and Chairman of the Midland Railway, of the Newarke, Leicester, by Emma, d. of the late Mr John Burgess, of Wigston Grange, Leicestershire, b. 1841, educated at the Friends' School, Kendal, and is a coal owner at Hucknall Torkard, Nottinghamshire. Is a J.P. for the county and borough of Nottingham and a D.L. and J.P. for the North Riding of Yorkshire. M., 1867, Maria, d. of the late Mr John Rowntree, of Scarborough. M.P. for Rushcliffe div. from 1885. 5,752 votes.

Mansfield. 12,345.

WILLIAMS, JOHN CARVELL (R.), of 21, Hornsey-rise-gardens, N., eld. s. of Mr John Allen Williams, of Stepney, by Mary, d. of Mr

John Carvell, of Lambeth, b. 1821, and in 1847 became secretary of the Society for the Liberation of Religion from State Patronage and Control, retiring in 1877, when he was appointed chairman of the society's Parliamentary Committee. Is chairman of the Hornsey Liberal Association. M.P. South Nottingham 1885–6, unsuccessful candidate 1886. M.P. Mansfield div. Nottinghamshire from 1892. 5,670 votes.

4·16 THE GOVERNMENT OF THE COUNTY AND 'THE GREAT UNPAID'

From F. W. Maitland, 'The Shallows and Silences of Real Life', in The Reflector, *February 1888.*

In 1888 Parliament passed the County Councils' Act which transferred responsibility for the administration of the counties from the Justices of the Peace to newly-elected bodies. The Justices had administered the counties since the fifteenth century and they had been largely men of the types of Shallow, 'in the county of Gloucester, justice of the peace and *coram ... custalorum ... ratolorum* and a gentleman born . . . who writes himself *armigero*, in any bill, warrant, quittance or obligation' and had 'done any time three hundred years' (*Merry Wives of Windsor*, I, i).

In 'The Shallows and Silences of Real Life' originally published in *The Reflector* of February 1888 F. W. Maitland attempted to write his epitaph and, implicitly, a eulogy of the English Ruling Class. The extract given here is reprinted from his *Collected Papers*, I, pp. 468–77.

But for the other side of the coin, see Cobden in 4·8 above.

An old form of local government which has served us for five centuries and more, is breaking up, and, to say the least, must undergo a great change which cannot leave even its essential character unaltered. A vital organ of the body politic must be renewed. Hitherto such government as our counties have had, has been government by justices of the peace – government, that is, by country gentlemen, appointed by the Lord Chancellor in the Queen's name, on the recommendation of the Lord Lieutenant of the county, legally dismissible at a moment's notice; but practically holding their offices for life. This institution has had a great past, we had almost said a splendid past; but Englishmen, unless they are taught by foreigners, seldom see its greatness, and to talk of splendour might therefore seem absurd. Our historians, even some who write what call themselves 'constitutional histories', are apt to spend all their energies upon describing the flashy episodes of national life, scenes in Parliament, tragedies on Tower Hill, the strife of Whigs and Tories, wars and rumours of wars.

To deal with the vulgar affairs of commonplace counties, to show what the laws made in Parliament, the liberties asserted in Parliament, really meant to the mass of the people, this was beneath their dignity or beyond their industry. . . . Some day it will be otherwise: a history of the eighteenth century which does not place the justice of the peace in the very foreground of the picture, will be known for what it is – a caricature. . . .

Certainly, to any one who has an eye for historic greatness it is a very marvellous institution, this Commission of the Peace, growing so steadily, elaborating itself into ever new forms, providing for ever new wants, expressing ever new ideas, and yet never losing its identity, carrying back our thoughts now to a Yorkist, now to a Lancastrian king, stamped with the sign manual of the Tudor monarchy, telling us of rebellion, restoration, revolution, of peaceful Georgian times, of the days of Bentham and the great reforms. Look where we may, we shall hardly find any other political entity which has had so eventful and yet so perfectly continuous a life. And then it is so purely English, perhaps the most distinctively English part of all our governmental organisation. The small group of country gentlemen appointed to keep the peace, to arrest malefactors, and lead the hue and cry, acquires slowly and by almost insensible degrees the most miscellaneous, multitudinous duties, judicial and administrative duties which no theorist will classify, for their rich variety is not the outcome of theory, but of experience. And all the while this group shows the most certain sign of healthy life; it can assimilate fresh elements of the most different kinds, and yet never cease to be what it has been. Aristocratic it has been from the first, but never oligarchic; always ready to receive into itself new members who would have the time, the means, the will to do the work, without inquiring into the purity of their pedigrees or their right to coat armour. Our justices have never been a caste, nor the representatives of a caste; there has been nothing feudal, nothing patrimonial in their title; they have represented the State, and yet no one would call them officials. They have adapted themselves to many changes in their environment; they may do so yet once more. . . .

Shallow, as they call him, is at worst an anomaly, and Silence is obviously an anachronism in this eloquent nineteenth century. It is not asserted that the justices, in administering the affairs of the county, have been corrupt or extravagant. Notoriously the fact is otherwise. For the last half-century we have been trying many experiments in local government: we have had municipal corporations, poor-law boards, boards of health, school boards, all constituted on different principles. The result of these experiments is simply this: that of all known forms of local government, government by justices of the peace is the purest and the cheapest. . . . The average justice of the peace is a far more capable man than the average alderman, or the average guardian of the poor; consequently he requires much less official supervision. As a governor he is doomed; but there has been no accusation. He is cheap, he is pure, he is capable, but he is doomed; he is to be sacrificed to a theory, on the altar of the spirit of the age.

Let it well be understood that a great change is absolutely necessary. Taken as a whole, our local government is a weltering chaos out of which some decent order has to be got. . . . Rightly or wrongly, we have determined to carry the principle of popular election into every department of Government. To regret this would be vain, and the control of the central Government having already been placed in the hands of the great mass of the people, it seems to us distinctly desirable that the control over the local government should be in the same hands.

The wisest advocates of representative government . . . have laid much stress upon the educational influence of the electoral franchise. Now, if ever the multitude of the newly-enfranchised is to be educated by having votes, it must be by having votes which they can exercise about matters fairly within the range of their intellect and their interests. It is possible, and we hope not treasonable, very seriously to doubt whether the issues of national politics are at the present day within that range. About local affairs the judgment of the average elector is already better worth having, and it would become still more valuable if local affairs were to gain new dignity and importance. As it is, we have begun at the wrong end; we have asked men to have opinions about extremely difficult questions, when they have never had a chance of forming effective opinions about simpler questions. . . . Perhaps the lesson of the parish should have been learned before the study of the county was begun, and the county should have been mastered before the kingdom was touched. Things have fallen out otherwise. This could hardly have been helped, and the mistake may not yet be irretrievable. By the commission of copious blunders in local business, the governing class may be taught to avoid more disastrous blunders in national business. . . . We trust men to decide the question of Home Rule whom we would not trust to try an action for slander. There seems nothing for it but to give them a sphere of action in which the consequences of their errors should be very obviously manifest. At present there is no such sphere. The various local boards which exist are too obscure; governmental powers have been too much macadamised; responsibility has been scattered about in fragments; not one man in a thousand knows under how many 'authorities' he lives.

The situation is critical; it should be faced boldly. If it is so faced there is a chance that out of a great deal of immediate evil some permanent good may come. There will be jobbery and corruption, incompetence and extravagance, very possibly there will be gross injustice. Then will come the cry for ever fresh interferences on the part of the central Government, for more State-appointed inspectors, accountants, auditors; but if the lesson of the past fifty years has really been of any good to us, the cry should be resolutely resisted. The local bodies should be left to flounder and blunder towards better things. . . . Give the local 'authorities' a large room in which, if they can do no better, they can at least make fools of themselves upon a very considerable and striking scale. Such is the counsel that we are inclined to give, and it is one which should be acceptable to all parties in the State. . . .

If the principle of government by elected representatives is to be extended, it should be extended frankly and courageously, otherwise there will only be fresh irritation and discontent. The hope of securing able and just administrators must now lie, not in the creation of fancy franchises, which at best are fleeting, rickety things, but in the character of the work. It must be made dignified and attractive. If possible, men of the same stamp as those who have hitherto been active at Quarter Sessions should be obtained; but no tinkering of the electoral machinery can assure this result. The old spirit, the spirit which century after century has moved the squires of England to work hard in their counties, doing justice and keeping order, is not yet extinct. Capable men there are, and it will be possible to attract them if the work to which they are called is interesting, important work, and not the mere registering of the orders of the central bureau. If they have patience they will be elected, if elected they will be heard; for even the most ignorant and careless electorate will at times be convinced that the foolishness of fools is folly.

4·17 SELECTION OF JUSTICES OF THE PEACE

From the Minutes of Evidence of the Royal Commission on the Selection of Justices of the Peace of 1909, Parliamentary Papers, 1910, XXXVII, 85 and from the Appendices (pp. 237/8).

The first extract gives the evidence of J. F. Watkins, Chairman of the Watford Bench and the second is a paper, handed in by the Lord Chancellor, Lord Loreburn, giving the text of a memorial which he had received in 1906 and his reply to it.

Even after the County Council's Act the position of the Justices of the Peace was important both by reason of their judicial functions and because of the prestige of the office. The power of appointment lay (and still lies) with the Lord Chancellor. Until 1910 (following the Royal Commission) suggestions reached him mainly via the Lords Lieutenant of the Counties and led often to bias in terms of party and consequently of class.

1775. With regard to your selections and recommendations, do the political views of any persons come into play? – Not at all. I may mention that when I first joined the bench I think the great majority of the magistrates were, I presume you would call them, Whigs or Liberals, and many of those who are now on the bench, although they were Whigs or Liberals when they were appointed, are now Unionists.

1776. I suppose that was in 1886? – Yes.

1777. In sending in recommendations to the Lord Lieutenant do you give particulars to the Lord Lieutenant of the qualifications of the persons you recommend? – In every instance, unless the persons are well known to the Lord Lieutenant himself. But I think I may say that in every case I, as chairman, for the last 20 years always wrote a letter to the Lord Lieutenant, and I gave the fullest particulars.

1778. Does the Lord Lieutenant always accept your recommendations? – Not straight off; in some cases he does, but in other cases he wants a little further information.

1779. (*Mr Henry Hobhouse*). What is the character of your division? Is it industrial or agricultural? – It has changed very materially during the last 10 or 12 years. Originally it was agricultural and brewing, and there were one or two silk mills. Those were almost the only industrial works that we had in our division. The population in Watford itself, when I first went there in 1867, was about 6,000; at the present time it is over 40,000.

1780. From what classes are your magistrates drawn? – I have a list of them.

1781. I do not want you, of course, to go to the individuals. I only want to know generally from what classes they are drawn? – Those magistrates who are living in the country, if I might call it so, are every one of them, I think, what you may call country gentlemen. . . .

1785. Could you tell us generally about what proportion are country gentlemen – more than half? – I should think about half.

1786. From what class are the rest of the magistrates drawn; are they manufacturers? – I will take the first name without mentioning it. I suppose you do not wish for the names?

1787. No? – I will take the first name I come to. It is that of a gentleman who is not a very active magistrate, but he is in a locality where he has easy access to the people residing around him, which is in rather a remote part of the division. He is a small landed proprietor. He would hardly perhaps come under the denomination of a country gentleman.

1788. I do not want to trouble you to go through the members of the bench. I only want to know generally the composition. Is the manufacturing interest represented? – No, I hardly think that it is. The trading interest is represented, and the banking interest (that is, the local banking interest) is represented.

1789. What trades are represented? – There is a large butcher on the bench, and there are two brewers on the bench.

1790. Any other trade? – There was a gentleman who was a medical man in the division, but he has now given up practice.

1791. That would not be a trade? – No.

1792. Are there any representatives of the lower middle class? – It is rather difficult to define them.

1793. Are there any small tradesmen? – No.

1794. You have told us that there are no artisans? – There are no artisans. We had one, who has just died. I was wrong in saying there were no tradesmen. It has just crossed my mind that there was one gentleman who was a Nonconformist and a very strong Liberal. He has just died. He was a chemist in the town.

APPENDIX II
Handed in by the Right Hon. Lord Loreburn, G.C.M.G.

Memorial to the Lord Chancellor on the appointment of magistrates, signed by 88 Liberal and Labour members of the House of Commons, and presented to his Lordship on their behalf by Sir John Brunner, M.P.:–

The Right Hon. Lord Loreburn,
Lord Chancellor.

My Lord, – We, the undersigned county Liberal and Labour members of Parliament, desire to communicate with your Lordship on the subject of the appointment of justices of the peace.

We desire to state:–

(1) That we believe the present system of appointment of the persons charged with the local administration of justice in county districts to be a wrong system, and would warmly welcome a proposal of the Government which would put it upon an entirely non-political basis.

(2) That we earnestly wish that all nominations of justices from whatever source should be strictly scrutinised by the Lord Chancellor and his staff.

(3) That while the present system continues, under which political influence is exercised in the appointment of justices, Liberal and Labour members, who desire to remedy the very great disparity in the numbers of Conservative and Liberal justices which has grown up under the long domination of the Conservative

Party, have found themselves unduly hampered by certain under-mentioned points, which have been the cause of much dissatisfaction:–

(*a*) The existence of a long-established custom of taking advice from exclusively Tory circles in a large majority of counties as to the nomination and appointment of the county justices.

(*b*) The acceptance of the nominations of the Lords-Lieutenant – such nominations being frequently made by them without due inquiry – in preference to those of Liberal members; and the absence of consultation with Liberal members interested, or of information to them of appointments intended.

(*c*) The absence of information as to the reasons for the refusal of members' nominations, which information would be useful to them for their future guidance.

(*d*) The frequent refusal of the nomination of the more active Liberal and Labour politicians, although otherwise qualified to be magistrates.

(4) That the passing of the recent Act of Parliament removing the property qualification indicates a general agreement that the administration of justice should no longer be the prerogative of a single class, and that particularly in view of the powers which should reside in the justices with regard to the drink trade, it is of the greatest importance to find, within a reasonable time, improved means for making the county benches more truly representative both of political opinion and of the different social classes of the community.

With a view to the settlement of this question, we ask that your Lordship will be pleased to discuss these matters either with the whole body of members of Parliament concerned, or with a small committee of ten persons which has been appointed by them.

[Signed by 88 members of the House of Commons.]

The Lord Chancellor's reply:–

> *8 Eaton Square, London, S.W.,*
> *December 1906.*

My dear Brunner, – The memorial signed by 88 members of the House of Commons which you handed me begins by expressing an earnest desire that under some new system the appointment of justices of the peace should become non-political. All the remainder of the document takes for granted that the existing system must necessarily be one of appointment under 'political influences', and in effect aims at making those influences more dominant and effective than hitherto while that system lasts. I agree in the initial aspiration, but cannot reconcile it with the remainder of the document.

It is indisputable that in many counties the immense preponderance of Conservatives on the bench amounts practically to an exclusion of others. Whatever the cause (and I think in many cases those who advise the Lords-Lieutenant, who cannot themselves know everyone, are the persons mainly responsible), the result is an indignity and threatens to become an injury to the credit of the bench. I will say the same thing and act in the same way whether those excluded are Liberal or Conservative or adherents of any other opinion or creed. Holding that view, I have pressed forward the selection of new justices. Since the end of February, when I first undertook this task, there have been appointed in ten months three times as many as have been appointed annually upon an average of the last ten years. . . .

I now come to a point which the memorial does not touch, but on which I must speak quite plainly. It is one thing to correct monopolies and open the bench to the honourable ambition of men of all parties. It is quite a different thing to treat the position of justice as merely or mainly a reward of party services. Yet this is what I am constantly and most importunately asked to do, not, indeed, by the great bulk of members, but by some of them and by many outside. And it is most significant that, with the exception of two or three names, I cannot recall any application from any Conservative member for the appointment of any person as justice of the peace. So widespread and so deeply rooted seems to be the persuasion that the bench of justices is the appanage of party, and the Lord Chancellor the mere registrar of party selections. Now this is, in my judgment, a serious danger. Justices of the peace in England and Wales deal with an immense proportion of the total number of criminal cases at one stage or another, and have a jurisdiction which ranges from long terms of penal servitude at quarter sessions to slight punishments at petty sessions, with practically little chance of appeal. I am certain that I ought not to allow an office which places in men's hands the liberty and reputation of their humblest neighbours to become the subject of political traffic.

The principle upon which I have acted and shall continue to act is that, if a man is suitable, the fact that he is a strong party man, on whatever side, is no objection. A great proportion of the ablest and most vigorous men are so; and justices, being unpaid, cannot be required, as judges are, to lay aside political activity. But I shall not allow a defect in the necessary qualities to be made good by political services or restrict the choice to those who have been politically active.

Believe me, my dear Brunner, always sincerely yours,

(Signed) *LOREBURN.*

4·18 THE CHANGING GOVERNMENT OF THE SHIRES

From T. H. S. Escott, Social Transformation of the Victorian Age, 1897, pp. 96–9.

A description of the changes in county government and life in the county town following the County Council Act of 1888 which Maitland had analysed in general terms.

If the machinery for establishing County Councils had been created in the era of the Corporation Reform Act, or during the first half of the present reign, it would have been premature, would at least comparatively have failed, instead of proving, as it has done, a signal success. How this institution works will best be judged by contrasting certain phases of County town life today and in the pre-County Council epoch. To visit such a town on a day when the magistrates were sitting at Quarter Sessions was like making an excursion into feudalism. One used to alight at the stable yard of the chief hotel to find no room for one's horse. The County's steeds had possession of the best stalls. They could not of course be displaced by, or consort with, the quadrupeds of less considerable riders. Inside the building, the same tale was retold and on every storey illustrated afresh. The apartment normally the coffee room was consecrated to the exclusive use of a select party of County justices who were still at luncheon. The drawing room on the first floor was in the occupation of the women kind of their relatives who were just about to refresh themselves after shopping with a cup of tea. The member of the general public who entered the chief shops of the place on the day devoted to County custo-

mers found himself and his patronage at a discount. The tradesman, in civil terms, profoundly regretted his inability to attend to
the chance comer until he had satisfied the needs of the County
justices' ladies who were expecting every moment to be called for
by their lords from the Sessions House.

Socially, not less than geographically, the County continues to
exist. The wives and daughters of the country gentlemen who are
County J.P.s set the fashion in their neighbourhood and are still
regarded as moulded out of a clay slightly superior to that of which
their neighbours consist. But as an object of fetish worship the
County has in most districts disappeared. The chief linen draper
in the town, as he watches the County ladies, in their dilatory
fashion, toy with one fabric after another, can scarcely suppress a
look of impatience on his well-disciplined face. He happens to be,
not less than the father and husband of these ladies, himself a
member of the new County parliament. He is exercised by a fear
lest the special committee of the body on which he is serving
should have decided the question of certain alterations in the
approach to the local capital in which he is interested, before he
has had time to get to the place of meeting. Unconsciously, perhaps, his manner towards the lady relatives of his council-colleague,
the squire and magistrate, has lost something of its old deference.
Still, the foundations of the social system remain the same. The
fusion between classes of which the County Council is the expression rather than the cause has not brought us appreciably
nearer the revolution and the Red Republic than had been done
by the earlier parliamentary reforms.

4.19 THE INNER CIRCLE OF POLITICIANS

From James Bryce, The American Commonwealth, *2 vols,
1889, I, pp. 24–6.*

THE POLITICIANS

What is one to include under this term? In England it usually
denotes those who are actively occupied in administering or
legislating, or discussing administration and legislation. That is to
say, it includes ministers of the Crown, members of Parliament
(though some in the House of Commons and the majority in the
House of Lords care little about politics), a few leading journalists,

and a small number of miscellaneous persons, writers, lecturers, organizers, agitators, who occupy themselves with trying to influence the public. Sometimes the term is given a wider sweep, being taken to include all who labour for their political party in the constituencies, as e.g., the chairmen and secretaries of local party associations, and the more active committee men of the same bodies. The former, whom we may call the Inner Circle men, are professional politicians in this sense, and in this sense only, that politics is the main though seldom the sole business of their lives. But at present extremely few of them make anything by it in the way of money. A handful hope to get some post; a somewhat larger number find that a seat in Parliament enables them to push their financial undertakings or gives them at least a better standing in the commercial world. But the making of a livelihood does not come into the view of the great majority at all. The other class, who may be called the Outer Circle, are not professionals in any sense, being primarily occupied with their own avocations; and none of them, except here and there an organizing secretary, paid lecturer, or registration agent, makes any profit out of the work. . . .

When in a large country public affairs become more engrossing to those who are occupied in them, when the sphere of government widens, when administration is more complex and more closely interlaced with the industrial interests of the community and of the world at large, so that there is more to be known and to be considered, the business of a nation falls into the hands of the men eminent by rank, wealth, and ability, who form a sort of governing class, largely hereditary. The higher civil administration of the state is in their hands; they fill the chief council or legislative chamber and conduct its debates. They have residences in the capital, and though they receive salaries when actually filling an office, the majority possess independent means, and pursue politics for the sake of fame, power, or excitement. Those few who have not independent means can follow their business or profession in the capital, or can frequently visit the place where their business is carried on. This was the condition of Rome under the later republic, and of England and France till quite lately – indeed it is largely the case in England still.

4·20 POLITICS AND THE CITY

From Lord Grantley, Silver Spoon, *1954, pp. 126–7.*

Lord Grantley, the sixth holder of the title, was a descendant of a family of landowners and MP's. After a business career he went into the film industry. Seaham Harbour was a solidly Labour constituency.

Seaham Harbour to Spain

In 1922 came my second incursion into the political world. It may be remembered that my first, as secretary to Almeric Paget before the war, had been a negligible affair. I was now asked to take on a candidature by Lord Londonderry, and the assignment he suggested was the loyally Labour coalmining constituency of Seaham Harbour, most of which he owned. The sitting member was the renowned Sidney Webb, later Lord Passfield, one of the founders of the Fabian Society.

Londonderry undertook to pay all my expenses, and Gordon Leith thought it might be useful for the firm if I went into politics, and said I could take the time it would need.

I was adopted as Tory candidate, and I am bound to say worked extremely hard. I went up to Durham at weekends and toured round making speeches and things off lorries and things, all the usual sort of business: which, for such a weak speaker as myself, was a great strain.

Of course I *was* a Tory; except in the most important matter of all where Seaham Harbour and Charlie Londonderry were concerned – coal royalties. I thought they were completely unjustified. I used to deliver my halting speeches carefully skirting the subject, but towards the end some miner would be sure to say 'Aye, but what about royalties?'; and I would try to shuffle out of it by telling a funny story. . . .

The sequel to my political campaigning came after a few months. By then Speyers had decided I was experienced enough to go abroad and try my hand as a principal in negotiating a foreign loan. Fortified by a secretary who knew all the ropes, I was to arrange a loan to the City of Madrid on behalf of a consortium of Speyers and Rothschilds. Being allowed to handle negotiations for a transaction involving two or three million pounds, and being permitted direct dealings with high officials of the City of Madrid, was a great chance for me. I also had instructions to see if, during what was bound to be a prolonged stay, I could get on friendly relations with the Ministry of Finance, in order that the consortium might have their finger in Spanish Government finance as well.

This assignment to Madrid of course made it quite impossible to go on with my candidature at Seaham Harbour, as it might last for weeks or months or even years. An election was expected quite soon, and much as I might have enjoyed it, I obviously would not be able to abandon my first important opportunity in business to come home and amuse myself playing politics in a hopeless constituency. So I went down to see Charlie Londonderry at the Turf Club and told him what had happened. He burst into flames at the idea of my pulling out, and started trying to governess me around. I pointed out that I had to earn my living, that I had a family to support, and that they had to come first: but he still went on shouting. Then I lost my temper too, and we had a noisy row such as the Turf Club had never seen before or since. The upshot was that I insisted on resigning my prospective candidature that same night, and my second unimportant incursion into politics came to an end.

4·21 POLITICAL CEREMONIAL

From Sir Edward Cadogan, Before the Deluge, Memoirs and Reflections, *1961, p. 174.*

The change in the character of political leadership and the entry of working class men into the House of Commons in considerable numbers resulted in partial adaptation, not in radical reform. Court Dress only disappeared with World War II. The author was Secretary to the Speaker.

At the commencement of each session the Speaker gave a series of five dinner parties in the large dining-room of the Speaker's House. They were glamorous affairs. The guests were under the obligation to wear full dress uniform and full dress was full dress in those days. An invitation to these dinners was held to be a command, a convention which is only shared by the Sovereign. On one occasion during the reign of Queen Victoria, King Edward, then Prince of

Wales, had asked a certain friend of his to dinner, but unfortunately the guest had accepted an invitation to the Speaker's dinner and pleaded this circumstance as an excuse to refuse His Royal Highness. There was much to do about it all, precedents were consulted and the upshot of it was that the Prince had to acknowledge that the excuse was a valid one.

The first of these dinners was given to the Cabinet and the rest of the Ministry, the second was given to the Opposition, the third to Privy Councillors, the fourth and fifth were given to those whom the Speaker delighted to honour.

After these official dinners the Speaker held his levees attended by the rest of the House of Commons, also in full dress uniform.

All these festivities gave me plenty to do and great care had to be exercised so that no one would be in any way offended or neglected.

I remember that by the time I had been with the Speaker some years the Labour party had grown to considerable proportions. The question then arose as to what was to be done about entertaining them, as it would have been embarrassing for members of that party who had no full dress uniform to take part in any function where it was *de rigueur*. The Speaker thought out a happy plan of afternoon parties, to which he could invite anyone without any regard to sartorial regulations. They proved a great success.

5   Education

5·1 THE THREAT OF A COMPREHENSIVE EDUCATION, 1820

From S. Butler, Letter to Lord Brougham, *1820, pp. 18–21.*

The occasion of this 'letter' was the proposal contained in a Bill sponsored by Brougham to establish a system of parish schools financed from the rates. Its author was then headmaster of Shrewsbury; later he became Bishop of Lichfield. (See also 8·6).

The intention of the founders of Grammar Schools appears to have been to diffuse as widely as possible the attainment of learning, by affording in most cases gratuitous, or at least cheap means of instruction in those languages, a knowledge of which is indispensable for academic education and the liberal professions. While the probability was, that what are generally called the middle classes of society would chiefly take advantage of these institutions, there was no exclusion either of the highest or lowest. But common sense evidently points out, that the lowest classes would not *wish* in many cases to bring up their children to liberal professions; and if they had this laudable ambition, would not be able, in many instances, even when their children had completed their school education, to support them at the universities, or place them out in liberal professions in life. It is equally obvious that the very highest classes would, from motives of pride, or even of conscience, generally decline to take advantage of eleemosynary foundations. – The probability therefore was, and has been confirmed by the experience of all ages since these institutions have been established, that the middle classes of society would *principally* be benefited by them. From hence we are supplied with our clergy, our lawyers, our physicians; and here by far the greatest part of the ordinary, and some of the highest order of the gentry of the realm receive their own education, and, as they advance in life, send their children to receive the same benefits. (I am not now speaking of boys who are educated at these schools without participating in the benefits of the foundation, but of those who claim and receive the provision made for them by the founder.) Now, Sir, as long as the decencies of life are kept up . . . as long, Sir, I say, as these decencies are kept up, parents will have some feelings about the associates of their children. They will not care if the son of a person greatly their inferior receives the *same* benefits of a learned education with their own children, – if they have common liberality, they will foster and encourage such a boy, if he is modest and deserving, well knowing that from such education, in such institutions, have arisen many of the brightest ornaments of their country both in church and state. But they will feel and apprehend a great deal, and justly too, if Grammar schools are to be made schools for teaching English reading, writing, and accounts, – in other words, Parish schools. They will know and feel, without the least ill-will or disrespect to the lowest order of society, that their children can learn no improvements in manners or morals by associating with all the lowest boys of the parish, and they will feel it necessary and inevitable, to forgo one of these two advantages, either the preservation of their children's minds from the contagion of vulgar example, or the benefits of an institution which they cannot enjoy without exposing them to so great a risk. Now, Sir, do you think that any sensible and affectionate parent will hesitate a moment, which of these two he should choose? Do you think that any pecuniary considerations would be sufficient to tempt him to sacrifice the morals and future respectability of his child? Would he not, if obliged to choose one of these alternatives, as undoubtedly he must, rather forgo the benefits of the foundation, than receive them at the risk of his child's moral habits becoming corrupted? If so, Sir, I beseech you to consider how great and valuable a portion of society you deprive of benefits, of which they have themselves participated, and which they have a right to expect for their children, for the sake of one class only, who can be better and more essentially benefited by instruction given them in schools appropriated for that purpose. Consider, Sir, what a numerous body of gentry, lawyers, medical men, merchants, naval and military officers, respectable tradesmen, and innumerable other descriptions of persons there are, in the middle classes of life, to whom these institutions, at present, afford the *only* means of giving their children educations suitable to their situation in life: all, or at least by far the greater part of whom, will be compelled to forgo these benefits, if Grammar schools are converted into schools for parish paupers. Above all, consider that large class of men of whom you have been pleased yourself to speak in high terms of approbation *in* the House of Commons – I mean the Clergy of the Established Church. What a great proportion of this body have been educated at these schools, and look to these schools for the education of their children! And thus far I have spoken only of those who have a *right* to the benefits of these foundations; but if we add those, who by usage and general consent have been in the habit of sending their children to such schools, paying a moderate sum for their education, and who, if these clauses pass, must place them elsewhere, probably at a greater expense and with less advantages of competent instruction – the injury which must result from the measure will appear indeed enormous.

5·2 THE ORTHODOX EDUCATION OF A GENTLEMAN

From E. G. Bulwer Lytton, England and the English, (1833), *1887, pp. 134–7.*

Lytton questions not only the academic value of a public school education but also the social opportunities which it is supposed to offer to the sons of socially less well-established families who thus forgo intellectual gain for the sake of spurious social advantage. (See also 1·5).

Writers in favour of an academical reform have not sufficiently touched upon the points I am about to refer to, for they have taken it for granted that men would allow education alone was to

be the end of scholastic discipline; but a great proportion of those
who send their children to school secretly meditate other advantages besides those of intellectual improvement.

In the first place the larger portion of the boys at a public school
are the sons of what may be termed the minor aristocracy – of
country gentlemen – of rich merchants – of opulent lawyers – of
men belonging to the 'untitled property' of the country: the smaller
portion are the sons of statesmen and of nobles. Now each parent
of the former class thinks in his heart of the advantages of acquaintance and connexion that his son will obtain, by mixing with the
children of the latter class. He looks beyond the benefits of education – to the chances of getting on in the world. 'Young Howard's
father has ten livings – young Johnson may become intimate with
young Howard, and obtain one of the ten livings.' So thinks old
Johnson when he pays for the Greek which his son will never
know. 'Young Cavendish is the son of a minister – if young Smith
distinguishes himself what a connexion he may form!' So says old
Smith when he finds his son making excellent Latin verses, although incapable of translating Lucan without a dictionary! Less
confined, but equally aristocratic, are the views of the mother. –
'My son is very intimate with little Lord John: he will get, when of
age, into the best society! – who knows but that one of these days
he may marry little Lady Mary!'

It is with these notions that shrewd and worldly parents combat
their conviction that their sons are better cricketers than scholars;
and so long as such advantages allure them, it is in vain that we
reason and philosophize on education – we are proving only what
with them is the minor part of the question, nay, which they may
be willing to allow. *We* speak of educating the boy, *they* think
already of advancing the man: *we* speak of the necessity of knowledge, but the Smiths and the Johnsons think of the necessity of
connexions. . . .

But calmly considered, we shall find that even this advantage
of connexion is not obtained by the education of a public school.
And knowing that this prevailing notion must be answered,
before the generality of parents will dispassionately take a larger
view of this important subject, I shall proceed to its brief examination.

Boys at a public school are on an equality. Let us suppose any
boy, plebeian or patrician, – those of his contemporaries whose

pursuits are most congenial to his become naturally his closest friends. . . .

Howard, the peer's eldest, and Johnson, the commoner's younger son, leave school at the same age – they are intimate friends – we will suppose them even going up to the same University. But Howard is entered as a nobleman at Trinity, and Johnson goes a pensioner to Emmanuel: their sets of acquaintance become instantly and widely different. Howard may now and then take milk punch with Johnson, and Johnson may now and then 'wine' with Howard, but they have no circle in common – they are not commonly brought together. Custom no longer favours their intercourse – a similarity of pursuits no longer persuades them that they have a similarity of dispositions. For the first time, too, the difference of rank becomes markedly visible. At no place are the demarcations of birth and fortune so faintly traced as at a School – nowhere are they so broad and deep as at a University. The young noble is suddenly removed from the side of the young commoner: when he walks he is indued in a distinguishing costume: when he dines he is placed at a higher table along with the heads of his college: at chapel he addresses his Maker, or reads the Racing Calendar, in a privileged pew. At *most* colleges the discipline to which *he* is subjected is, comparatively speaking, relaxed and lenient. Punctuality in lectures and prayers is of no vital importance to a 'young man of such expectations'. As regards the first, hereditary legislators have no necessity for instruction; and as to the last, the religion of a college has no damnation for a lord. Nay, at Cambridge, to such an extent are the demarcations of ranks observed, that the eldest son of one baronet assumes a peculiarity in costume to distinguish him from the younger son of another, and is probably a greater man at college than he ever is during the rest of his life. Nor does this superstitious observance of the social grades bound itself to titular rank, it is at college that an eldest son suddenly leaps into that consequence – that elevation above his brothers – which he afterwards retains through life. It usually happens that the eldest son of a gentleman of some five thousands a year, goes up as *a Fellow Commoner*, and his brothers as *Pensioners*. A marked distinction in dress, dinners, luxuries, and, in some colleges, discipline, shows betimes the value attached to wealth – and wealth only; and the younger son learns, to the full extent of the lesson, that he is *worth* so many thousands less than his elder brother. It is obvious that these distinctions, so sudden and so marked, must occasion an embarrassment and coldness, in the continuance at college, of friendships formed at school. . . . This is the common history of scholastic 'connexions' where there is a disparity in station. It is the vulgar subject of wonder at the University, that 'fellows the best friends in the world at Eton are never brought together at college'. And thus vanish into smoke all the hopes of the parental Johnsons! – all 'the advantages of early friendship!' – all the dreams for which the shrewd father consented to sacrifice, for 'little Latin and *no* Greek', the precious – the irrevocable season – of 'the sowing of good seed', of pliant memories and ductile dispositions – the lost, the golden opportunity, of instilling into his son the elements of real wisdom and true morality – the knowledge that adorns life, and the principles that should guide it!

5·3 COST, RESULTS AND ETHOS OF EDUCATION AT ETON

From Report *and* Evidence *of Royal Commission on the Public Schools,Parliamentary Papers, 1864, XXI, pp 92, 100* (Report) *and pp. 185, 302* (Evidence).

The evidence is that of E. Warre, Assistant Master at Eton, and of Mr J. Walter, MP.

School charges and annual expenses of a boy at Eton.
The expenses of a boy in a tutor's house are as follows:

Annual Payments	£	s.	d.	*Single Payments*	£	s.	d.
Board and tuition ..	120	0	0	Head Master, entrance	5	5	0
Books and washing, about...........	10	0	0	Ditto, leaving present	10	0	0
				Tutor, leaving present	15	0	0
Head Master	6	6	0				
Mathematics	4	18	0				
Sanatorium	1	4	0				
Petty school charges	1	3	0				
Library (above Lower Fifth)	0	12	0				
	£144	3	0		£30	5	0

Extras	£	s.	d.	Extras	£	s.	d.
Extra mathematics ..	10	10	0	French, entrance	1	1	0
French	10	10	0	German, ditto	1	1	0
German	12	12	0	Drawing, ditto	1	1	0
Drawing and materials	14	14	0				
Fencing	8	8	0				

A boy, therefore, who has extra mathematics and learns French, costs annually 165*l*. 3*s*. exclusive of his clothes, journeys, pocket-money, and other petty expenses. If he also learns drawing, it would be 179*l*. 17*s*. The average amount of the annual bills sent in by a tutor are computed by Mr Eliot at about 175*l*.; by Mr James at 65*l*. a school-time, or 195*l*. a year; by Dr Goodford, at from 150*l*. to 210*l*. The amount of the 'leaving-presents' to Masters is not fixed precisely; some Assistant Masters, we believe, do not take them from all their pupils, and the ill-defined character of these payments is felt to be unsatisfactory by the masters themselves.

Of the results of an Eton education considered as a preparation for the Universities we can only form a very general opinion. The distinctions gained at the Universities by Eton men, when compared with the numbers of the school, do not certainly entitle it to rank among those which are most successful in this respect; but it sends out a fair number of good and well-instructed scholars. Within the ten years ending in 1861, during which probably 500 or 600 Eton men have gone to the Universities, it has had at Oxford 18 classical and two mathematical 'Firsts', eight in law and modern history and one in natural science, and at Cambridge 17 Wranglers and 19 in the first class of the Classical Tripos; has twice gained at Oxford the Ireland and Hertford University Scholarships and the Craven Scholarship at Cambridge, besides other distinctions. . . . As to the mass of young men who enter at Oxford and Cambridge, and who do not try for honours, it has been already seen that the mental training which they bring from the schools where they have been educated cannot be rated high; and in this respect Eton can claim, at the least, no advantage over the rest. According to the evidence of the Dean of Christ Church and of Mr Hedley, it is rather below the common level. The wealthiest, it is true, and therefore on the whole the idlest men, go to Christ Church; but Christ Church and University College contain one-half of all the undergraduate Etonians at Oxford, and one-third of the total number at Oxford and Cambridge.

Of 36 Etonians who entered the army by direct commissions within the three years above mentioned, 16 came direct from Eton, and 20 had been afterwards at other schools or under private tutors. Eight others failed to pass the necessary examination, of whom three came direct from Eton. Of those who succeeded, coming direct from Eton, all passed in mathematics, English, history, and Latin, and all but one in French, eleven in drawing, only six in Greek. Among the unsuccessful candidates the largest number of failures was in Latin and French. It is remarkable that of all the 42 Eton candidates, only 27 took up Greek, and of these 12 failed in it. In history, Latin, the natural and experimental sciences, and drawing, those who came direct from Eton appear to have succeeded better than those who did not. In French and German the balance is slightly the other way. The conclusion from these figures is, that this examination requires, in the case of boys of ordinary intelligence and moderate industry, no special teaching which may not be had, either in the school course or as an extra, at Eton.

E. Warre, Esq.

5360. Can you tell us whether or not boys who excel in games are commonly pretty good at the school work? – I have only been there two years now, so that I could not tell what was a good average, but I think you could not say that there was a regular tendency of intellectually distinguished boys to come to the top in other things; I do not think you will find that; but at the same time, I do not think you will find that the eight and the eleven were particularly stupid fellows, or that they did not care about intellectual distinction.

5361. Is there any difference between games in that respect? Cricket, we understand, takes a great deal more time. Do you think the cricketers are less well up in the school work than others? – No, I do not think so; I think they are on a par with the others....

5365. (*Lord Clarendon*). As to the general habits of expense at the school, are not some boys very extravagant, and is not their example rather prejudicial to others? – I think it is less so now than it was in my time. The idlers are always the most expensive fellows. Those who work hard in the boats and at cricket have not the time to think about the adornment of their persons very much; but the idlers who lounge about have got nothing else to think about but that.

5366. Do you think that the principal cause of extravagance there is the adornment of their persons? – I think it used to be. I do not think they think so much of it now.

5367. That used to be the great cause of expense? – I think so. It followed them to Oxford and Cambridge. I do not think it is so much as it used to be.

5368. Extravagance in jewellery, for instance? – Yes; wealthy parents encouraged their sons to some extent, I think. In my own house a boy was ill with the measles; I moved him to another room. He said 'Will you get me my money?' I said, 'Where is it?' He said, 'You will find it in the pill-box in my bureau'. There were two 10*l.* notes wrapped up in the pill-box besides the gold. He had 24*l.* or 25*l.*, and I have heard of others having 50*l.* If the parents let them have that sort of thing, it makes it very difficult for the master.

5369. (*Lord Lyttelton*). There are several parents who give enormous pocket money, are there not? – Yes, they are generally people who are *nouveaux riches*.

5370. (*Sir Stafford Northcote*). What should you think would be the average sum with which a boy would go up to Eton? – I think he brings up 3*l.* or 4*l.*, and he writes home if he wants more. They get most things by orders, but I discourage that as much as possible. I think the rifle corps has done some good, or has had a share in having done good to the school.

J. Walter, Esq., M.P.

What I conceive to be the great object of all education which is to enable men to deal with their fellow-citizens in certain different relations, and that, after all, a thorough mastery of their own language, which, I maintain, is best acquired by a classical education, is what most fits a man for dealing with other men. Take the House of Commons, take the leading men on both sides of the House, take the men on the Treasury Bench; you have Mr Gladstone, Sir George Cornewall Lewis, both, I think, Eton men. Sir

Charles Wood is an Eton man, Sir George Grey is not; and Lord Palmerston is a Harrow man, and the late Sir Robert Peel was a Harrow man. Although it is the fashion to say that a great number of Eton men do not go to Parliament, there are still the best men and the best speakers in the House of Commons who have received that peculiar training, and those who have not generally wished for it. I think that, with all Mr Cobden's genius, he would have been a more effective speaker if he had been a better scholar.

5·4 BOYS OF NOBLE BLOOD

From William Sewell, Sermons to Boys, preached in the chapel of Radley College, *2 vols. Oxford, 1854–49, 2, pp. 238–51.*

Sermons extolling the virtues of a hierarchical social order and the value of hereditary distinctions for society are not uncommon, although perhaps more typical of the earlier years of the century. The significance of this sermon lies as much in its provenance as in its theme. Delivered in what was then one of the new public schools which had been designed, as its founder head tells us in his sermon, for 'the sons of the upper classes' it seeks to instil, even in this exclusive, though probably largely *arriviste* group, a proper feeling of deference for those of hereditary rank.

My Boys,

If I were living in a separate establishment, like the Heads of other Schools and Colleges, I should like sometimes in the Term to have parties of you to dine with me. And I could give you many reasons for this usual practice; many much deeper reasons than at first sight you would think possible for such a trifling observance of common laws of hospitality. . . . I cannot at present enter into these considerations. They have induced me, however – since, keeping no separate table, I cannot have you to dine with me myself – they have induced me to tell the Senior Prefect that he may now and then do for me, what I cannot do for myself, and invite some of you to dine with him at his table. . . .

Now you can all understand that one difficulty in such parties is, to select those who are to be asked. He cannot invite all at once; and he must take care not to draw partial or invidious distinctions.

Few things require more thoughtful care and Christian consideration for the feelings of others, than drawing the line which is necessary when we give a party; asking some persons and omitting, as we must, others. . . .

And I think also that the line drawn in the invitations for today is very unintelligible to you all. I can imagine you all not a little surprised to find who have been asked, and who have been omitted. This is the subject on which I am going to preach to you this morning. . . .

I will tell you, then, that when this College was first planned, I was thinking chiefly of one class of boys. There are earnest, munificent, zealous Christian-minded men, who are devoting their best energies to the education of the poor; who are going out into the lanes and alleys of our crowded and demoralized cities, and gathering from them their wretched, famishing, tattered outcasts, without parents, without home, without a hand to save, or an eye to guide, or a heart to love them. . . . My thoughts and my anxiety have been for other boys – boys born to rank and fortune; nursed up in comfort and luxury; tended with over care, and over fondness; safe indeed from temptations of hunger, and poverty, and neglect, but exposed to the equally fatal dangers of flattery, pride, self-indulgence, indolence, and arrogance. This College, and all its system, was planned, as I have often told you, for the sons of the upper classes. . . . And now I need scarcely remind you, that there is great difficulty in the education of boys of rank, simply because they have rank. And the difficulty is peculiarly great in this country, from the light in which rank is here regarded.

If a boy is sent to a small inferior school, it is almost certain that he will be flattered, indulged, humoured, made conceited and consequential, in one word, be spoiled, by the vulgar, extravagant, selfish, and criminal deference both of master and boys. And from the dread of this, noblemen of whom I am now thinking, very wisely prefer sending their sons to one of our great public schools, and especially to Eton. And there, instead of rank and title being recognised by the public tone of the school as any passport to superior privileges, all such pretensions are immediately put down by a very summary process. Most of you are familiar with such stories as that of a young duke being asked by a boy, on his first coming to Eton, who he was. 'I am the Duke of A.', was the answer. And the reply to this was a blow and an insult. . . . And yet I think you will all agree with me, that neither of these modes of treating rank can be right, can be Christian.

Low, contemptible, vulgar sycophancy, courting obsequiously the notice of persons of rank, degrading ourselves by seeking for invitations to their houses and parties; suffering mere title to be an excuse for sin and folly; talking about persons of rank as if we were intimate with them; imitating them when we cannot afford it; coveting to be seen in their company; making it the object of our lives to gain admittance into certain sets, or to obtain distinctions of rank ourselves, from mere personal vanity – we all know to what an extent this degrading, contemptible spirit pervades every part of English society; what mischief it does to those who pay, and to those who receive, such homage. God grant in this place you may learn even as boys to loathe and abhor it! And yet God also grant that you may loathe and abhor as much that sour, envious, jealous, malignant temper, which abhors all that is superior to itself; which will allow of no privilege which it cannot share; no distinction of rank, no prerogatives of birth, no inheritance of blood – the spirit of a vulgar, selfish, heartless, degrading democracy, which has no respect for others because it has no respect for itself, and which is as sure to be accompanied with an odious sycophancy, as a democrat is sure to be a tyrant.

Shall I tell you, my boys, how a Christian gentleman, such as all of you without exception are here, feels towards rank and blood, especially to noble blood? . . .

A gentleman, then, and a Christian, whether boy or man, both knows, and is thankful that God, instead of making all men equal, has made them all most unequal. Every one possesses something more than another of some particular advantage. Among these is birth or blood. It is God's ordinance that the reverence due to a father extends to his son. We love, we respect, we honour even the infant in the cradle for the father's sake. . . . Hereditary rank, nobility of blood, is the very first condition and essence of all our Christian privileges; and woe to the nation, or the man by whom such a principle is disdained, who will honour no one except for his own merits and his own deeds!

And a Christian also knows that this hereditary nobility of blood, rightly directed, and worthily employed, is one of the main-springs of human goodness. . . . A boy who inherits blood ought to be proud of it; so proud of it, as to be ashamed of any act, which would disgrace a noble ancestry. And he will learn betimes the lessons and the duties of government, as he is accustomed from his childhood to be respected and obeyed by others. And thus he will escape from the follies and vanities of men, who only arrive at distinction late in life, and then become conceited, overbearing, and ostentatious. And they will also be humbled by the knowledge, that their distinction and honour is not due to any merit of their own – that they owe it entirely to others. And they will learn kindness and gentleness to their inferiors, and attachment to all that is settled, old, and venerated. The whole tone of their character will be elevated by this one fact, that they have been accustomed from their childhood to be honoured and obeyed for the sake, not of themselves, but of their parents. . . . Examine into the temper of any nation from which hereditary rank, and an hereditary nobility is excluded, and compare it with the high, chivalrous, generous, gentle, self-sacrificing spirit which is the true character of an ancient aristocracy; and then you will understand one at least of the reasons, why God has established nobility of blood as an essential condition of society, and why Christians delight to recognise, and to honour, even though they do not possess it themselves. These are but a few words on a vast subject; but they contain the substance of those considerations which make me so anxious that, amongst ourselves, in this place, rank and nobility of blood should be recognised and valued as it should be. Almost all the old and great places of education provide some mode of marking it, of showing respect to it. The mode selected may seem to us more or less judicious, but the principle is asserted. And for the same reason that the Constitution of the country gives titles of honour, and precedency, and distinction to noble blood, I suggested to the Senior Prefect that the first invitations which he gave should include all the boys, now here, between twenty and thirty, who had in them noble blood, as sons, nephews, or grandchildren of noblemen, or what the English Constitution ranks as noble, of bishops. Be assured, my boys, that this little act and sign, petty as it is asserts and establishes among us a grand principle for our own welfare here, as a great place of education, and for our future conduct in the world. I have said little on it, but I have thought much.

And I will add only one more word at present to those who have been thus selected, and then to the rest.

The former know already the lesson which it is to impress upon them: that if they bear the blood of nobility in their veins, they must bear its spirit in their hearts. Everything which is great, noble, high-minded, brave, generous, liberal, delicate, unselfish, God, who gives nobility, and men who honour nobility, expect from noblemen, and from all who have within them the blood of noblemen. Anything that is petty, mean, contemptible, selfish, disgraceful, or immoral, is in a nobleman infinitely worse than it is in a beggar. Noblemen, like Christians, are to be the salt of the earth. Read history, and scarcely will you find an instance of a great name famed for his solid benefits to mankind, but he has in him noble blood. . . .

And now I will turn to all the rest of you, who look on upon these earthly distinctions, and in whose mind rises up the natural feeling, it may be of regret, it may be of discontent, it may be of jealousy, it may be, in darker minds, of sullen, bitter, factious resentment, and mean ambition; craving to beat down every eminence on which they do not stand themselves; that spirit which, in proportion as it grows into habits and actions, shatters society to its centre. I am speaking only to boys; but those who know the hearts of boys, are well aware that there is scarcely any feeling in a public school more widely spread, more deeply seated, more permanently affecting the character and the life of boys, for good and for evil, than their ideas on the subject of rank. Boys long for it more than for any other distinction, and long for it the more earnestly because so hopelessly. To gain it is beyond their reach. . . . You who have, and you who have not, in your veins the blood of an earthly nobility, think of that which you all possess alike; of the royal blood, that life of God's Spirit within you, which makes you a new creature, as kings and priests unto the Lord, nobler in your calling, vaster in your hopes, more glorious in your nature, than all the sovereigns upon earth – children of God, members of Christ, inheritors of the kingdom of heaven. This is the thought to temper, and balance, and sanctify, and render safe that recognition and respect for worldly rank which I long to impress upon your minds, while I know at the same time too well, that unless it be thus balanced and sanctified, it will lead you into serious evil. . . . Look on the boys who will dine together today – many of them very young – many of them with no personal claim to any particular respect, not with jealousy and contempt, but with manly, honourable elevating respect for rank. And that feeling carried out into the world will save you alike from the vulgarity, the contemptible vulgarity, and degradation of the tuft-hunter; and from the sullen, malignant meanness of the democrat and the republican.

5·5 BREEDING AND EDUCATION

From J. H. Newman (Cardinal Newman) 'Rise and Progress of Universities', Historical Sketches, *3 vols, 1876, vol 2, ch. 2.*

Even Newman, despite his enthusiasm for the liberal influences of a university education thought that truly gentlemanly behaviour could only be acquired in the surroundings of established 'society'.

For instance, the polished manners and high-bred bearing which are so difficult of attainment, and so strictly personal when attained, – which are so much admired in society, from society are acquired. All that goes to constitute a gentleman, – the carriage, gait, address, gestures, voice; the ease, the self-possession, the courtesy, the power of conversing, the talent of not offending; the lofty principle, the delicacy of thought, the happiness of expression, the taste and propriety, the generosity and forbearance, the candour and consideration, the openness of hand; – these qualities, some of them come by nature, some of them may be found in any rank, some of them are a direct precept of Christianity; but the full assemblage of them, bound up in the unity of an individual character, do we expect they can be learned from books? Are they not necessarily acquired, where they are to be found, in high society? The very nature of the case leads us to say so; you cannot fence without an antagonist, nor challenge all-comers in disputation before you have supported a thesis; and in like manner, it stands to reason, you cannot learn to converse till you have the world to converse with; you cannot unlearn your natural bashfulness, or awkwardness, or stiffness, or other besetting deformity, till you serve your time in some school of manners. Well, and is it not so in matter of fact? The metropolis, the court, the great houses of the land, are the centres to which at stated time the country comes up, as to shrines of refinement and good taste; and then in due time the country goes back again home, enriched with a portion of the social accomplishments, which those very visits serve to call out and heighten in the gracious dispensers of them.

We are unable to conceive how the 'gentlemanlike' can otherwise be maintained; and maintained in this way it is.

5·6 SOCIAL AND INTELLECTUAL PERVERSIONS OF UNIVERSITY EDUCATION

From Evidence *of the Royal Commission on the University of Oxford, Parliamentary Papers, 1852, XXII, p. 121.*

Sir Charles Leyell, F.R.S., argued for reforms in curriculum and mode of life which would make Oxford more attractive to the middle classes and more useful to the nation.

The aristocratic notions, and class prejudices which the neglect of useful knowledge engenders, is fostered and exaggerated by several old customs and institutions of the place. I allude particularly to the distinctions referred to by the Royal Commissioners, between compounders and ordinary graduates, and between noblemen, gentlemen commoners, and commoners. A peculiar costume assigned to the possessors of mere rank, or, what is if possible even more objectionable, to mere wealth, or the power of paying higher fees, is calculated to enhance in the eyes of young men the importance of these adventitious advantages. All academical honours and distinctions should be reserved exclusively for the successful cultivation of talent coupled with good moral conduct. How can we expect to cherish a proper feeling of equality among gentlemen, or to guard against the worship of mere riches in a mercantile community, if marks of personal favour and external privileges are conferred at the University, not for merit, but for the mere accident of birth and fortune? I speak from personal experience of what has happened within the circle of my own friends and acquaintances, when I affirm, that parents possessing ample pecuniary means are often deterred from sending their sons to Oxford by a well-grounded apprehension, that after a residence of a few years, they will contract from the social atmosphere of the place, notions incompatible with the line of life to which they are destined, although that professional line may be one peculiarly demanding a liberal education. They wish, for example, to bring them up as attorneys, publishers, engineers, surgeons, or as merchants in some established house, and naturally turn their thoughts to Oxford as a safe and good training place, till they are warned by those who know the working of the system, that the youth, however well satisfied with the honourable calling proposed for him, (which, perhaps, he has chosen himself), will discover at the end of a few terms, that such occupations are vulgar and beneath his dignity. How much vulgarity of feeling and want of true independence of mind may lie at the bottom of such fine notions it is superfluous to inquire here. The remedy is, I think, as obvious as the cause; – a large accession to Oxford of the representatives of the professions alluded to, would make such class-prejudices disappear at once, without the accompaniment of an evil so much dreaded by many advocates of the state of things as they are, namely, a diminished attendance of men of rank and fortune. These, on the contrary, might be tempted to come in larger numbers, if their time at the University was spent more profitably in learning, not simply Classics and Mathematics, but the history, laws, and constitution of England, and a variety of information respecting modern literature or physical science, which might accord with their individual tastes. By application to such studies they would be far better prepared than at present to fill the stations into which many of them are destined immediately to enter as legislators, magistrates, or country gentlemen.

5·7 UPPER CLASS HABITS AT OXFORD

From Evidence *submitted to the Royal Commission on Oxford University, Parliamentary Papers, 1852, XXII, p. 52.*

The evidence of the Reverend David Melville, an Oxford Tutor and later Canon of Worcester Cathedral.

In a state of society such as that which exists in England, it is very clear that unless some strong check was put upon its development, any congregation of young men representing all the upper orders, would carry the false features of that society into an excess; the youth is not likely to correct the undue display, or the weak emulation of the parent, and thus given the means for their indulgence, nay, it may be the temptation to that indulgence, and the consequences are very apparent. In Oxford this explains a great deal of that vicious extravagance which now and then startles the public attention, and explains it not only with regard to what finds the spendthrift in himself a likely victim, but also with reference to that which is wanting to correct this tendency to fall. So far as Colleges directly countenance, or do not directly prevent by all possible means the indulgence of those expenses called *unrecognised*, through a foolish vanity for the distinction of men able to so indulge, or any other ground for weak concession; so far they help on the evil deplored, and a University edict is powerless as long as there is this sort of pride in College display. The virtual recognition then, of what is professedly unrecognised, co-operating with the evils of an artificial state of society, make in the University that extravagance in things obviously illicit, which colours the whole question of expense, within or without the College walls, and consequently a remedy must be looked for (a remedy extending far beyond the immediate effect of its own sterner rule) in a system directly at variance with such lax concession. Ambition and energy are the necessary results of young men's minds and character acting on each other, as they must in the Universities. There is an ambition, almost an energy in profligate expenditure and display, and if in any degree such habits seem to find favour or even not disfavour in the eyes of constituted authority, we ought not to wonder at the phenomena they present. It would seem almost imperative, in order to regulate expense in those particulars where some freedom of action must obtain, viz., those which we have denominated *recognized*, though not directly controlled, that the *unrecognized* should be strictly forbidden, and as much prevented as vigilance and binding rule can command, and that matters directly under control, which make up the common experience of daily College life, should be conducive to habits of self-control and economy. Everybody seems to understand the evil to be a liberty of action in the matter of expense, tempted from without, undisciplined from within the College walls. To afford as few occasions to expenditure, and withdraw all encouragement from it, I conceive to be the primary step in the correction of this evil. So to shape the educational course that the social relation of members shall not seem the ruling idea of their congregation, or not to leave great vacuums of members shall not seem the ruling idea of their congregation, or not to leave great vacuums of time so objectless (apparently) that *vis inertiae* adopts extravagance perforce as a pursuit, immediately follow on as auxiliary measures. Compared to these, laws on tradesmen, or mere directions to members of the University touching their relation to tradesmen, are very secondary.

5·8 CLASS DISTINCTIONS AND UNIVERSITY EDUCATION

From the Report *of the Royal Commission on Oxford University Parliamentary Papers, 1852, XXII, p. 28 and from the* Evidence *given to the Commission by Professor James Ogle, ibid. p. 40.*

In the nineteenth century, Oxford and to a lesser extent Cambridge revealed distinctions by rank in the student body which reflected the divisions in society. Some reformers thought that these distinctions and the discrepancies in style of life were inimical to the aims of a true University. Archbishop Whateley opposed such notions, and so did Ogle, the Professor of Clinical Medicine.

Several of those who have given us evidence lay stress on the bad effect caused by the distinctions of rank and wealth which the University still retains among the Students. Young noblemen wear a distinctive academical dress, take precedence of their academical superiors, are permitted to take Degrees at an earlier period than other Students, and in general are treated in a way that seems to indicate too great a deference to rank in a place of education. The sons of Baronets and Knights are also permitted to graduate earlier. This is a relic of a past state of things, when the different orders of society were much more widely separated than they are at present. Among the Fellows and Tutors of Colleges, whatever may be their birth, their fortune, or their social position out of the University, a perfect equality subsists. This is very beneficial, and among the junior members of the University it might at least be expected that there should be nothing in the institutions of the place to encourage an opposite feeling.

If distinctions of birth, even where they are in some measure warranted by the law of the land, are objectionable in a place of education, those made on the ground of mere wealth are still more objectionable; and the distinction between Gentleman-Commoners, as they are called, and Commoners, rests on no other ground. We are here, however, bound to quote the argument by which Archbishop Whately has defended the existing usage:–

'I am not for abolishing the distinction (or something amounting to it) between Commoners and Gentleman-Commoners. If restrictions as to expense are laid down, such as are suitable to men who can only afford to spend from 100*l.* to 200*l.* per annum, or even considerably less, it can hardly be expected that these will be conformed to by men of ten or twenty times that income. Why should a man not be allowed a valet, or a horse, who has been always used to such luxuries, and to whom they are not more extravagant luxuries than shoes and stockings are to his fellow-students?

Answers from James Adey Ogle, M.D., Aldrichian and Clinical Professor of Medicine in the University of Oxford.

. . . That the benefits of our national institutions should be extended to all members of the community without any restrictions, other than such as the nature of the institution itself demands, is an undeniable axiom of state policy, imposing on the state authorities, among other obligations, that of placing academic education within reach of the very many, who would be prompt to secure, but are, from adventitious causes, constrained to forgo its advantages. Among such causes excessive cost is perhaps that of most extensive operation. The *necessary* expenses of University life at Oxford are not however unreasonably large; the *ordinary* expenses certainly exceed the means of the middle classes of society, to whom, for obvious reasons affecting the common weal, it is of the highest importance, that sound learning and high moral discipline should be freely and systematically imparted. Idle expenses are natural to young people of large possessions or expectations when removed from the immediate control of parents or guardians; yet such as are immoderate in the case of one individual may not be so in the case of his companion; hence positive sumptuary enactments with a view to restrain extravagant habits would seem to be inexpedient, not simply because they are for the most part inefficient, but that they are in principle unjust. Extravagant habits at school or college ordinarily have their origin in the unequal worldly condition of the young men, and the more sure mode of preventing them is the severance of the parties by distinctions or order, college, and the like. That all students should be on a footing of equality in regard to academic privileges and rights is perfectly consistent with that accidental inequality which rank and wealth occasion, and far from there being any offence in distinctions based on such inequality, it is greatly to be desired, since indeed they must always exist, that the minds of young people should be disciplined to recognise them without any sense of degradation in so doing; content in knowing that, under the free institutions of their country, the attainment of such distinctions is, under Providence, as open to themselves as it was to those who have already been successful; and happy in the practice of a duty, to which as good citizens and Christian men they are unquestionably bound.

5·9 COST OF A UNIVERSITY EDUCATION

From Report *and* Evidence *of the Royal Commission on Oxford University, Parliamentary Papers 1852, XXII, pp. 33 and 23 respectively.*

The costs of a stay at Oxford which were given in evidence before the Commission show clearly that in the majority of the colleges the expenses incurred in taking a degree were such as to restrict attendance to a small section of the population.

On the whole, we believe that a parent, who, after supplying his son with clothes and supporting him at home during the vacations, has paid for him during his University course not more than 600*l.*, and is not called upon to discharge debts at its close, has reason to congratulate himself. Those who allow their sons a private Tutor should add proportionably to their estimate. Private Tutors usually charge 10*l.* a term, or 30*l.* a year, for three hours a-week; 17*l.* 10*s.* a term, or 50*l.* a-year, for six hours a-week. Private Tutors of high standing expect 20*l.* a term: 30*l.* is usually paid by young men who join a reading party during the long vacation.

Rev. J. D. Collis, M.A.

The following bona fide list of expenses may be of use in estimating the *real* cost of a degree at Oxford. Of the sum there mentioned, I received about 120*l.* first from a Post-mastership at

Merton, and afterwards from a Scholarship at Worcester College.
I was matriculated June 1834, and took my degree October 1838:–

	£	s.	d.
College battels	237	5	0
University fees (Matriculation, B.A. degree, &c.)	32	4	0
College servants	33	7	6
Private Tutor	33	10	0
Loss on furniture of rooms	21	5	0
Groceries	21	8	0
Wine, desserts, occasional expenses for dinners, &c.	38	12	6
Books	40	7	8
Letters, parcels, &c.	6	5	11
Subscriptions, and private disbursements	22	13	6
Boating and amusements	10	17	0
Washing	18	19	6
Tailor	85	7	6
Boots, &c.	23	2	0
Various	29	19	6
Total cost of degree	655	4	7
Add travelling	69	18	0
	£725	2	7

This is a low sum for Oxford; I should say the usual cost of a
degree is 800*l.* at least; to very many it is as much as 1,000*l.*

5·10 HEADS OF HOUSES

From *J. W. Burgon*, Lives of Twelve Good Men, *2 vols,
1889, I, p. 71.*

Although the academic world provided some avenue of upward
mobility, the successful don, like the majority of his students, was
often a member of families from the older gentry.

*RICHARD LYNCH COTTON: The humble Christian [A.D. 1794–
1880]*

One of the oldest of the surviving Heads of Houses disappeared
from the familiar scene when, on the 8th of December, 1880, the
revered Provost of Worcester College departed, – 'full of days',
being already in his eighty-seventh year.

Richard Lynch Cotton was born on the 14th of August, 1794, at Walliscote in Oxfordshire, being descended from a very ancient family settled in Shropshire (it is said) from Saxon times. He was the third son of Henry Calveley Cotton, esq., (youngest son of Sir Lynch Salusbury Cotton, fourth Baronet), and Matilda, daughter and heiress of John Lockwood, esq., of Dews Hall, Essex. He therefore stood in the relation of first cousin to Sir Stapleton Cotton who was created Baron Combermere in 1814, – Viscount, in 1827. His mother bore to her husband fourteen children: – three daughters and eleven sons, of whom three entered holy orders, and six attained high rank in the army and navy, – viz., General Sir Sydney Cotton, G.C.B., Colonel Hugh Calveley Cotton, E.I.C.S., General Sir Arthur Cotton, K.C.S.I., Major-General Sir Frederick Cotton, and Admiral Francis Vere Cotton.

5·11 SOCIAL SELECTION OF THE PUBLIC SCHOOL SYSTEM

From R. H. Tawney, 'The Problem of the Public School', Political Quarterly *1941,* Reprinted in *R. H. Tawney,* The Radical Tradition, *(ed. R. Hinden), 1964, pp. 58–61.*

While not necessarily out of place in the nineteenth century with its rigid social division, Tawney argues that an exclusive public school system is out of place in the more democratic society of the twentieth century.

Educational policy is always social policy. In the England of the later nineteenth century, when the public school system was in the making, it could plausibly be argued that the recruitment of educational institutions on the basis of wealth, if in itself unedifying, was not out of tune with the temper of the day. In their subservience to money and social position, and the tranquil, unsophisticated class-consciousness which that subservience bred, the public boarding-schools, it might be said, did not rise above the standards of their generation, but neither did they fall below them. Their virtues were genuine and their own; their vices were of a piece with those of the society about them. Whether convincing, or not, in the past, that defence is clearly out of date.

Since the public school system assumed its present shape,

England has become a political democracy. The public boarding-schools continue to serve much the same tiny class as in the days when Lord Balfour was at Eton and Lord Baldwin at Harrow. A national system of education has not only been created in the interval, but has revealed unanticipated possibilities of growth. It is hardly an exaggeration to say that, as far as the contact with it of the great majority of the public boarding-schools goes, it might as well not exist. Institutions so immune to the stresses and demands of a changing environment may enjoy some of the advantages of an old régime, but they suffer also from its weaknesses. It is not primarily a question of the attitude of headmasters, or even of governing bodies; for representative figures among the former have expressed themselves strongly, if with reservations, in favour of reform, and the latter, however opaque their prejudices, could not prevent it, once it had become the national policy. It is a question of the reluctance of a small, but influential, class to acquiesce in interference with institutions which it has come to regard as peculiarly its own; of its fears of the keener competition for posts of profit and distinction which will result from a diminution of educational inequalities; of a temper which values the more exclusive public schools, not only as organs of culture, but as instruments of power; of public indifference; of the refusal of Governments, for each and all of these reasons, to take a thorny subject up. As a consequence the public boarding-schools have been permitted to live in isolation from the educational needs of the mass of the population and from the system which serves them. What are the results of that policy?

Its first result is obvious. The rising generation is submitted in youth to a somewhat rigid system of educational segregation, which is also a system of social segregation. Whether Disraeli's famous epigram is still applicable or not to the adult population, it certainly remains true of the young, though, thanks to the development of public education, it is less true than in the recent past. Given the existing economic order, sharp class divisions exist independently of educational organization and policy. It is unreasonable, therefore, to speak of the public boarding-schools as creating them. But education ought to be solvent of such divisions. It is difficult to deny that the tendency of those schools is to deepen and perpetuate them. 'The very existence of the public schools, as they now are,' writes Mr Simpson, himself formerly a master at one of them, 'helps to keep the different social classes ignorant of one another, and aggravates misunderstanding to an extent which public school men commonly do not realize.' Is it possible convincingly to challenge that criticism? . . .

There is nothing whatever to be said for preserving schools whose distinctive characteristic is that they are recruited almost exclusively from the children of parents with larger incomes than their neighbours. That infliction on the young of the remorseless rigours of the economic calculus is mischievous for two reasons. It is unfair to them, and it is injurious to society. Children learn from each other more than the most skilful of masters can teach them. Easy, natural and unself-conscious contacts between young people of varying traditions and different social background are not the least valuable part of their education. They are not only a stimulating influence in youth, but the best preparation for an attitude which makes the most of life in later years. An educational system which discourages them is, to that extent, not a good system, but a bad one.

The predominantly one-class school is not favourable to them. Not only is an obvious injustice when children are excluded by financial barriers from the schools in question, but the pupils admitted to them are themselves injured. They are taught, not in words or of set purpose, but by the mere facts of their environment, that they are members, in virtue of the family bank-account, of a privileged group, whose function it will be, on however humble a scale, to direct and command, and to which leadership, influence, and the other prizes of life properly belong. The capacity of youth to protect itself against the imbecilities of its elders is not the least among the graces bestowed on it by Heaven; but that does not excuse us for going out of our way gratuitously to inflict our fatuities upon it. If some of the victims continue throughout life, as unhappily they do, to see the world through class spectacles, a policy which insists on their wearing them at school must bear part of the responsibility. Insolence and servility in the old may well be incurable, and are a subject for pity rather than for indignation. But why persist in transmitting the bacilli to the young?

Nor, of course, is it only individuals who suffer from our erection of educational snobbery into a national institution. The nation, as a whole, pays a heavy price for it. The complicated business of democratic government demands, with the world as it is, a high capacity of co-operation; and co-operation, in its turn, depends on mutual understanding. A common educational background fosters such understanding. An organization of education which treats different sections of the population as though they belonged to different species is an impediment to it.

5·12 MAKING PUBLIC SCHOOLS MORE 'PUBLIC'

From the Board of Education's Committee on Public Schools, Report, *1944, pp. 53–5.*

The report had considered the advantages as well as the difficulties of a gradual widening of the entry to the public schools which it favoured. It then turned to the wider issue of the social selectivity of this sector of secondary education.

145. We pass now to the wider and more serious objections which are raised to the admission of pupils from the Primary Schools to the Independent Public Schools – objections based not on anticipation of the failure of the experiment, but upon the belief that there is something radically wrong with the Public Schools as such. There is undoubtedly a very widespread belief that the Public Schools originate in, and still tend to increase, the cleavage between social classes – and particularly between rich and poor – which is deplored by all men of goodwill and not least by the Governing Bodies of the Public Schools themselves. It is true, roughly speaking, that the Public Schools were part of a social order which existed until the beginning of the present century and in which little attempt was made to provide any but elementary education for the children of manual and industrial or even of the less well-paid clerical workers. One of the consequences of this was that all those posts which demand a higher education in Church and State and in some of the professions, went almost inevitably to persons educated in the Public Schools and the older Universities; those who by force of character rose from other beginnings to these positions were rare though notable exceptions. Moreover, such a state of things was bound to persist to a great extent even after the introduction of secondary education for a large number of the pick of Elementary School children. Such posts of power and responsibility are not usually awarded to anyone before middle

life; it could hardly be expected that any considerable number of men who were educated in Secondary Schools (from 1902 onwards) and in the newer Universities (nearly all created in the present century) would find their way to the higher positions earlier than the last fifteen years or so, and the process would still be retarded by the natural tendency of the dispensers of patronage to select persons of the same type and outlook as themselves. From some tables submitted to us by the Workers' Educational Association, it appears that, in 1939, out of 830 Bishops, Deans, Judges and stipendiary Magistrates, highly-paid Home Civil Servants, India Civil Servants, Governors of Dominions, Directors of Banks and Railway Companies, 636, or about 76 per cent, were drawn from the Public Schools, and of these 394 (or about 47·5 per cent of the total) from twelve of the more important Public Schools – a result which is approximately the same as was worked out by Professor R. H. Tawney twelve years earlier.

146. We see some signs of gradual change in the evidence submitted to us by the Civil Service Commissioners. In the examinations for the Administrative Class of the Home Civil Service, between 1925 and 1937, there was a decrease of about 13 per cent, as compared with the period 1904 to 1914, in the proportion of successful candidates who had been previously educated in Public Schools. Even in the later period, three-fifths of the successful candidates had been at Public Schools as defined in our terms of reference, but it must be remembered that the term 'Public School' in this sense includes a number of well-known and successful Direct Grant Day Schools and a number of important Scottish Day Schools; in both the earlier and the later periods mentioned there was a majority of successful candidates from Day Schools as compared with Boarding Schools. In the examinations for the Indian Civil Service, between 1921 and 1938, the proportion of successful candidates both from Public Schools and from Boarding Schools was about the same as for the Home Civil Service during the same years, i.e. rather less than half from Boarding Schools and about three-fifths from Public Schools; no comparable figures were available for the Indian Civil Service during the earlier period. In examinations for the Consular and Diplomatic Services, between 1923 and 1938, a majority of the successful candidates came from Boarding Schools and an even larger majority (in the Diplomatic Service an overwhelming majority) from Public Schools. In

examinations for admission by Special Entry to the Royal Navy in 1942 and 1943 there was, among the successful candidates, a bare majority of boys from Boarding Schools and a considerable majority (over three-quarters) from Public Schools.

147. These figures do not afford a substantial basis of comparison between recent and less recent times, and such changes as they do reveal are small and gradual, though perceptible. They do, however, establish the considerable extent to which the higher branches of the public service are, and have for some time been, dependent on the Day Schools and they show also that, in the Home and Indian Civil Services at least, boys from the grant-aided schools generally (and not only from the better known Direct Grant and Scottish Day Schools) are obtaining an increasing share of responsible posts in the public service. Other figures supplied by the Commissioners show that such entrants are successful in holding their own with others in subsequent progress in the service. But changes of this kind make themselves felt slowly, and a natural impatience with what many people regard as unfair advantages has been accentuated by the experience of the war, in which all classes of society have contributed without distinction of origin to the number of gallant and successful officers in all the Services, and many men whose career began in Elementary Schools have filled high offices of State with great efficiency and distinction. A full solution of this problem, which is not a purely educational one, does not lie within our power to devise, but the proposals we make for enabling boys and girls of all classes to enter the Public Schools will go far, we hope, to ending the social exclusiveness of these schools, and so to ending, also, any unfair or undeserved advantages which their pupils may have enjoyed from the mere social reputation of their schools.

148. We realise the possibility that just as some parents now send their sons to Public Schools partly, perhaps mainly, for the sake of social or economic advantages, so our proposals may attract some other parents who are interested mainly in the same narrow advantages. This is a risk that must be taken, but it can be watched and reduced, if not entirely eliminated, from the start, and should eventually disappear as the Public Schools become representative of all classes of the community. We recognise also that if a number of Primary School boys were admitted to the Public Schools, the privileges for the rich and the inequality of opportunity would not

immediately disappear. Indeed some of our witnesses tell us that nothing would happen beyond a slight extension of the privileged class through the addition of a few poorer boys who would absorb its prejudices and failings. There would certainly be some risk of this if the number admitted were small; but the number need not be small, and we emphasise again that the ultimate object of our proposals is to make these schools accessible to all classes irrespective of wealth and social position.

149. Finally, it has been very freely stated to us that Public School men generally show a lack of sympathy with, or even understanding of the lives and difficulties of the other classes in society, from which they are said to be wholly segregated, and particularly of those engaged in manual and technical work; and that they are out of touch with social realities and incapable of grasping modern social conditions. It is difficult to prove or disprove sweeping statements of this kind, but it may be admitted that in so far as social classes exist, the members of one class, especially while they are young, are bound to know more about the life and conditions of work and the outlook of their own class than about those of another, and that in so far as Schools exist which are accessible only to those who can pay high fees, there is a real danger that the outlook of those who are less well off should be insufficiently understood. It must not be forgotten, however, that those Public Schools which are attended by boys whose parents are wealthy or aristocratic are very few out of the whole number, and in all schools there are boys whose parents have only been enabled to send them there by a hard struggle; there is in the Public Schools much less economic exclusiveness than is often supposed. But so long as degrees of wealth and poverty and a diversity of functions in the social organism exist, all men of goodwill must desire increased mutual understanding, and the question before us, once more, is how this aim is most likely to be furthered. We hope that, as a result of our proposals, any exclusiveness and lack of understanding that may be associated with the Public Schools may be diminished, but, as we said earlier, the problem is part of a wider one, the solution of which will call for broadmindedness and good sense outside as well as inside the Public Schools.

6 The Civil Service

6·1 *PLACEMEN AND PENSIONERS*

From John Wade (ed.), The Black Book, *1835 ed. pp. 492–3 and 497–9.*

The Black Book, John Wade's industrious compilation of known abuses and wastes, devoted much space to the benefits accruing to Civil Servants. Ministers and their servants used the power of patronage which they had for the benefit of their favourites and relations, making certain that this élite would be self-perpetuating.

Salaries and Pensions exceeding one thousand pounds

Great as are the salaries, pensions, and emoluments of individuals, it must be constantly borne in mind that these constitute the smallest part of the advantages, or perhaps we may term it corruptive influence, to which official men are exposed. The most important, the most seductive, and most tempting adjuncts to public offices of the higher grade are the vast patronage, the power and personal consideration they confer on the possessors. In this consists the great difference between government employments and the pursuits of trade and commerce. There are, we doubt not, individual merchants and manufacturers who do – or at least have – realized an annual profit equal to the salaries of a first lord of the Treasury, Secretary of State, the Chief Justice, or even the Lord Chancellor. But observe the difference in their respective situations; observe the dazzling and glittering elevation of the state functionaries; observe the good things they have at their disposal – the benefices, bishoprics, commissionerships of customs and excise; the clerkships, registrarships, and secretaryships, worth from £1000 to £10,000 a-year – and think of the opportunities afforded by these splendid gifts for enriching their families and friends – and think, too, of the delightful incense of adulation and obsequiousness the dispensers of such favours must inhale, and of the host of fawning sycophants, expectants, and dependents, they must everywhere raise up around them. Here are the real *sweets* of *office*, the delicious flavour of which can never be tasted by a mercantileman, however successful in his vocation. . . .

In considering, therefore, the salaries of civil and judicial officers, it is always necessary to bear in mind that they form only a single element in the multifarious advantages of their situations. The patronage of most public officers would be ample remuneration; and were it limited to that alone, we have no apprehension there would be a dearth of candidates for official employments, no more than there are for the magistracy, shrievalties, *custos rotulorum*, lord lieutenancies, and other unpaid services.

We have been drawn into these observations from reflecting on a singular public document before us, and of the contents of which we shall give the reader some account. We have hitherto spoken of placemen and pensioners generally; we shall now direct attention to the highest class, whose emoluments *exceed* £1000 *per annum*, and of which a return has been made to parliament. . . .

It comprises 956 individuals whose incomes amount to £2,161,927, averaging £2261 each; there are *forty-two* persons whose incomes are not less than £5000 each, and whose united incomes amount to £339,809; and there are ELEVEN individuals whose incomes are not less than £10,000 each and who altogether receive £139,817 per annum. Of the whole 956 names the following is a classification, showing the total income of the several classes, and the average income of each individual. . . .

226

Classification of 956 Placemen and Pensioners whose Salaries, Profits, Pay, Fees, and Emoluments exceeded, January 5, 1830, £1000 per Annum.

No. of Officers	Description	Total Emoluments	Average Income
350	Civil Officers	£698,805	.... £1997
50	Court of Chancery	137,216	 2744
112	King's Bench and other Judicial Officers	338,651	 3023
100	Ambassadors and Consuls	256,780	 2567
134	Military Officers	240,847	 1794
36	Ordnance and Artillery	50,155	 1390
19	Naval Officers	39,835	 2076
147	Colonial Officers	387,996	 2578
8	Officers of the House of Commons	20,642	 2567

It is not, however, by *averaging* the incomes of public functionaries that we see the iniquities of the System in its most conspicuous light. In the state, as in the church, the most flagrant abuse consists in *pluralities*, in the power which individuals of title, influence, and connexion have to heap upon themselves, families, and friends, a multiplicity of offices. Next to this abuse is that of patronage. We know that the direct income of a lord of the Treasury, or a secretary of state, is very considerable, and that of a lord chief justice or lord chancellor is enormous; but what is that to the value of their patronage. All their immense patronage is so much direct revenue, and we know that it is applied as such in making provisions for sons, sons-in-law, and collaterals. We might cite the Bathursts, Manners, Abbotts, Scotts, and others; but we think the subject has been already sufficiently illustrated, and further proof will be found in our *Place and Pension List.* ...

Having explained the origin and principle of the Pension Act, let us next glance at some of the worthies who, up to this time, under the designation of 'high and efficient public men', have fastened their greedy talons on the earnings of the industrious. First on the list is Lord Sidmouth, £3000 a year for life: his lordship, besides, has Richmond-park Lodge, and for many years has been receiving, as deputy-ranger, from £1000 to £2000 per annum, out of the rents and profits of the crown lands. The sinecure of clerk of the pells was many years held by his son; and there are several other Addingtons in the church, and on foreign missions. Altogether £5000 a year may be put down as the reward of the famous circular, the memorable *letter of thanks*, to the Manchester magistrates, for the massacre of the 16th of August, and other high and efficient public services of Henry Viscount Sidmouth. . . .

The right honourable Henry Goulbourn £2000, the Duke's luminous and most efficient chancellor of the Exchequer. Then follows a Mr Hamilton £1000, of whom we know nothing, unless he be a late consul or clerk of the Treasury. Afterwards we have Thomas Peregrine Courtenay, M.P. for Totness, colonial agent for the Cape of Good Hope, and late secretary of the India Board. This is the 'family man', with a wife and fourteen children, for whom Canning once made so melting an appeal to the guardians of the public purse; they must be provided for. Mr Courtenay is the cousin of a peer – let him be put down for £1000, and his sons have the first vacancies in the Mint, the Treasury, or Exchequer!

Now, right honourable John Wilson Croker, come forth; don't be ashamed; who can begrudge anything to the paymaster of the widows' charity, and a twenty-one years' secretary of the Admiralty, with £3000 per annum. Put John down for £1500 a year for life – but stop; do not let him receive his pension, any more than his brother pamphleteer, Peregrine Courtenay, if he hold offices yielding £3000 a year. . . .

We pass over Canning and Huskisson; at the time of their death, each was down for £3000; they were amongst the most greedy and audacious of corruptionists; but they are gone to their audit elsewhere; – not, however, without leaving long trails of calamities behind, of which more hereafter.

Next is a Hobhouse £1000; but we pass over him also to come to the last and greatest of our 'high and efficient public men', the right honourable Lord Bexley. How ought a statesman like this to be rewarded: the great Sieur Vansittart, the steadfast coadjutor of the 'Thunderer', the astounding financier, the man of infinite resource, who, in the period of our greatest tribulations, did, by the mere force of native genius, make a pound note and a shilling equal to a guinea, when the former was depreciated thirty per cent. Put Nicholas down for £3000 a year for life, and make him a Lord!

There is another description of pensioners whom we must shortly touch – the noble and learned lords: Here is Lord Eldon still preying upon us, at the rate of £4000 a year. Surely £15,000 a year, and upwards, for more than a quarter of a century, and a disposition naturally parsimonious, afforded the means of making a comfortable provision for old age. Lord Manners, another ex-chancellor, draws £3892 a year; Wynford £3756. Then there is lord Tenterden impending, and Bayley and others menace us in the distance. Lyndhurst for a time hung out a flag of distress, but, after receiving £505 14 11¼ . . . as temporary relief, he retreated into the court of Exchequer. Brougham, or his friends for him, have put in a claim for £6000 as a retiring pension, – but avast there, good lord! Surely such doings must have an end! At this rate the whole Bar may file through the judgeships, and come upon us, after a quarter's service, for pensions for life, each of which, at the present rate of labourers' wages, would maintain eight hundred persons.

6·2 THE RATIONALE OF LINKING HIGH OFFICE TO HIGH STATUS

From Sir Henry Taylor, The Statesman, 1836, H. J. Laski's edition, with introduction, 1927, pp. 98–101.

Taylor, the son of a gentleman farmer, had an uneventful career in the Colonial Office which lasted for nearly half a century until 1872. His book was conceived as a guide to Civil Servants and Ministers and was subtitled 'An ironical treatise on the art of succeeding'. In defending the tradition of giving high office to men of high rank he shows considerable insight into the basis of politics of deference.

Concerning Rank as a qualification for high office

It may be thought that the function would carry the rank. If this were so, still social and extrinsic rank would be desirable, as coming in aid of official. But it is not so always. For it often happens that the functions of statesmanship are performed by one who has neither social nor much of official rank. The evil of this is that parties who transact business with him do not feel the value of his time, and a considerable part of the public property invested in his labour is lost.

Such a person, through the want of better titles, will commonly obtain that of a 'Jack in office'; and *his* insolence and presumption will be contrasted with the natural courtesy of a man of high rank and station. The truth is, however, that the one, being scrupulously approached and charily occupied, can afford to be courteous; whereas, if the other were to be equally so, it must be at the cost, not only of his personal convenience, but of his duty and essential utility as a public servant. No suitors tread timorously in *his* approaches; none sit upon thorns in his presence, pricked by the consciousness that they are stealing the golden minutes. He is understood to be active and influential in the transaction of business, and every stranger, therefore, who has anything to solicit, knocks hardily at his door, not reflecting that his influence and activity depend upon his shutting himself up and applying himself uninterruptedly to his business. His remedy is to be cold, dry or harsh, – not for his personal relief, but in order that he may be allowed to do his duty to the public. His reward is to be called a 'Jack in office'; and the common remark is repeated, 'How unassuming are the highborn, the highbred, the men of rank, the men of station – how insolent are the understrappers!'

Further, adventitious rank goes well with office, in respect that it tends to smooth over an inherent disparity the wrong way, when it occurs (as it must and will occasionally) between those in command and those under command. To see reason over-ruled . . .

> 'And strength by limping away disabled,
> 'And art made tongue-tied by authority'*

will doubtless be disagreeable, let it be warranted as it may; but it will be less odious when done by a prince or a duke, than when it is the act of a man raised from a lower rank in society to a high official station. Were it possible that preferment should always go by merit, other elevation might be better dispensed with; but looking at life and human nature as they exist, and to the influence which established orders and degrees of society obtain over the imaginations of men, it may be said that the influence is well applied when it helps to render less obnoxious an inevitable official subjection of the superior intellect. That is no insignificant part of the philosophy of government which calls in aid the imaginations of men in order to subjugate the will and understanding; and so long as man shall continue to be an imaginative being, it will be expedient that those who are to enjoy pre-eminence or to exercise power, should be invested with some ideal influence which may serve to clothe the nakedness of authority.

*Shakespeare's Sonnets, 66.

6·3 BIRTH AND ASPIRATION FOR ADMINISTRATIVE OFFICE

From J. C. Henderson, The Parent's Handbook; a guide to choice of the professions, *1842, pp. 127–8.*

The advice given here was only a statement of fact.

The offices of the Secretaries of State and the Treasury rank higher than any other in the public services, and a man of inferior birth and education would be regarded as presumptuous in asking for appointment in either of them. Other departments it might be invidious to classify; but the superiority of those above mentioned is universally acknowledged, and ought therefore to be stated here to prevent any person who may think that he has a claim on the minister possessing the patronage of either of such offices, from soliciting an appointment for which the person on whose behalf the solicitation is made may happen to be ineligible.

6·4 THE SYSTEM OF PATRONAGE

From (1) the Report *on the Organisation of the Permanent Civil Service (Northcote-Trevelyan Report) and (2), (3) and (4) from* 'Papers relating to the Re-Organisation of the Civil Service', *both Parliamentary Papers 1854/5, XX (1) p. 7, (2) p. 74, (3) p. 263, (4) pp. 44–5.*

After the reforms introduced into the system of recruitment to the East India Company on the advice of Macauley, the Reform of the Home Civil Service began with the Northcote-Trevelyan Report. Together with this the government published a series of essays by eminent Civil Servants and educators which commented, in part, on the report.

6·4·1 FROM THE REPORT

It is of course essential to the public service that men of the highest abilities should be selected for the highest posts; and it cannot be denied that there are a few situations in which such varied talent and such an amount of experience are required, that it is probable that under any circumstances it will occasionally be found necessary to fill them with persons who have distinguished themselves elsewhere than in the Civil Service. But the system of appointing strangers to the higher offices has been carried far beyond this. In several departments the clerks are regarded as having no claim whatever to what are called the staff appointments, and numerous instances might be given in which personal or political considerations have led to the appointment of men of very slender ability, and perhaps of questionable character, to situations of considerable emolument, over the heads of public servants of long standing and undoubted merit. Few public servants would feel the appointment of a barrister of known eminence and ability to some important position, like that of Under Secretary of State, as a slight or a discouragement to themselves; but the case is otherwise when someone who has failed in other professions, and who has no recommendation but that of family or political interest, is appointed to a librarianship, or some other such office, the duties of which would have been far better discharged by one who had been long in the department, and to whom the increased salary attached to the appointment would have been a fair reward for years of faithful service.

6·4·2 SIR JAMES STEPHENS

The members of what I have described as the 'third class', usually entered the office at the age of 18 or 19, coming directly from school, and bringing with them no greater store of information, or maturity of mind, than usually belongs to a boy in the fifth form at Eton, Westminster, or Rugby. What they so brought they never afterwards increased by any private study. Finding themselves engaged in the actual business of life, they assumed that their preparation for it was complete; and (as far as I could judge), they never afterwards made or attempted any mental self-improvement.

It would be superfluous to point out in detail the injurious results of such a composition of one of the highest departments of the State. Among the less obvious consequences of it, were – the necessity it imposed on the heads of the office of undertaking, in their own persons, an amount of labour to which neither their mental or their bodily powers were really adequate – the needless and very inconvenient increase of the numbers borne on the clerical list – the frequent transfer of many of their appropriate duties to ill-educated and ill-paid supernumeraries – and the not infrequent occurrence of mistakes and oversights so serious as occasionally to imperil interests of high national importance. . . .

In reliance on much uniform, concurrent, and credible evidence from others, and in reliance of what I myself knew and observed at the Board of Trade, I believe that the state of the Colonial Department, as I have described it, is no unfair example and illustration of the state of the other great departments of the Government as they existed during my personal connexion with the Public Service.

6·4·3 EDWARD ROMILLY (Chairman of the Board of Accounts)

Another idea that has been suggested is, that the examination should be of a very high order; – that the higher this standard the greater the degree and quantity of ability that will present itself for the public service. But is not this a delusion? Will not this rather depend upon the Civil Service itself than upon the nature of the examination for admission to it? If that service offers high prizes, attainable by superior intellect alone, superior intellect will be tempted into it. If it does not, no examination, however difficult, which is to be ultimately and comparatively barren of result, will have any such effect. It may however be said, in order to enlarge the field of competitors, Government patronage may be abandoned, and the public generally admitted into the lists. But even this expedient, supposing it to be practicable and desirable, would not have the desired effect as long as other modes of life offered better chances for attaining wealth and fame. It should also be borne in mind that moral qualities and social position are often as important elements in the character of a public servant as great facility and intellectual power. Good sense and judgment, good manners and moral courage, energy and perseverance, a high sense of honour and integrity, a wholesome fear of public opinion, and the desire of being well thought of by a circle of friends, are more important qualities and motives in public officers, for the practical business of official life, than familiarity with classical and modern literature, science, and history. The latter may be tested by examination, the former cannot; and the lower you descend in the scale of society the less the guarantee that candidates for the Civil Service will possess those moral and social qualifications, which are so indispensable for the practical business of official life.

6·4·4 ARCHIBALD CAMPBELL TAIT

The principal objection which I have heard urged against such a system of promotion by merit as your report advises is that appointments now conferred on young men of aristocratic connexion will fall into the hands of persons in a much lower grade of society, and that the tone of honourable feeling, which at present exists among those holding such appointments will be endangered. To this argument I attach no importance whatever. I feel certain . . . that the highest classes . . . are quite capable of maintaining their own in any competition . . . and I cannot think that any real favour is done to young men of these classes by putting them out of reach of such stimulants to exertion and good conduct as might exercise a most beneficial influence on their whole character.

(Later Archbishop Tait, then Dean of Carlisle and formerly Tutor of Balliol and Headmaster of Rugby)

6·5 PATRONAGE – A POSTSCRIPT

From Anthony Trollope, An Autobiography, *(1883) Oxford, 1963, pp. 30–34.*

Writing about his own entry into the Civil Service over forty years later Trollope sought to justify this method of recruitment by referring to the gentlemanly qualities needed for some posts.

On reaching London I went to my friend Clayton Freeling, who was then secretary at the Stamp Office, and was taken by him to the scene of my future labours in St Martin's le Grand. Sir Francis Freeling was the secretary, but he was greatly too high an official to be seen at first by a new junior clerk. I was taken, therefore, to his eldest son, Henry Freeling, who was the assistant secretary and by him I was examined as to my fitness. . . . I was asked to copy some lines from the *Times* newspaper with an old quill pen, and at once made a series of blots and false spellings. 'That won't do, you know,' said Henry Freeling to his brother Clayton. Clayton, who was my friend, urged that I was nervous, and asked that I might be allowed to do a bit of writing at home and bring it as a sample on the next day. I was then asked whether I was a proficient in arithmetic. What could I say? I had never learned the multiplication table, and had no more idea of the rule of three than of conic sections. 'I know a little of it,' I said humbly, whereupon I was sternly assured that on the morrow, should I succeed in showing that my handwriting was all that it ought to be, I should be examined as to that little of arithmetic. If that little should not be found to comprise a thorough knowledge of all the ordinary rules, together with practised and quick skill, my career in life could not be made at the Post Office. Going down the main stairs of the building, – stairs which have I believe been now pulled down to make room for sorters and stampers, – Clayton Freeling told me not to be too downhearted. I was myself inclined to think that I had better at once go back to the school at Brussels. But nevertheless I went to work, and under the surveillance of my elder brother made a beautiful transcript of four or five pages of Gibbon. With a faltering heart I took this on the next day to the office. With my calligraphy I was contented, but was certain that I should come to the ground among the figures. But when I got to 'The Grand', as we used to call our office in those days, from its site, St Martin's le Grand, I was seated at a desk without any further reference to my competency. No one condescended even to look at my beautiful penmanship.

That was the way in which candidates for the Civil Service were examined in my young days. It was at any rate the way in which I was examined. Since that time there has been a very great change indeed; – and in some respects a great improvement. But in regard to the absolute fitness of the young men selected for the public service, I doubt whether more harm has not been done than good. And I think that the good might have been done without the harm. The rule of the present day is, that every place shall be open to public competition, and that it shall be given to the best among the comers. I object to this, that at present there exists no known way of learning who is best, and that the method employed has no tendency to elicit the best. . . . When it is decided in a family that a boy shall 'try the Civil Service', he is made to undergo a certain amount of cramming. But such treatment has, I maintain, no connection whatever with education. The lad is no better fitted after it than he was before for the future work of his life. But his very success fills him with false ideas of his own educational standing, and so far unfits him. And, by the plan now in vogue, it has come to pass that no one is in truth responsible either for the conduct, the manners, or even for the character of the youth. . . .

The desire to examine the efficiency of the young men selected, has not been the only object – perhaps not the chief object – of those who have yielded in this matter to the arguments of the reformers. There had arisen in England a system of patronage under which it had become gradually necessary for politicians to use their influence for the purchase of political support. A member of the House of Commons, holding office, who might chance to have five clerkships to give away in a year, found himself compelled to distribute them among those who sent him to the House. In this there was nothing pleasant to the distributor of patronage. Do away with the system altogether, and he would have as much chance of support as another. He bartered his patronage only because another did so also. The beggings, the refusings, the jealousies, the correspondence, were simply troublesome. Gentlemen in office were therefore not indisposed to rid themselves of the curse of patronage. I have no doubt their hands are the cleaner and their hearts are the lighter; but I do doubt whether the offices are on the whole better manned.

As what I now write will certainly never be read till I am dead I may dare to say what no one now does dare to say in print, – though some of us whisper it occasionally into our friends' ears. There are places in life which can hardly be well filled except by 'Gentlemen'. The word is one the use of which almost subjects one to ignominy. If I say that a judge should be a gentleman, or a bishop, I am met with scornful allusion to 'Nature's Gentlemen'. Were I to make such an assertion with reference to the House of Commons, nothing that I ever said again would receive the slightest attention. A man in public life could not do himself a greater injury than by saying in public that commissions in the army or navy, or berths in the Civil Service, should be given exclusively to gentlemen. He would be defied to define the term, – and would fail should he attempt to do so. But he would know what he meant, and so very probably would they who defied him. It may be that the son of the butcher in the village shall become as well fitted for employments requiring gentle culture as the son of the parson. Such is often the case. When such is the case, no one has been more prone to give the butcher's son all the welcome he has merited than I myself; but the chances are greatly in favour of the parson's son. The gates of the one class should be open to the other; but neither to one class or to the other can good be done by declaring that there are no gates, no barrier no difference. The system of competitive examination is I think, based on a supposition that there is no difference.

6·6 THE SOCIAL BACKGROUND OF VICTORIAN CIVIL SERVANTS

Table from the Third Report *of the Civil Service Commission, Parliamentary Papers, 1857–58, XXV, p. 48.*

NOMINEES

Table showing the Social Position occupied by the Fathers of 493 Nominees to Clerkships in certain of the Principal Departments.

Social Position of the Father of Nominee	Number of Nominees
Peers	11
Members of Parliament	7
Other persons of title	12
Officers in the Army, Navy, and Militia	67
Civil Service, –	
Superior Officers (including Judges, Magistrates, &c.)	39
Clerks	21
Other Officers	9
Professional Men, viz.,	
Clergymen	65
Dissenting Ministers	3
Barristers	9
Attorneys and Solicitors	10
Physicians and Surgeons	27
Others (viz., Architect, Artist, Astronomer, Author, Civil Engineer, Comedian, Editor, Engraver, Schoolmaster, Teachers, &c.)	32
Officers of Public Bodies	7

Social Position of Father of Nominee	Number of Nominees
Clerks to Attorneys, Bankers, &c.	5
Merchants, Tradesmen, &c., viz., –	
Bankers	3
Brewers	6
Farmers	11
Others (including Accountant, Auctioneer, Bath Proprietor, Bleacher, Broker, Builder, Carpenter, Cardmaker, Chemist, Chairmaker, Coachbuilder, Coal Merchant, Corn Broker, Draper, Goldbeater, Hatter, House Agent, Innkeeper, Jeweller, Land Agent, Land Surveyor, Printer, Nurseryman, Sailmaker, Shoemaker, Stationer, Stockbroker, Tailor, Upholsterer, Underwriter, Wine Merchant, &c.)	72
'Gentlemen', Miscellaneous, &c.	77
	493

6·7 THE COMPETITION WALLAH

From 'Competitive Examinations' Quarterly Review, Vol. 108, 1860, pp. 572–9.

Concentrating on the formal aspect of the proposed system of selection by examination, the *Quarterly Review* defended the patronage system for Civil Service appointments. Above all, public morality could not be in advance of private morality.

But, after all, is this 'stern morality' true morality, or not? Is it an evil that in the administrative departments, as well as in other departments of the public service ... a certain prima facia preference should be conceded to a man who is connected with those who are already known and trusted; that the advantage which society at large confers upon him in its own affairs should be extended to the business of administration? Why should favour and friendship, kindness and gratitude, which are not banished by men from private life, be absolutely excluded from public affairs? All exercise of patronage under the influence of such motives is not abuse of patronage. No doubt, abuse must be guarded against. As soon as it becomes a recognised fact that the odium of an unfit appointment will do more to shake a minister's position than the gratitude of a favoured partisan can do to strengthen it, the abuse of patronage will be at an end. . . . If those who are anxious for amendment in this matter would apply themselves to the education of public feeling on the subject, they will obtain a security from abuse which they will vainly seek from legislative provisions; and the remedy applied by public opinion will not only be the most effective, but it will be the most safe. It will distinguish between the true abuses of patronage, and those which only exist in the minds of theorists. So long as no unfit person is appointed, it will not care to inquire whether the patron has consulted his own interests or gratified his own feelings in the choice of his nominee; and it possesses the still more peculiar advantage that it will only demand improvement precisely in proportion to the ability of the nation to bear it. . . .

It is possible, as the celebrated dictum of Tacitus records, that a nation may not be strong enough to bear the immediate remedy of even intolerable evils. . . . Sir Robert Walpole's bribery saved his country; Necker's purity ruined his. Though the general improvement of the age has operated powerfully upon the tone of our representative system, yet private interest, in some form more impalpable than actual bribery, still goes for a great deal in the machinery by which such an heterogeneous assembly as the House of Commons is organised, and anything like stability of government is obtained. . . .

There are politicians who must have sharper remedies than a cautious philosophy can promise, just as there are impatient invalids who prefer the speedy and treacherous relief of patent medicines to the slow cure of a careful diet. A school of theorists, whose natural home is in Laputa, have fastened on the present movement as an unhoped-for opportunity for giving effect to certain *doctrinaire* crotchets of their own. They are warm and enthusiastic, and cannot wait till the slow unseen breathings of public opinion shall have dried up the miasmata of jobbery. They have a new, patent, self-acting machine, which will do it all at once. . . . They find that all shortcomings of the public departments have arisen from abuse of patronage, and that the abuse of patronage has arisen from the hopes, fears, or loves of the human patron; therefore they seek a mechanical patron that has no hopes or fears, or loves. Because patrons have not selected (as they think) well, they have had recourse to an automaton which will not select at all. . . . It is evidently an idea of Lancashire inspiration, derived from a constant contemplation of the power-loom. If a mechanical contrivance could really be discovered with such wonderful capabilities, of course the remedy would be perfect. We think it will not be difficult to show that there is no other way of detecting the qualities which go to make an efficient civil servant than that which men employ to find out a good butler or a good cook. But the theorists think they have discovered such a machine in a system of literary examinations. . . .

The problem of finding the right man for each employment is nothing new in England, as some advocates of open competition seem to imagine; nor is it a difficulty confined to the Government. Those who conduct the enormous and varied commerce of Great Britain, and indeed of every other European country, have always contrived – apparently with satisfactory results – to fill up the vacancies in their vast army of subordinates without the help of this new machine. Even the Directors of Companies, who do not carry on their business on their own behalf, but, like the Government, on behalf of a vast body of constituents to whom they owe their power, have found the system of simple nomination perfectly efficient. They use their own judgment in the choice of a servant, or they rely on the judgment of subordinates or of friends. . . . But not only have they never, within the memory of man, thought of examining their candidate in philology, Greek verse-making, and the differential calculus, but even now, when the theory has become familiar to the world, they utterly decline to accept, in the slightest degree, these qualifications as a recommendation for their choice. The system is new in this Government, unknown to other civilized governments, and unknown to men of business anywhere. . . .

The truth is, that the defects alleged against the Civil Service, assuming them to be proved, are wholly beside the question in making out a case for literary competition. A test-examination rigidly limited to the kind and amount of knowledge that each office requires, will be a perfect guarantee against the appointment of ignorant men. . . . It is perfectly possible to get a man who can spell without getting a philologist. There is no logic in appointing an astronomer because you want a man who can cast up an addition-sum. Competition gives you undoubtedly the man who is able to produce at short notice the greatest amount of knowledge in the great variety of sciences and languages of which your examinations consist. But what the departments want for their clerks, in the way of learning, are in great perfection the homely accomplishments of reading, writing, and cyphering, and certain further special acquirements which differ in various offices. These a test examination will give them with absolute certainty. Competition can do no more. Indeed, as we shall presently show, it will give them a great deal less; for it will tend to exclude qualifications that are far more important than any literary acquisitions.

6·8 THE BEGINNINGS OF CIVIL SERVICE REFORM

From T. B. Macauley (Speech in the House of Commons of 10 July 1833) Speeches, 1854, pp. 149–51.

Macauley was the chief architect of the reform of the system of recruitment to the service of the East India Company.

One word as to the new arrangement which we propose with respect to the patronage. It is intended to introduce the principle of competition in the disposal of writerships; and from this change I cannot but anticipate the happiest results. The civil servants of the Company are undoubtedly a highly respectable body of men; and in that body, as in every large body, there are some persons of very eminent ability. I rejoice most cordially to see this. I rejoice to see that the standard of morality is so high in England, that intelligence is so generally diffused through England, that young persons who are taken from the mass of society, by favour and not by merit, and who are therefore only fair samples of the mass should, when placed in situations of high importance, be so seldom found wanting. But it is not the less true that India is entitled to the service of the best talents which England can spare. That the average of intelligence and virtue is very high in this country is matter for honest exultation. But it is no reason for employing average men where you can obtain superior men. Consider too, Sir, how rapidly the public mind of India is advancing, how much attention is already paid by the higher classes of the natives to those intellectual pursuits on the cultivation of which the superiority of the European race to the rest of mankind principally depends. Surely, in such circumstances, from motives of selfish policy, if from no higher motive, we ought to fill the magistracies of our Eastern Empire with men who may do honour to their country, with men who may represent the best part of the English nation. This, Sir, is our object; and we believe that by the plan which is now proposed this object will be attained. It is proposed that for every vacancy in the civil service four candidates shall be named, and the best candidate selected by examination. We conceive that, under this system, the persons sent out will be young men above par, young men superior either in talents or in diligence to the mass. It is said, I know, that examinations in Latin, in Greek, and in mathematics, are no tests of what men will prove to be in life. I am perfectly aware that they are not infallible tests: but that they are tests I confidently maintain. Look at every walk of life, at this House, at the other House, at the Bar, at the Bench, at the Church, and see whether it be not true that those who attain high distinction in the world were generally men who were distinguished in their academic career. Indeed, Sir, this objection would prove far too much even for those who use it. It would prove that there is no use at all in education. Why should we put boys out of their way? Why should we force a lad, who would much rather fly a kite or trundle a hoop, to learn his Latin Grammar? Why should we keep a young man to his Thucydides or his Laplace, when he would much rather be shooting? Education would be mere useless torture, if, at two or three and twenty, a man who had neglected his studies were exactly on a par with a man who had applied himself to them, exactly as likely to perform all the offices of public life with credit to himself and with advantage to society. Whether the English system of education be good or bad is not now the question. Perhaps I may think that too much time is given to the ancient languages and to the abstract sciences. But what then? Whatever be the languages, whatever be the sciences, which it is, in any age or country, the fashion to teach, the persons who become the greatest proficients in those languages and those sciences will generally be the flower of the youth, the most acute, the most industrious, the most ambitious of honourable distinctions. If the Ptolemaic system were taught at Cambridge instead of the Newtonian, the senior wrangler would nevertheless be in general a superior man to the wooden spoon. If, instead of learning Greek, we learned the Cherokee, the man who understood the Cherokee best, who made the most correct and melodious

Cherokee verses, who comprehended most accurately the effect to the Cherokee particles, would generally be a superior man to him who was destitute of these accomplishments. If astrology were taught at our Universities, the young man who cast nativities best would generally turn out a superior man. If alchymy were taught, the young man who showed most activity in the pursuit of the philosopher's stone would generally turn out a superior man.

6·9 AN OPEN OR A CLOSED ÉLITE

From Minutes of Evidence *of the Select Committee on Civil Service Appointments, Parliamentary Papers 1860, IX, pp. 224, 228.*

The evidence is from Sir R. M. Bromley and H. Chester respectively.

3213. Then what system do I understand you to recommend upon the whole. Are you in favour of simple nomination, with a test examination, or of limited competition between a certain number of candidates? – *Sir R. M. Bromley.* I am in favour, certainly, of nomination. I trust that the system will never be carried to open competition. At this stage of my examination I may, perhaps, be allowed to express my own feeling upon the subject. As an old public servant, I hope never to see that kindred feeling or tie which exists between Members of the House of Commons and the public service severed. My belief is, that if you carry the system forward to open competition, Members of the House of Commons will in time lose that interest in the civil service which they now in a great degree feel for it. But I should state that I am not merely in favour of a simple nomination. I think that a patron should still nominate three or more persons, but I would have the number limited. I think that even six is too many. I should prefer that there should be three men of nearly the same age.

3214. When you say that you are in favour of nomination, do you mean nomination to compete, which is what we here understand as limited competition? – Yes, to compete; but with the proviso that you should make such arrangements as I have suggested with respect to the ages and the test. . . .

3217. When you speak of the feeling that exists between members of the civil service and Members of the House of Commons, and which you think the system of entirely open competition would tend to destroy, do you mean that that feeling is created by the power of recommendation which exists in Members of the House of Commons? – In a very great measure; and moreover it is introducing into the public departments the sons and nephews and friends of Members of Parliament, which creates that interest in the civil service.

3218. Your fear is, that if you dissociate from the House of Commons, the members of the civil service in the way which you think would follow from open competition, there would be a strong *esprit de corps* among them, tempting them to consider themselves as a distinct power in the State, acting rather antagonistically to the Parliamentary institutions of the country than acting with and under them? – Yes, I believe so; and my impression is that nothing would so much tend to give rise to a system of Bureaucratic Government as the system of open competition.

4046. Mr *Maguire*. I understand that you consider the system of direct appointment by a political officer very vicious? – *H. Chester*, Esq. The final appointment, I think, ought to be in the head of the office, but not the original selection.

4047. You wish the power of nomination to be taken out of the hands of the political officer? – Yes.

4048. You cannot conceive that that gives any guarantee to the department for either intellectual qualifications or moral qualities? – No.

4049. And you look at it merely as giving to a certain class the power of conferring reward for political service? – Commonly so; some men, of course, exercise more care than others in making their nominations.

4050. But you being no longer in the public service, can no doubt take a more liberal view of the subject than while you were a mere officer? – No, I think I take the same view that I took then; I always expressed the same opinion.

4051. You cannot apprehend any injury to the public service from taking the patronage away from the Treasury, and throwing open those departments to the public? – None whatever.

4052. You cannot conceive that any evil would arise from it? – None that would not cure itself.

4053. There could, of course, be no injury to the public in getting the services of highly intelligent and able men? – Quite the contrary.

4054. And inasmuch as those men would rise from the humbler grades in the office to the higher, would not there be a greater necessity for intelligence and ability? – That is merely with some appointments; others stop at a certain line.

4055. But as a general rule, that is so? – Yes.

4056. Then as the man does rise from the lowest office to the highest, greater intelligence, and greater abilities are necessary in the discharge of his duties? – Yes.

4060. Have you ever considered that those appointments are not only political but one-sided? – Yes.

4061. And commonly given by the Government of the day to their own friends? – Yes.

4062. Are you of opinion that nothing can be more unfair than that those who do not belong to the party of the day should find it impossible to obtain those appointments on the ground of possessing ability and character? – It is very unfair and corrupting, both to Members of Parliament and their constituents, in my opinion.

4063. And you cannot anticipate any possible injury to the public from throwing open those public offices to young men of ability and intelligence of all classes? – None that cannot be guarded against by judicious regulations.

4064. Have you any apprehension of a mob of candidates rushing forward and deserting all other methods of progress in life? – None whatever.

6·10 VICTORIAN DIPLOMATS

From Minutes of Evidence *of the Select Committee on the Diplomatic Service, 1861, from* Hansard, *3rd Series, vol. 138, columns 2061–2. (15 June, 1855) and from E. C. Granville Murray,* Sidelights of English Society, *1883, pp. 96–101.*

Lord Clarendon had held diplomatic office before entering the government. He was Foreign Secretary from 1853 to 1858 and in 1865. The Royal Commission on the Civil Service of 1912 quoted his evidence in its report on the Foreign Service. Layard, the discoverer of Nineveh, had been in the diplomatic service. He later became a radical MP. Granville Murray wrote from inside experience, as a dismissed member of the Diplomatic Service, but his account though caustic did not exaggerate wildly.

6·10·1 LORD CLARENDON

In general they (the applications) were from persons who were what is, in common parlance, called the upper ranks of society; persons who could afford to give their sons the necessary income while they remained unpaid attachés at a foreign Court. I always took care to inform the persons applying ... that (they) might remain four or five years unpaid; that during that time he must depend upon the assistance of his parents or his friends, and that, at the expiration of that time, the salary that he might receive either as a paid attaché and subsequently as a Secretary of Legation, would be very small and that I considered that as a profession it did not offer much attraction or inducement to enter it.

6·10·2 A. H. LAYARD

Recent events have shown us of what importance our diplomatic service is, and what important questions are committed into its hands; and yet, if there is one service more than another which is made the vehicle of favouritism it is our diplomatic. Here is a little book published annually by the Foreign Office, which gives a list of those who are employed in our diplomatic service. I open it at random and I read – Hanover – Minister, the hon. John Duncan Bligh, C.B.; Secretary of Legation, hon. G. Edgcumbe; First Attaché, hon. W. Nassau Jocelyn. Then I go to Austria. There the Minister is the Earl of Westmorland; the Secretary of Legation, hon. Henry G. Elliot; First paid Attaché, hon. Julian H. C. Fane. I turn to Berlin, and there I read – Minister, Lord Bloomfield; Secretary of Legation, Lord Augustus Loftus; First paid Attaché, hon. Lionel S. Sackville West; Second Attaché, hon. William G. C. Elliot; and so on throughout, showing what a complete monopoly the service is. From this little book I have made the following analysis of the composition of the service – Heads of Missions: 7 lords, 9 honourables, 2 baronets, 3 noble families; 7 gentlemen – nearly all small missions; 21 against 7. Secretaries of Legation – 2 lords, 9 honourables, 1 baronet, 5 noble families; 7 gentlemen: 17 against 7. Paid Attachés – 1 lord, 7 honourables, 6 noble families; 10 gentlemen: 14 against 10, but the 10 include Turkish or Persian

Mission. Unpaid Attachés – 2 lords, 5 honourables, 9 noble families; 17 gentlemen; 16 against 17. My hon. Friend the Member for Stafford (Mr Wise) the other night mentioned the case of Mr Stanley, who had been a précis-writer in the Foreign Office, and who, after six days' service as second attaché, was made first attaché; and, after three years' service as first attaché, was promoted to the post of secretary of legation. Certainly I should have thought that that family had had enough – two peerages and a bishopric, besides other things, ought to have sufficed for them. Then, on the other hand, there is the case of Mr Alison – emphatically a man of genius – who has been kept in the embassy at Constantinople since 1839; an abler man does not exist; yet the Government, though they have made him Oriental Secretary, will not allow him to rank as a secretary of legation or to claim increase of pay; he is kept under such men as Mr Stanley, and others who have been put over his head.

6·10·3 GRANVILLE MURRAY

AMBASSADORS

A few years ago there were only five of these august creatures going about on the face of the earth as representatives of the majesty of Great Britain. One started in his ennobling life as a lawyer's clerk; one was a Scotsman who married a title; and the other three were titled born. None of them had ever written, done, or said anything remarkable, or they never could have risen to their conspicuous eminence – for promotion came slowly to all of them. Even the Scotsman spent thirty-seven patient years in climbing to the gilded rank of Excellency. The way to promotion was, of course, made easier to the persons of title; but even the most popular member of the greatest ducal family of the governing Whigs could not do the ambassadorial thing in less than twenty-two years. Indeed, it must be thoroughly well known and understood by all whom it concerns – and their name is legion – that there is nothing in a man before he is honoured with the most brilliant reward in the public service. Lord Dalling was the last person of real ability who was appointed English Ambassador, and he has had no successor. Indeed, candid politicians in the confidence of Government admit that he would never have obtained such an honour save by a miracle, and never have kept it under any circumstances but for the fortunate chance that he happened to be an invalid, who was nearly always on leave of absence, and who was steadfastly believed to be upon the point of death.

The place of a British Ambassador at a foreign Court would indeed be intolerable to any man of average energy and mature intellect. He has no power of initiative in any business; and his public conduct is absolutely under the control of telegraph wires, which are for ever instructing him, night and day. By his own countrymen he is considered as a peg on which to hook complaints. The courtiers of the country where he resides treat him with civil scorn if he gives himself airs, and as a Jack Pudding if he does not. The Ambassadors of Russia, who are entrusted with real powers, and are commonly the intimate personal friends of their Sovereign, feel an unfeigned contempt for him; and the Ambassadors of other constitutional States regard him as a fellow-actor in the performance of a heavy farce, which has ceased to attract public notice. In truth, the Ambassadors of constitutional States have an uncomfortable sensation that they are all pretending to be what they are not. . . .

A deal of envy has been expressed in news-sheets and elsewhere about the preference given to titles over merit in the diplomatic service. Titles, however, make a goodly show in all Courts, while they are still more favoured in Republics. A very small lord looks larger and more important in the esteem of rich and idle societies than a very great philosopher. This fact being indisputable, however moralists may carp at it, no Minister should be lightly blamed for taking it into account when making his promotions. A lord will do far better for a lay figure than a man of genius or a man of business; and as it is now universally acknowledged that Ambassadors have no rights and no duties, dull empty folk with sounding names can fill, with peculiar decorum, so meaningless an office. . . .

There seems to be no certain rule for mounting to the topmost rung on the ladder of British diplomacy. Men as brave and unselfish as Lord Lyons have tumbled off from unexplained causes. Each step is made by the help of patronage, and therefore depends on luck. A perfectly colourless well-behaved nobleman, who has been brought up by an experienced mother, holding a good place behind the scenes of the political stage, will always have a nice chance, if he and his mamma live long enough to make use of their

friends and experience. She will teach him to be patient and courteous; never to tread on anybody's toes or heels; never to be eager,
or apparently desirous, of promotion; till even rivals and competitors do not hesitate to cry out that his professional advancement
has been fairly earned. . . .

There are few Ambassadors on the pension-list, and their retiring allowances are not large, considered as the ultimate end of so
much ambition and such vaulting hopes. They are generally lords,
however, poor souls, if that is any consolation to them; and they
cost the nation, when lumped together, no more in superannuation
doles than half, or maybe a third, of the yearly earnings of a
country solicitor in moderate practice. Possibly they really want
nothing.

They are great lights at their clubs, these frail and worn-out
wrecks and spars of forgotten vessels, freighted with forgotten
schemes, that have gone down in the ocean of time. They are in
earnest request at christenings and weddings. Their names are
thought to look well in the trust-deeds of marriage settlements;
they are often fished for, but seldom hooked, by promoters of
public companies, for they sink heavily into silent pools like large
tench, as soon as they have carried off the bait held out to them,
They may be met in fashionable neighbourhoods during the season,
strutting grandly homewards, with feeble knees, from pompous
dinners, where they have been honoured guests. Their orders and
decorations are firmly sewn on to their dowdy dress-coats by the
hands of loving women, who firmly believe that they are the centre
of the universe, round whom all other men are in duty bound to
revolve. They have small select companies, who admire them
fervently once, or even twice, a week, over weakish tea, and who
listen to the favourite stories of their youth as to the oracles of a
prophet.

6·11 PREREQUISITES OF A CIVIL SERVICE CAREER

From Report of the Select Committee on Civil Service
Expenditure, *1873, Parliamentary Papers 1873, VII, p. 292.*

In spite of the rationalization of entry achieved by the Reforms of
the eighteen-fifties the high cost of educating young men to the

standards required effectively restricted entry. The quotation is from a memorandum of T. H. Farrar, who was Assistant Secretary and later Secretary to the Board of Trade.

Another point in the scheme referred to is the aristocratic or rather plutocratic character. It selects men by competitive examination, demanding an expensive education in high subjects which only the rich can afford. It offers no opportunity to those who cannot afford this early education of afterwards making good their way. It professes to carry out the principle *'La carrière ouverte aux talents'*. But while it follows this principle in the original selection by competition . . . it ignores a far more important and practical means of carrying out this principle.

6·12 'THE OUTDOOR RELIEF OF THE BRITISH ARISTOCRACY'

From R. T. Nightingale, The Personnel of the British Foreign Office (*Fabian Society Tract 232*) *1930, pp. 6–11, 16–17.*

The above phrase was coined by John Bright; in one of the first social analyses of a group of administrators and policy-makers, we have clear evidence of the correlation between aristocratic and upper-class background and high office.

The reason why the democratic principle has been extremely slow in permeating the methods of recruitment for the British Foreign Office and Diplomatic Service is to be found in the theory by which foreign affairs have been conducted. 'There is,' wrote Bagehot in the 1860s, 'one kind of business in which our aristocracy have still, and are likely to retain long, a certain advantage. This is the business of diplomacy. . . . The old-world diplomacy of Europe was largely carried on in drawing-rooms, and, to a great extent, of necessity still is so.' Diplomacy was thought to require a breeding and finesse that could be found only amongst the aristocracy and the gentry. It was a branch of public affairs in which suitable administrators could be secured only if the democracy continued to select them according to the aristocratic principle. To associate on equal terms with the Ministers of foreign Governments, a diplomatist should possess the elegance and refinement of manners which result from gentle birth and aristocratic upbringing. Thus, until 1919, the Foreign Office and Diplomatic Service remained as a relic of the régime which had first begun to crumble in 1832. It was almost a century after the first step had been taken towards democratisation of the State when the career of diplomacy was opened unconditionally to ability. . . .

*TABLE 1**
(a) Parental Occupation

	F.O.	D.S.	Total
Aristocrats	17	82	93
Rentiers	6	36	39
Foreign Office	1	3	4
Diplomatic Service	4	10	12
Consular Service	1	5	6
Other Civil Service Departments	4	6	7
Church	2	11	13
Law	3	8	10
Army	5	19	24
Navy	1	3	3
Medicine	—	4	4
Parliament	4	3	6
Business	2	9	10
Literature	—	2	2
Academic	—	1	1
Stage..	1	—	1
Unclassified	6	8	14
	57	210	249

(b) School

	F.O.	D.S.	Total
Eton	27	67	85
Harrow	6	23	27
Leading Public Schools	6	36	38
Lesser Public Schools	4	22	26
Other Schools	—	9	9
Military and Naval Colleges	—	5	5
Privately	1	18	18
Abroad	2	9	10
Unclassified	11	21	31
	57	210	249

(c) *University*

						F.O.	D.S.	Total
Oxford	..	..	..	..	..	15	62	72
Cambridge	..	..	..	..	..	9	31	36
London	..	..	..	..	..	—	2	2
Edinburgh	..	..	..	..	..	—	3	3
Glasgow	..	..	..	..	..	—	1	1
Dublin	..	..	..	..	..	—	5	5
Belfast	..	..	..	..	..	—	2	2
Foreign Universities		..	..	..	..	3	5	7
No University	..	..	..	..	..	24	100	115
Unclassified	..	..	..	..	..	7	5	12
						58	216	255

*[*This table refers the holders of the following offices in the Foreign Office and the Diplomatic Service respectively: Permanent, Deputy and Assistant Under-Secretaries, Chief Clerks, Counsellors and Assistant Secretaries, Ambassadors and Envoys – who served between 1851 and 1929.*]

The above table provides a broad picture of the nature of the personnel of the Foreign Office and the Diplomatic Service during the last eighty years. The most striking deduction is that 53 per cent belong to the aristocracy or the gentry. Twenty-two per cent were sons of men following one or other of the professions, but only 4 per cent came from business families. Among parents dependent on their own efforts for a livelihood, civil servants and soldiers form easily the largest categories. . . .

Attendance at one or other of the great English public schools is the hall-mark of a high social position. Sixty per cent went to the eleven most exclusive schools. Of the remaining 40 per cent, well over one-half attended the lesser public schools, received a military or naval education, or were educated privately or abroad. Only nine men out of 249 have been traced who went to schools other than the recognised public schools and the military and naval colleges, and of these five were not diplomatists *de carrière*. Forty-five per cent of the personnel of the Foreign Office and the Diplomatic Service went to the two foremost schools in the country, and over one-third were Etonians. . . .

A comparison of the two services shows that the Diplomatic Service is the more socially exclusive. The aristocratic and rentier classes form 56 per cent of the Diplomatic Service, but only 40 per cent of the Foreign Office. This fact is probably due to the attraction to men of noble birth of service abroad in an environment of Courts and aristocratic society, and equally no doubt to the necessity until recently for ample private means to supplement the diplomatist's official salary. A perceptibly higher proportion of the Foreign Office personnel consists of public-school men, and indeed no member of the Foreign Office has been traced who has attended any school in this country other than the public schools. In contrast, 13 per cent of diplomatists have been educated either privately or abroad. This is due to the important part which foreign languages play in diplomacy, and to the exacting linguistic tests imposed on entrants to the Diplomatic Service. It is notable that among men trained at British universities every member of the Foreign Office without exception went either to Oxford or Cambridge, while 6 per cent of diplomatists went elsewhere. . . .

The broad conclusion indicated by the statistics hitherto tabulated is that the British Foreign Office and Diplomatic Service are wholly unrepresentative of the general community whose accredited delegates they are. Their members are drawn to the extent of 37 per cent from the aristocracy, which consists of no more than about one thousand families, and to the extent of 86 per cent from the aristocratic, rentier, bureaucratic, and professional classes – classes which form a mere fraction of the total population.

It is important to discover whether, during the seventy-nine years under review, any change in the character of the personnel has taken place, and whether the reforms in the procedure of recruitment which have from time to time been effected, have enlarged the circle from which entrants are drawn.

Attention must be given mainly to the pre-war period, because, although far-reaching reforms in the examination system were carried out after the War, their effect during the last decade is as yet difficult to estimate. The system that the reforms of 1919 supplanted was recruitment by what has been called 'limited competition'. In the Foreign Office 'limited competition' replaced patronage as early as 1857, but in the case of the Diplomatic Service there were two landmarks in the reform movement. In 1857 pure patronage was supplemented by a 'qualifying test'. No competitive element was, however, introduced into the test, and it was not until 1880 that 'limited competition' was set up. . . .

During the epoch of patronage two out of three diplomatists were aristocrats. After the reform of 1857 the proportion declined to one in two, and when competition was inserted in the examination in 1880, to less than one in three. The percentage of men whose fathers earned their own livelihood rose from 20 in the first to 37 in the second, and 44 in the third period. The proportion of sons of civil servants increases perceptibly after 1880, and the parental categories of professional and business men show a marked expansion over the whole period. The percentage educated at the eleven most exclusive public schools rises from 49 in the first to 67 in the second and 76 in the third period. The higher proportion of public-school men in recent years may be attributed to the fact that Roman Catholics, who have always been numerous in both the Foreign Office and the Diplomatic Service, were formerly debarred from going to English public schools, and were educated, as investigation bears out, either at Catholic schools in England or abroad, or privately at home. Since the abolition of patronage there has been a discernible increase in the proportion of academically trained men. Moreover, it is noteworthy that not a single diplomatist of distinction who has entered the service since 1880 has been trained at any university other than the two premier ones.

The unchallengeable conclusion that emerges from this statistical analysis is that the British Foreign Office and Diplomatic Service have been a preserve for the sons of the aristocratic, rentier and professional classes. For this reason their personnel is not a fair sample of British society as a whole. This was the view of the Macdonnell Commission: '. . . the Diplomatic Service is effectually closed to all His Majesty's subjects, be they never so well qualified for it, who are not possessed of private means. The official conditions of entry into this Service fix the amount of the private means required at a minimum of £400 a year. The effect is to limit candidature to a narrow circle of society.' The bureaucracy in foreign affairs has been one of the last strongholds in which the aristocratic principle has withstood the advance of democracy.

Men who have been nurtured in the British upper class have lived in a world secluded from the common people. Education at a great public school and one of the older universities provides a liberal education that fits men to be good administrators, but it is also a process of initiation into a social caste. Those so reared and trained are imbued with the peculiar prejudices of their walk of life. They are too far removed from the common people to comprehend their point of view. Their perspective is not characteristic of the nation as a whole.

In a democracy the Foreign Service ought firstly to represent to peoples abroad the mental attitude of the nation it stands for, and secondly to convey to the Government at home the mind of foreigners. It is not qualified to perform either of these functions if it is representative only of a very small section of the life of the nation. With the best intentions, it can accurately interpret neither the broad lines of policy laid down by statesmen nor the inclinations of the people they represent. Unless the diplomatic personnel is typical of all classes, it will not work with a constant sense that it is the servant of the whole body politic.

In former times the practice of diplomacy was restricted to Courts and the highest social circles, and this was the reason Bagehot gave as justifying the predominance of the aristocracy in British diplomacy. But today aristocratic society is in most countries divorced from government. Familiarity with aristocratic habits is no longer a necessary qualification for the diplomatist. Indeed, the problems that have faced the world since 1919 demand treatment by men with qualities entirely different from those associated with the aristocratic frame of mind. The successful diplomatist needs in this age the capacity to mix with men of all classes and standpoints, a capacity which is not to be acquired from an upbringing in British upper-class society.

6·13 THE CLOSED WORLD OF DIPLOMACY

From the Report *of the Royal Commission on the Civil Service, 1912, Fifth Report, Parliamentary Papers, 1914–16, XI, pp. 9, 10, 45, 46.*

In its Fifth Report the Royal Commission turned its attention to the Diplomatic Service for which different and more restrictive conditions of entry applied than for the rest of the Civil Service. The majority report recognised implicitly that the existing process of selection gave scope for the exercise of social bias, but it only sought to eliminate one of the hurdles in the process by which appointments were made; the minority of the Commission sought more radical changes. A note of dissent defends the traditional ties between the Foreign Service and an exclusive social class.

Chapter II. RECRUITMENT

1. We have described in the preceding chapter the earlier methods of recruitment and the successive changes which have led up to the system now in force. We now proceed to explain in detail what this system is, and what alterations we consider should be introduced into it. . . .

The Board, which meets twice a year, interviews the candidates who have received permission to appear, and carefully scrutinises their credentials. It then frames its recommendations and submits them to the Secretary of State, whose decision is final. We were informed that the Secretary of State accepts the recommendations of the Board unless he sees any strong reason to the contrary. In this way he is to some extent relieved from political or personal pressure in favour of any particular candidate.

Candidates who have been passed by the Board of Selection, and have been finally 'nominated' by the Secretary of State, are placed upon the list for examination, and, subject to the prescribed conditions as to age, &c. are allowed to state the year in which they may desire to compete. There is no limitation of the number of competitors for any particular vacancy or vacancies.

The examination is conducted by the Civil Service Commissioners, and though, as already explained, there is no longer any difference in the tests applied for admission to the Foreign Office and the Diplomatic Corps, the candidates for the one branch of the service do not compete against the candidates for the other, the names being kept on separate lists, and competition being limited to those included in each list. . . .

2. With the existing practice, as thus described, we find fault on two points. We consider, in the first place, that the preliminary permission required from the Secretary of State to appear before the Board of Selection is undesirable.

We have been told that neither political influence nor considerations of birth and family contribute in any degree to the decisions of the existing Board of Selection, and that the proportion of rejections is very small – 'roughly speaking, about 2 per cent'. It is said, in fact, that the system of nomination through the Board has been reduced to a system of eliminating, in the least objectionable or obtrusive way, those candidates whose previous records or personal qualities render them unsuited for a diplomatic career.

This appreciation of the existing system seems to lose sight of the necessity under which the candidate lies of obtaining the Secretary of State's permission to appear before the Selection Board. If this preliminary stage is retained, the Board of Selection must lose much of its usefulness, for all candidates who do not conform to a pre-determined type may have been already eliminated. And this view borrows confirmation from the percentage of rejections referred to above. This fact was cited before us as proof of the Board's impartiality and freedom from prejudice. But it is also open to the interpretation that little scope is allowed the Board to perform the duties for which it is ostensibly appointed. We recommend accordingly that the names of all applicants for nomination should be submitted direct to the Board of Selection. . .

4. We consider the Board of Selection to be an essential part of the organisation for recruiting the diplomatic establishment of the Foreign Office and the Diplomatic Corps.

It is true that in regard to the appointments in the Civil Establishments we expressed the view that 'all such limitation as depends on personal selection by a Minister or an official should be abolished, and that the examinations should be thrown open to all candidates who fulfil the prescribed conditions. Thus there will remain only such proper and legitimate "limitation" as confines candidature to those persons who can produce evidence of 'possessing prescribed qualifications, and certain kinds of training and experience which are desirable or requisite in a given situation.'

While we adhere to these views in regard to the General Civil Establishments, we are clearly of opinion that the conditions of a diplomatic career call for certain qualities which are not equally essential in other branches of the Civil Service. It is impossible to describe in detail the qualities demanded by the peculiar conditions of the Diplomatic Service, but among them are powers of observation, good address, readiness to take responsibility, and above all the capacity to mix on easy terms with men of all classes in the countries to which diplomatists may be sent.

We share the opinion that has been expressed or implied by all the previous Committees or Commissions appointed to inquire into the subject, that the test of competitive examination by itself is an insufficient means of selecting the men whom we require for our Diplomatic Service. There is needed in addition some process by which, without favouritism or hardship to the individual, candidates who are unsuited to the Diplomatic Service may be eliminated. We can conceive no process better adapted to the purpose than a well constituted and properly empowered Board of Selection.

This Board should not be precluded from making the fullest inquiry into the antecedents and the up bringing of candidates, for these factors as well as those emerging from the person interviewed are relevant in the estimate of their probable suitability for a diplomatic career.

RESERVATION BY MR BECK, MR CLYNES, MR HOLT, MR GRAHAM WALLAS, AND MRS DEANE STREATFEILD

While agreeing with the Report generally, we desire to express our dissent from the proposal (in Chapter II.) that no candidate shall be allowed to offer himself, at the Class I. examination, for the Foreign Service, unless he has received, before that examination, a nomination from the Secretary of State, based on a report from the Board of Selection; and that intending candidates shall be allowed to present themselves before the Board of Selection 'at any time after they had reached (say) their nineteenth year of age'. . . .

Under the particular circumstances of the Foreign Service, we do not propose that it should be treated exactly like every other branch of the Civil Service in respect to the assignment of those candidates who come highest in the examination, and whose characters are approved of by the Civil Service Commissioners, at once to the offices of their choice. In a large Government department, including many different kinds of work, it is comparatively easy to give to every official who enters by open competition a position corresponding to his individual ability and interests as they develop. But every officer in the Foreign Service will be called upon during his career to assume some measure of personal responsibility abroad. We agree, therefore, that a suitable Board of Selection should exist, and that it should take such steps as are possible to ascertain before the appointment of any candidate to the Foreign Service that he is fit for that kind of responsibility.

At the same time we think it desirable that the presumption should be in favour of those candidates who offer themselves for the Foreign Service, are successful in the open competition, and pass the scrutiny of the Civil Service Commissioners into their character.

Our reason for this is that we believe it to be extremely important to secure for the Foreign Service not only the widest possible area for the selection of young men of ability, but also a large variety of type in the officers appointed. One of our witnesses told us, 'I think your Board of Selection will generally take what we may call, perhaps, one type of man, because he is the type of man who is fit for the international career called diplomacy. All of this type of men, speaking metaphorically, speak the same language; they have the same habits of thought, and more or less the same points of view. . . .' This expresses very exactly the danger which we desire to avoid; and we think that that danger will be more easily avoided if the Board of Selection has before it able young men of twenty-four, who, after educational careers of different kinds followed by success in a great examination, offer themselves as candidates for the Foreign Service, than if, as we believe would normally be the case under the scheme proposed in the Report, nominations are given to schoolboys of eighteen. The boys who, at eighteen, seem most likely to become fit candidates for the Foreign Service will belong to a more uniform social type than the young men who, five or six years later, may have made themselves fit for that service.

DISSENT BY MR HOARE
The Foreign Office and the Diplomatic Corps

. . . But with the general tenor of the Report I am in disagreement. Its implication seems to me to be that our Foreign Service, particularly the Diplomatic Corps, is still what it was said to be in 1869, 'a close and inefficient service, regulated by favouritism'. In support of this view my colleagues quote figures showing how large is the number of old Etonians in diplomacy. If it could be shown that Eton were producing inefficient diplomats, this would be a relevant statistic. In point of fact every witness of experience, who came before us, was firm in the opinion that our Ambassadors and their subordinates are universally respected for their ability as well as their integrity. A public service does not exist for the purpose of providing careers for a number of young men; its sole purpose is the efficient administration of the country's affairs. If men with a certain kind of upbringing and education make the best diplomats, it is their services which the country should seek for its diplomatic affairs. ... If foreign policy is to be democratised, it is not by turning municipal scholars into Ambassadors that the end will be reached. As it is, although my colleagues make no mention of the fact, our diplomats are doing their work at small cost but at great advantage to the country. Why then, except to provide careers for other young men – an object which the Commissioners have already disowned in our last Report – should drastic changes be recommended?

I will deal with what I consider to be the three most important changes which they propose:–

Firstly, they recommend that the Foreign Secretary should be deprived of his power to select the candidates for the Diplomatic and Foreign Service who are to go before the Departmental Board of Selection. In actual practice the Foreign Secretary seldom exercises his veto. None the less his power of selection seems to me to be a useful safeguard against the intrusion of alien or unsuitable candidates, and I see no reason to abolish it. ...

The third important group of changes which the Report proposes is concerned with the question of pay. I agree with these proposals so far as they recommend an immediate salary of 200*l.* a year for what are now attachés but in future to be Third Secretaries, the recoupment of travelling expenses for all diplomats and a distinction between the salary and *frais de représentation* of Heads of Missions. I cannot, however, support the general view which seems to me to underlie my colleagues' recommendations that a living wage should be provided for every member of the Diplomatic Service. The Commissioners state that one of the first duties of a diplomat is to move on terms of perfect equality and freedom with the best society in foreign capitals. No Government inquiry can define how much this duty will cost in a small service working under widely variable conditions. The Diplomatic Service will always be an expensive service, just as a Guards Regiment is more expensive than a Line Regiment. The only result of appearing to offer a living wage will be to attract into it young men who will make failures of their own careers, and, what is much more important, their country's concerns.

6·14 SELECTION WITH A BUILT-IN BIAS

From the Evidence *and* Report *of the Royal Commission on the Civil Service, 1929–31. 6·14·1 Evidence, Q. 1419 (Evidence of R. S. Meiklejohn, a Civil Service Commissioner); 6·14·2* Report, § *253, Parliamentary Papers 1930–1, X.*

Critics of the Civil Service had long suggested that an element of social bias entered its selection procedure, especially in the interviewing.

6·14·1 A CIVIL SERVICE COMMISSIONER

There are five of us and directly the young man comes in I try to put him at ease, by looking at his record and saying 'You were at Rugby; you went from there to Corpus; you got a scholarship there'. Then I should say 'What Schools did you read?' He says 'Great and Mods'. I ask 'have you any preference for history or Philosophy' and he says which he has a preference for. I do not want to take all the questions myself, so one of the others says 'have you been abroad?' He may say 'I have been to Germany'. Then he is asked did you notice any difference between Bavaria and Saxony?' then other people ask him has he done any social work in the East End, or has he been interested in Boy Scouts. Then we might try to find whether he has any interest in Natural History. Has he read much German or Italian literature. . . . You may ask him almost anything which occurs to you, to find out what his interests are and how he reacts to other people and other things. It is as wide as we can make it.

6·14·2 OBJECTIVITY OF INTERVIEWS

We received a considerable amount of evidence (on the interview). In the first place it was suggested that it offered scope for the display of class prejudice. No evidence was adduced in support of this criticism and the competition results support the view that no such prejudice exists. We are satisfied that there are no grounds for any suspicion of this kind.

6·15 DECLINE IN STATUS AND PRESTIGE OF THE HIGHER CIVIL SERVICE

From the statement submitted in evidence by Association of First Division Civil Servants to The Royal Commission on the Civil Service, *Minutes of Evidence, Appendix VIII, H.M.S.O., 1930.*

The statement quoted here shows how the Civil Servants themselves saw the effects of the decline of prestige which the service had suffered. The continued exclusiveness in the recruitment was thus threatened not only by demands for greater prospects for promotion from the ranks. It remained for the next Royal Commission on the Civil Service, which sat after the war, to draw the practical conclusions from this change in bringing Civil Service salaries into line with those pertaining in the world of commerce, industry and the like.

82. During the nineteenth century and to a lesser extent in the early years of the present century the First Division of the Civil Service undoubtedly enjoyed a prestige which was an important attraction. It was one of the comparatively small number of professions which were regarded as suitable for men of a certain social standing, while business employment was not so regarded. The State was thus able to obtain at a relatively low rate of remuneration the services of men of ability who were debarred by custom or social prejudice from entering more lucrative occupations. The gradual decline of aristocratic traditions, a process accelerated by the economic changes resulting from the War, and the great development of the importance and prestige of business undertakings have, however, transformed the situation. The old prejudice against business employment has disappeared and, as was indicated in the evidence given to the Royal Commission by the Civil Service Commissioners, University graduates who have been educated at the leading Public Schools now show a marked preference for such employment.

83. But concurrently with this rise in the status of business

employment, which would in any case have affected the comparative status of the Civil Service, there has been a marked decline in the prestige of the Civil Service itself. Whereas it was formerly regarded as a dignified profession, somewhat remote from the ordinary life of the community, it has now, by reason of the great expansion of the functions of Government, been brought more directly under the public eye. Moreover, the hostility to that expansion which exists among certain sections of the public has, by a natural though illogical process, found expression in hostility to the Service which is responsible for carrying into effect the policy of the Government, with the result that the Civil Service has become the subject of incessant attacks by sections of the Press and by certain public writers as a result of which but little of the prestige of the Service remains. . . . The Civil Service does not claim to be perfect and does not resent fair criticism, but many of these attacks are grossly unfair and distorted and there can be no doubt that their cumulative effect has been to lower the prestige of the Service in the eyes of the public and to prejudice recruitment. . . .

84. It has been suggested that the idea of public service as distinct from employment in profit-making industry or commerce has in itself an attraction to many young men to which weight should be given in the present connection. We recognise that this source of satisfaction exists, but we believe that the value to society of business enterprise is now so fully accepted that the attraction of direct service to the State can no longer be regarded as a substantial factor in weighing the advantages of the Civil Service against those of other occupations.

85. To sum up, therefore, we submit that the Civil Service no longer enjoys the superior prestige which it formerly possessed as compared with business employment, and that men who enter the Administrative Class find themselves at no advantage, whether as regards social position or professional status, compared with their contemporaries who have entered other occupations. This important element of attractiveness, which formerly enabled the State to compete on favourable terms with external employers, has therefore disappeared, while the other advantages commonly attributed to the Civil Service are shared by a large range of outside occupations which now compete with the State for the services of University graduates.

6·16 *MAKING YOUR WAY*

From Sir John Arrow Kempe. Reminiscences of an old Civil Servant, 1846–1927, *1928, pp. 28, 59, 60.*

Kempe's career ended as Comptroller and Auditor General.

I left school for Trinity College, Cambridge, in 1864. I had intended to read for the Classical Tripos, but in 1867 I had the good fortune to be nominated by Lord Derby for limited competition for a vacancy in the Treasury.

Downing Street,
Nov. 2, 1866

My dear Sir,
    I will with pleasure direct that your son's name shall be placed on my list of candidates to be admitted to competitive examination for a clerkship; but it is fair to say that there are others on the list to whom I should be bound to give priority, and vacancies at the Treasury are of such very rare occurrence that I cannot encourage you to be very sanguine.

I am, dear Sir,
Very truly yours,
DERBY.

The Revd. J. E. Kempe.

    I succeeded in the examination and accordingly left Cambridge in that year before completing my full term of residence for a degree. . . .

In 1874, after the defeat and resignation of Mr Gladstone's Government, I received a communication from Sir Stafford Northcote, who had accepted office as Chancellor of the Exchequer, offering me the post of his assistant Private Secretary, his son, Walter Northcote, taking the chief post; the work to be shared, he to take the Parliamentary and general work, I the financial and Treasury side of it.

    Of course I gladly accepted the offer, and took up the work at once.

11 Downing Street,
March 2, 1874

My dear Sir,

Mr Mowbray wrote to me a few days ago to say that he heard you were desirous of filling one of the Private Secretaryships now vacant at the Treasury.

I have decided to follow Mr Lowe's example and to appoint two secretaries. My son will be one, and I hope that you may join me as the other. Your salary would be the same as that of Mr Hamilton when he was with Mr Lowe: but I hope you would not find the work disagreeable and that you and my son would manage it easily between you. In the event of your accepting my proposal I should be very glad to make your acquaintance some time tomorrow.

I remain,
Yours faithfully,
STAFFORD H. NORTHCOTE.

J. A. Kempe, Esq.

My father had, at the same time, a letter from Mr W. H. Smith, who throughout my career was always a good friend to me.

11 Downing Street.
March 3, 1874

My dear Mr Kempe,

I did not reply to your note of the 17th ulto. because I really did not expect at the time to come here. At this moment I am not Secretary and the old Board is still in office, but in a day or two we shall be regularly at work; and it is now arranged that Mr Kempe will become an additional Secretary to the Chancellor of the Exchequer and that Mr Primrose will be my Private Secretary. If Sir Stafford Northcote had not taken Mr Kempe I should have done so, but it is perhaps better that I should retain the services of Mr Primrose, who is Mr Dodson's Private Secretary, as he is acquainted with everything which has been done in the office for the past year.

Believe me,
Yours very sincerely,
WILLIAM H. SMITH.

6·17 CORRIDORS OF POWER

From Sir James P. Grigg, Prejudice and Judgment, 1948, pp. 174-7.

As Grigg shows, the power of an even comparatively junior Civil Servant can be great. On the other hand the position of ministerial Private Secretary often serves as a stepping stone to higher things as Grigg's own career was to testify. Later he became Finance Member (i.e. Minister) in India and Permanent Secretary at the War Office. In 1941 Churchill made him Secretary of State for War.

Winston walked into the Treasury in November 1924 carrying the seals of office which he had just received, and which he showed the greatest reluctance to entrust to anyone less than the Permanent Secretary. It was not at all certain that he would wish to continue me as his Principal Private Secretary, for it could be taken for granted that he would resume the partnership which had started in 1906 with Eddie (now Sir Edward) Marsh. However, he made us joint holders of the office, and I looked after the more mundane problems of finance and administration, while Eddie was his confidant in all the humaner matters. The other members of the private office were Donald Fergusson and Lord Wodehouse (afterwards the Earl of Kimberley). . . .

One of the jobs of the more specifically Treasury private secretary was to suggest to his master that not all of these were worthy of serious examination or that to investigate so many at the same time would place an impossible burden on the officials concerned. Occasionally I was allowed, after argument, to suppress his minutes, but more often than not, Winston refused to abandon a project until the departmental experts had convinced him that it was worthless or inexpedient. And quite a number of them were never abandoned but survived, though perhaps modified considerably, to become part of his adopted policy. . . . On one occasion I recall having been provoked into retorts which went far beyond the latitude allowed to equals let alone subordinates, but instead of my getting the sack, as I deserved, all that happened was a somewhat pained look over the top of his spectacles and the mildest of exhortations: 'Don't be so controversial'. It was an extremely effective retort, for the unexpectedness of it immediately deflated both my anger and the injudiciously truculent expression of it.

This habit of 'all in' argument between the Chancellor of the Exchequer and his private secretary must have continued throughout his term of office for I discover, among the few of my papers which have survived, the following letter under the date March 6th, 1928:

P.J.: Always be assured that our friendship is proof against all minor tiffs. But make allowances for the effect of suddenly pulling me up with a round turn, and forcing me to some measure of self-defence – however mild. 'Cet animal . . . etc'. Yours ever.   W.

Here again, as far as I can remember, the treatment was successful. Altogether, nothing can take away from the gratitude for the frank and equal intimacy which Winston allowed me. When I say equal, I mean only that the master did not attempt to take advantage of his position of authority and that he conceded the utmost freedom of speech. On the other hand he also exercised the utmost freedom of speech and as he was a magnificent rhetorician, the servant was very often worsted – sometimes even when he was right. Hence, no doubt, the attacks of rage or sullenness which led to 'minor tiffs'.

7 The army

7·1 *THE MID-VICTORIAN OFFICER CLASS*

From the Report *of the Commissioners appointed to enquire into the purchase of Commissions in the Army, Evidence. Parliamentary Papers, 1857, Second Session, Vol. XVIII, pp. 254, 49, 177, 79–80, 333.*

The experience of the Crimean War led to a number of investigations into Army affairs. The enquiry into the purchase of commissions which determined entry into the Army in peacetime and largely governed promotion was regarded by many as an obstacle to Army efficiency. Such questions apart, the evidence reveals to us the character and attitudes of the Officer Corps. Of the witnesses here quoted the Earl Grey was a Whig politician who had been Secretary-at-War. Sir J. Scarlett had commanded the Cavalry in the Crimea. Mr Hammersley was an Army Agent and Mr M. J. Higgins was a journalist. Purchase of commissions was not abolished until 1871. The actual scale of charges for the sale of commissions was laid down by the Army Council in 1766, and later revised, and was reprinted as an appendix to the Report.

7·1·1 *EARL GREY*

4112. With respect to examination for young officers entering the army for the first time, is it your opinion that the examination should be left very much as it is at present; or that any competitive examination should be introduced? – I have a very strong opinion of the impolicy of introducing the system of competitive examination. I do not think that any examination can test the qualities which are most important. . . . You test nothing but the acquirements of a man by examination, and what you want in an officer far more than any specific amount of acquirements is, that he should possess certain moral qualities, such as courage, high spirit, the feeling of a gentleman, energy, judgment, and the power of thinking and acting for himself. These things cannot be tested in the slightest degree by examination, and it is very possible that by a competitive examination you may even interfere with a man's acquiring those qualities; because I believe there is nothing more certain than that by over education . . . you weaken the powers of the mind. . . . I find in a very interesting work by Sir Benjamin Brodie, that over-forcing the youthful mind is extremely injurious to its vigour in after life; and I am told that in France this inconvenience is already found, that so many of the employments both in the army and in the civil service of the state are given by competitive examination, that there is a tendency in the different schools to vie with each other in the amount of knowledge which, within a limited time, they can force into the heads of their pupils . . . and the consequence is, in the opinion of eminent men in France, a very serious increase of brain disease among the young. . . . Then I am also bound to say that I think the theory of conducting a government without means of reward is essentially a false one. . . . The reward of able service is one of the principal means which the government can use in order to encourage zealous exertion in those who serve under it; and we know that in the army one of the rewards most looked to by good officers is, obtaining commissions for their sons, and to take away all that power from the government, and giving it merely by competitive examinations, would in my opinion be a great mistake. And there is this also to be said, the tendency of that system would be to make the army a poor body, and the officers of the army to consist generally of persons looking to the army as a mere profession and having no other means of existence; but if that came to be generally the case, . . . you must either very largely increase the pay of the army and the advantages upon retirement, which would be a great burden to the public, or else you must incur the great hazard of having a large body of officers of very high qualifications, and who feel themselves always in difficulty and not remunerated in proportion to advantages which men enjoy in other occupations in life. That, as it seems to me, would be very dangerous. You would have a strong feeling then in the whole army, and they would always be desirous to force the country into war in order that they might get the distinctions and the great rewards which would be the only compensation that could be given to them to make that profession equal in advantages to all other professions in life. At this moment a large proportion of the officers in the army do not look to it entirely as their means of existence. They trust to private fortune to a very considerable extent; and the existence of a large number of persons of that kind in the army, as I said before, seems to me to be a very great political advantage, and to render the maintenance of a considerable standing army much more safe than it would otherwise be.

7·1·2 CHARLES HAMMERSLEY, Esq.

922. (*Chairman*). You belong to the house of Mr Cox, the army agent? – Yes.

923. In cases of promotion in the army, it is, I am informed, usual for the money to be paid into the army agents before the promotion takes place? – Yes, that is the case.

924. Upon payment being made the agents certify that the money has been paid, and then the promotion takes place? – The agent certifies to the Commander-in-Chief that the regulated price is lodged, and then the promotion takes place.

930. (*Sir De Lacy Evans*). Could you give us an estimate as to the percentage usual on the average, in time of peace, that is given beyond the prescribed amount? – Yes, I could give you a pretty good estimate, I believe, of what is done. Of course it is entirely derived from private and confidential communications. We do not officially know anything but the regulation price, but it is quite notorious that larger sums are given.

931. Might it be 40 per cent on the average? – A great deal more than that. In the cavalry, anything under double the regulation is considered very reasonable; for instance, in the case of a lieutenant-colonel of the cavalry, the regulation is 6,175*l.*; the common price is 14,000*l.*

932. In the guards what might be the regulation price of a

captaincy? – It varies in different regiments. The regulation price of a company in the guards is 4,800*l.*; 9,000*l.* is commonly given in two of the regiments. In the other regiment 8,200*l.*

935. (*Chairman*). Seeing that the prices are not at all adhered to, do you think, . . . that it would be better to have no system of price at all fixed? – I think there is a convenience in having a regulated price.

936. What is the advantage of it? – There are instances in which officers are only allowed, and only receive, the regulated price.

937. (*Mr Sidney Herbert*). In the case of a compulsory sale? – Yes; if the officer is not in a situation to make terms with those below him, then he receives the regulation price and no more.

938. (*Chairman*). Then it acts as the minimum and not as the maximum? – Yes.

939. (*Mr Sidney Herbert*). In the war it has practically acted as the minimum? – The war has brought everything down to regulation.

940. Supposing the regulation price had been lower, would it have gone down lower? – Yes.

941. So that the regulated price has operated rather disadvantageously against officers during the war? – Yes.

942. In time of peace it has no effect at all? – No.

7·1·3 MAJOR GENERAL SIR J. SCARLET

3122. With regard to the composition of the officers generally in the cavalry, are you satisfied with the style of persons who enter the cavalry? – Yes; upon the whole.

3123. Have you any objection to a man of high rank coming in for a short time and going out after remaining for a limited period? – Not the slightest objection.

3124. You think that no inconvenience has occurred to the service from that practice? – No; provided they attend to their duties. On the contrary, I should prefer men of high rank in the service.

3129. (*Mr G. Carr Glyn*). Does not the introduction of officers of that description tend very much to increase the expensive tone of the regiment? – Yes. No doubt men of fortune always make the service to a certain extent more expensive than it otherwise would be.

3130. That is rather a characteristic of the cavalry regiments? – I think it is necessary to have a larger income in the cavalry than in some of the infantry regiments, but I think that a prudent man, with a very moderate income, may live in the cavalry – a man having from 200*l*. to 300*l*. a year.

3134. (*Mr G. Carr Glyn*). Are the Commissioners to assume then that upon general grounds that you think it always an advantageous thing to have the officers composed generally of all classes of society in this country? – I think, from the aristocratic and higher classes, – the same classes of men that send their sons to the law and to the profession of the church, – it is desirable to have that class of men in the army.

3135. (*Mr E. Ellice*). In short, the army must, more or less, bear the tone, and have the character, of the social condition of the country? – Yes.

3136. It would be impossible by any regulations to prevent the habits of military life being in sympathy with those of the civil life of the country? – I consider whatever the life of civilians is, to a certain extent it must influence the army.

3137. As the habits of expense in the country increase, however unfortunate it may be, still it must have an influence upon the habits of officers in the service? – No doubt; I do not think that you can separate officers from civil life.

3138. (*Chairman*). Have you heard of many non-commissioned officers being promoted to the rank of officers in the cavalry? – Yes; lately.

3139. Does it answer? – I do not see that it is a great benefit to the men.

3140. Are they able to bear the expense? – No; I do not think they can without some small income, unless they become adjutants or riding masters.

7·1·4 M. J. HIGGINS, Esq.

1423. (*Sir G. Carr Glyn*). I understood you to say, that the system of purchase chiefly prevents the middle class from entering the army, is it not the fact that the greatest amount of money paid for commissions in the army comes from the middle class? – When I said the middle class I meant the class below the gentry – I meant the class that our civil engineers and our merchant captains come from; that is the class that I alluded to, and all classes below that.

1424. (*Lord Stanley*). In point of fact it is not a question of class, but a question of purse? – It is to a certain degree a question of class, I think. The wording generally is, that an officer shall be the son of a gentleman, a gentleman being understood to mean a man who has plenty of money, and does not exercise any retail trade or any mechanical profession.

1425. (*Colonel E. R. Wetherall*). You are aware that that is not very strictly attended to? – I think that there are a few cases in which it has not been attended to, but those exceptions have not been made in consequence of the superior merit of the candidates, but because their parents happened to have unusually good interest with influential people. If you see a horsedealer's son or a shop-keeper's son in the army, you may be certain that the rule has been relaxed because his father had contrived to ingratiate himself with the class above his own, and not on account of the personal merit of the candidate.

1430. (*Sir H. J. W. Bentinck*). Would it be desirable to diminish the number of officers in the army from the class you named as gentlemen, and increase the number from the other class? – I do not think it much matters what class the officers come from if you take the precaution to select the best that present themselves. My opinion is, that if you increase the educational test you will get better gentlemen than you do now.

1431. Would not the people who possess money be better able to procure that education for their children than the poorer class? – They will always have that advantage, and I think it is a most legitimate advantage, to which no reasonable person can object.

1432. (*Lord Stanley*). Is there not a very large number of persons, take for instance the mass of the country clergy who are educated men, and gentlemen in every sense of the word, but who are men though educated, yet of very small fortunes, who under the present system could very seldom obtain admission into the army for their sons? – The sons of that class of men are almost excluded from our military service, partly by the difficulty of obtaining a commission, and partly by the expensive tone of the army when they have got in.

1433. Although they are all persons whose parents would be in many cases perfectly competent to give them the requisite education? – Certainly.

7·1·5 THE PRICE LIST

We, the undersigned General Officers, having had a meeting thereupon, and it appearing to us, upon due investigation, that the Pay of Officers of certain branches of the Army has been increased since the above-mentioned Regulation of 1766; that the Rates of Half-pay have, in like manner, been increased; and that Commissions in the Army are of a higher value than that fixed for them by the aforesaid Regulation; we consider it to be expedient to revise the Prices of the several Commissions in the Army, as fixed by such Regulation of 1776, as well as the difference between Full and Half-pay in the Dragoons and Infantry, with a view of adapting the same to the present circumstances, and the general interests of the Service.

And we do accordingly most humbly offer to Your Majesty the following Estimate, wherein the sum proper to be given for each of the Commissions referred to our consideration, is, according to the best of our judgment, apportioned: And we are unanimously of opinion, that the same, if it shall meet Your Majesty's Royal approbation, should be uniformly observed in the respective Corps, whenever Your Majesty shall, in Your good pleasure, permit such Commission to be sold.

We have further humbly to report our opinion to Your Majesty, with respect to the difference between Full and Half Pay, and upon full consideration, the following appears to us to be a just scale of difference to be paid in the several cases of exchange from Half to Full Pay; and we humbly recommend the same for Your Majesty's consideration.

We beg leave to add, that the principle upon which the difference between Full and Half Pay in the Dragoons and Infantry, as here settled is, that the Officer going upon Half-pay, above the Rank of Cornet and Ensign, shall receive a Sum of Money for the Pay he loses, calculated at eight years purchase.

Commissions	Prices	Difference in Value between the several Commissions in succession
Royal Horse Guards		
Cornet	£1,200	—
Lieutenant	1,600	£400
Captain	3,500	1,900
Major	5,350	1,850
Lieutenant Colonel	7,250	1,900
Life Guards		
Cornet	£1,260	—
Lieutenant	1,785	£525
Captain	3,500	1,715
Major	5,350	1,850
Lieutenant-Colonel	7,250	1,900
Dragoon Guards and Dragoons		
Cornet	£840	—
Lieutenant	1,190	£350
Captain	3,225	2,035
Major	4,575	1,350
Lieutenant-Colonel	6,175	1,600
Foot Guards		
Ensign	£1,200	—
Lieutenant	2,050	£850
Captain, with rank of Lieutenant-Colonel	4,800	2,750
Major, with rank of Colonel	8,300	3,500
Lieutenant-Colonel	9,000	700
Marching Regiments of Foot		
Ensign	£450	—
Lieutenant	700	£250
Captain	1,800	1,100
Major	3,200	1,400
Lieutenant-Colonel	4,500	1,300

7·2 THE PURCHASE SYSTEM AND MILITARY EFFICIENCY

From Sir Charles Trevelyan, The Purchase System of the British Army, *1867, pp. 2–7.*

Trevelyan looked at the methods by which the Officer Corps of the Army was selected in the same light as he had investigated the recruitment to the Civil Service.

The large and important class of well-educated young men who depend for their advancement upon their own exertions, and not upon their wealth and connexions, and who constitute the pith of the Law, the Church, the Indian civil service, and other active professions, are thus ordinarily excluded from the army. Well-educated poor men are notoriously those who throw themselves into their work with the greatest energy and perseverance, and the army would soon reform itself if it had its fair share of them. On the other hand, idle young men, who dislike the restraints of school, and desire to lead an easy, enjoyable life, are attracted to the army as the only profession in which advancement depends, not so much upon personal qualifications as upon a certain command of money. ... The encouragement which the purchase system gives to young men of fortune to enter the army as a fashionable pastime aggravates the pecuniary embarrassments of those who desire to follow it as a profession. The style of living is pitched so high by the former class ... that it would be impossible for the younger officers to live upon their pay, even if they received it unencumbered by purchase. ... The original commission is usually purchased by an advance of family property, which has to be secured by a life insurance. Therefore, besides the loss of the interest upon the advance, the premium upon the life insurance has to be deducted from the officer's pay. Then, the young officer, in the struggle to get on and to avoid being passed over, is tempted to borrow further sums, which are secured by further life insurances. ... And all this time they have to keep up an appearance of equality in their expenditure with associates belonging to rich landed, commercial and manufacturing families, who do not look upon the army as a profession, but only desire to spend a few years pleasantly in good society, with the prestige which belongs to the military character. ... A general desire exists to raise the army in the scale of professions; to make its ranks attractive to a better class of men, and to increase the inducements to self-improvement and good conduct; but these natural and wholesome aspirations are repelled by the purchase system, which has built up a wall of separation between the officers and privates. Persons promoted from the ranks have not the means of buying themselves on, and they cannot stand the expense of messing, and of the general style of living among the officers. . . .

When it is remembered that our army is recruited on the voluntary principle, it must be admitted that this is a serious state of things. If the system were so modified that every man in the ranks who, by previous education and subsequent cultivation, and through good conduct, had acquired the necessary qualifications for an officer . . . could look forward to promotion, numerous enlistments would take place with the hope of obtaining the higher promotion, and those persons best qualified for it would have the greatest inducement to enlist. As it is, a great gulf is fixed between the ranks of the army and the higher grades of the profession, and the consequence is, that the army has to be recruited in public-houses from the class of society least suited, from education and manners, to associate with gentlemen. Persons in a high position connected with the recruiting system are ashamed of it. Persons in an inferior position are corrupted by it. There cannot be a more decisive proof of the unsoundness of the principle upon which our army is based than the fact that, in order to recruit it, we are compelled to shut our eyes to practices altogether inconsistent with the morality of the present generation.

7.3 THE SOCIAL EXCLUSIVENESS OF SANDHURST

From the Report *of the Select Committee on Sandhurst Royal Military College, Evidence, Parliamentary Papers, 1854–5, vol. XII.*

The Committee examined General Sir H. Douglas, Bart., Commandant of the College, who started his evidence with an expression of regret that the College, which had been originally, that is prior to 1803, primarily an institution for the training of orphan cadets or others of limited means, had increasingly become a school for the sons of gentlemen. After the war the parliamentary grant was gradually reduced and eventually it ceased altogether.

SIR H. DOUGLAS, Bart. (at the time Inspector General of Instructions)

2224. You have attached great importance to the original charitable foundation of the college, and you have stated that you think it necessary that the original foundation should be regarded? – I attach very great importance to it.

2225. You think it a misfortune that it has been departed from? – A very great misfortune.

2226. Originally the expense was borne by the State? – Originally the expense was borne by the State. In the year 1815 there were four companies of cadets, containing 103 each. The original endowment of the college was that there should be 30 orphans of officers, free of expense; 20 sons of officers on service at 40*l.* a year, 30 sons of noblemen and gentlemen at 94*l.* 10*s.*, and the cadets of the East India Company were at the rate of 20*l.* a year. . . .

2228. From your knowledge of the college, should you say that 94*l.* at that time was remunerative; that those sons of gentlemen who paid 94*l.* a year cost the public nothing? – I consider that they cost the public nothing.

2229. That being so during the war, when prices of all kinds and salaries were at their highest point, should you conceive it likely that the cost of a cadet who was the son of a private gentleman would be as much now, making allowance for the great depreciation of prices? – No, I do not think it would. I should like to say, that in 1824 the number of cadets had diminished from 216 to 190. At that time the orphan class had been entirely abolished. There were 20 cadets of the first class, at 20*l.* each. The subscriptions to the second class, which in 1816 were respectively 20*l.*, 30*l.*, 40*l.*, and 60*l.*, were raised to 30*l.*, 40*l.*, 70*l.*, and 80*l.*; and the subscriptions of the third class were raised to 125*l.* each, there being 75 of those cadets. . . . In 1816 the charge [on the public funds] was diminished to 33,819*l.*; in 1817 to 27,664*l.*; all these diminutions compelling the Commissioners to make some corresponding alterations in the endowment of the college, that it might gradually, as the persistence of Parliament determined it should, become ultimately self-sustaining. . . . In 1832, up to March 1833, it was 2,638*l.*, when the Parliamentary votes entirely ceased, and

the college became self-sustaining. In proportion, as these reductions went on, it became necessary to diminish more and more,
first, the orphan establishment, and then the number of cadets
who did not pay anything like the cost of their education; afterwards to increase vastly the number of the sons of private
gentlemen, and to augment their rates of subscription to a
great deal more than the education of their sons individually cost.
So that, in order to make the college self-sustaining, the chief
expense of the establishment is contributed by the sons of private
gentlemen, who pay about one-half more than their education
actually costs, and the excess is carried to the aid of the college
funds to educate those who cannot afford to pay the cost of their
education. . . .

2231. You attach great importance to a sound military education
being given to an officer? – Very great.

2232. Do you think that the fact of charging, in round numbers,
double the cost for the education of a gentleman's son tends to
exclude from the benefits of a military education the sons of
gentlemen of smaller means? – Certainly, by so much.

2233. In fact, it throws the military education into the hands of
the very wealthy class, and not into the class of orphans and the
sons of officers of subordinate stations, who receive an education
partly gratuitously from the surplus funds furnished by the sons of
the wealthy gentlemen? – Applying that with respect to the College,
it is clear that the effect of the pecuniary economy was to introduce
the sons of a great number of persons who could afford to pay that
high price for their education, and to exclude by so much, those
who could not so well afford it, but who had been admitted under
the former plan. . . .

2243. [Mr Hardinge]. You stated that the sons of noblemen and
gentlemen had gradually excluded the sons of officers, and also
orphans; is not the third class limited in number? – Yes; but it was
much less numerous originally than it is now; what I mean to say
is, that the number of the third class is, for financial reasons
consequent on the cessation of the Parliamentary Grant, increased
to 114, out of 170.

2247. Do you see any objection to introducing into the ranks of
the army a larger number of poorer officers who have nothing to
live upon except their pay? – I do not admit that the difficulty of
living in the army should be conceded as sufficient to exclude

those destitute young men from entering into the service. . . . The great evil, the bane of the service, is the expense, the extravagance I may call it, of military messes. How to cut them down, may be difficult; but I do think that there is no higher or more important duty imposed upon us all, whatever our places may be, than to cut down the luxury and extravagance of messes. When I first entered the service, the officers' mess was very much what the sergeants' mess is now. Subalterns could live on their pay, and did in every regiment live on their pay; but in this long peace things are very much altered; the rates of subscription are high; the whole style of a mess-table is magnificent; the *cuisine* even is *recherché*; the wines expensive, and it is utterly impossible, I think, for any young man, excepting one who is endowed with a very rare and almost scarcely-to-be-expected degree of self-denial, to live at the mess without some resource besides his pay.

2248. It has been stated that the history of those orphan cadets has been rather a lamentable one; that they have got into debt, and so forth; are you aware of that? – I have heard of many such cases; I think it should excite our pity and commiseration; I think it may arise from their having been imperfectly educated for want of means; I have known a great many turn out well. . . . I think that the cases alluded to are no reason why we should refuse to those young men the benefits of the institution, but rather a reason why we should grant them.

2249. [*Mr M. Milnes*]. Would you not think it a great misfortune for any service, that its social condition was such as to make it impossible for any but rich men to live in it? – Certainly.

2250. You think, therefore, that an extension of the system of giving good military education and gratuitous commissions to the sons of men who have fallen in the service of their country, or who have served their country dutifully, is one that would tend not only to the advantage of those young men themselves, but to the general advantage of the service? – Certainly.

2251. [*Mr Rich*]. Do you think that the encouraging of the sons of gentlemen and professional gentlemen of smaller means to enter the army would tend to reduce the tone of extravagance which you have just named takes place in the messes in consequence of the preponderance of men of large fortunes? – I think it would to a considerable extent.

2259. [*Mr M. Milnes*]. Would there be any fear, supposing the admission of the poorer men into the army was facilitated by these and other means, of the army losing the gentlemanly tone which perhaps at present distinguishes it? – I do not think there would be the least fear of that; I think the college in its original state had not that effect; it provided for the poorer, but it did not exclude the wealthier classes; and the college, when it existed in that purely military form, in which it was first established, had no such effect as that.

2260. Do you think that the introduction of more men of very moderate means into the army would have either the effect of reducing the gentlemanly tone of the service, or of excluding from the army so many of the higher classes as now enter into it? – No, I do not think it would. I think, independently of the college, they would work their way into the service; and I should be the last to lay any difficulty in the way of the entrance into the service of the aristocracy, or the wealthy part of the country. I think it is a very great advantage to the army that they are introduced, and a very great advantage to the country in every respect.

7·4 SANDHURST IN THE NINETEEN-FIFTIES

From the Report *of the Advisory Committee on Recruiting, Cmnd. 545, Parliamentary Papers 1958/59, vol. VIII.*

To balance the picture of an officer class still predominantly recruited from the Public Schools it must be remembered that not all officers are recruited from Sandhurst cadets. A certain proportion is recruited via Woolwich and some are promoted from the ranks.

SANDHURST ENTRANTS, 1947–1958

							%
Total Entries ..	..	..	..	..	..	6,171	
Public Schools	..	..	..	..	..	4,116	67
Other Schools	..	..	..	..	..	2,055	33
Number of Schools sending Cadets							
Public Schools	..	..	..	..	..	195	20
Other	..	..	..	..	..	795	80

Schools with 50 or more Cadets

Wellington	..	..	..	..	..	399
Eton	..	..	..	..	..	302
Marlborough	..	..	..	..	..	114
Sherborne	..	..	..	..	..	114
Cheltenham	..	..	..	..	..	105
Winchester	..	..	..	..	..	97
Haileybury	..	..	..	..	..	93
Bedford	..	..	..	..	..	69
Radley ..	..	..	..	..	..	67
Harrow	..	..	..	..	..	66

(*And 11 others of which only one – Portsmouth Grammar School – was not a Public School*)

7.5 'UNGENTLEMANLY' OFFICERS?

From T. H. Escott, The Social Transformation of the Victorian Age, *1897, p. 310.*

In this book Escott – a Conservative journalist – deals with many social and economic aspects of life.

Intellectual quality is not the only respect in which there has been lately witnessed a change among the officers of the army. The Crimean War was followed by many promotions to the grade of officers from the ranks. Since then the average number of commissions given in this way seems to have been about twenty-five a year. Of this number 16 have gone to infantry, 4 to cavalry, and the remainder to other branches of the Service. These promotions, suitable as they are to the day of democracy, cannot of course affect sensibly the tone or the *personnel* of the officers of the Queen's army, who will continue to be, as they have been, men born to the social advantages of gentle station. The social fusion and personal intimacy of men whose antecedents and interests differ, though their rank be identical, is not likely ever to be more complete than between English and native officers in the Indian Staff Corps regiments; though the difficulty in the way of amalgamation proceeds probably less from the exclusiveness of the older officer than from the indisposition of the new to avail himself of the social opportunities placed technically at his disposal.

7·6 *INFLUENCE* VERSUS *PROFICIENCY*

From Appendix II of the Report *of the Select Committee on Military Education, 1901, Parliamentary Papers 1902. vol. X.*

The following are two replies by commanding officers to the question 'Do you consider that under the existing system sufficient inducements are held out to the young officer to study his profession seriously?' All thirteen replies were in the negative but not generally as revealing as those quoted here.

(*l.*) I do not consider that there are sufficient inducements held out for young officers to study their profession. An officer may be very keen to get on, and do his best to pass all his examinations as well as it is possible to do so, and be looked upon by his commanding officer as a thoroughly good officer and soldier in every way, and be known in his regiment as above the average. Yet, unless one of three things happens to him, he is never known beyond his regiment. The three things to which I refer are (1) a considerable amount of private interest outside his regiment to push his interests; (2) getting a P.S.C. Certificate; (3) some unforeseen piece of good luck on active service, when commanding a detached post, &c. I think commanding officers should be more consulted as to the qualifications of officers taken to fill staff appointments. Officers are too often taken to fill appointments without the opinion of their Commanding Officer being asked for, outside influence being the only thing that carries weight. Officers are thus often taken for appointments, when it is well known in their regiments that they have no qualifications for such appointments. The effect of this is that officers who have no outside interest to bring to bear get disheartened and disgusted, and cease to take interest in their profession.

(*m.*) Decidedly no. It has long been recognised that, unless supplemented by private means, in the junior ranks at any rate, an officer cannot live on his pay and allowances. The money question, however, is invariably burked whenever raised, being distasteful to the authorities. A young officer on joining, who aspires to become Adjutant to the battalion, has to find himself with a horse, and the forage allowance is totally inadequate to keep the animal, being based on the lowest estimate, apart from the fact that no storage exists to admit of fodder being bought wholesale. Shoeing and payment of a batman or groom comes out of the officer's pocket, though the extra duty pay pertaining to the appointment is, presumably, intended for the additional work entailed upon an Adjutant and not as part of his 'allowances'. . . . The facilities or encouragement provided by the State for a lad to study are nil, opportunities for travel in order to study campaigns or manoeuvres abroad are withheld from the impecunious youngster whose pocket is being continually touched by pinpricks more or less acute. The officer who is content to pass his service with his regiment is by no means encouraged, and, less fortunate than his comrades on the staff, has borne the heat and burden of the day unrecognised and unrewarded. This want of encouragement to regimental officers causes many to look anywhere rather than to their own regiment and to merely consider their corps as an accommodation, 'faute de mieux', at such time as extra-regimental employment is not forthcoming. The lad who joins cannot fail in a short time to realise this; he becomes restless, and, if possessed of sufficient means or backers, aspires to outside employment, not invariably for purposes of study or professional improvement, but in hopes of more pleasant occupation than the regimental routine provides.

7.7 WIDENING THE FIELD OF SELECTION FOR ARMY OFFICERS

From the Report *of the Committee on the Education and Training of Officers, Parliamentary Papers, 1924, vol. VII.*

In 1924 the Government appointed another committee on military education with Lord Haldane as chairman. The committee felt that recruitment to the army was still unnecessarily restrictive.

The Committee began its work by considering the real nature of the difficulty in the way of obtaining an adequate supply of officers for the Army. The impression it formed was that this difficulty was in part at least due to the belief of the public that the profession of officer in the Army was not one which called for as high qualities as that to be found in the analogous profession of the Navy or in many other professions. The somewhat paradoxical inference presented itself that in order to increase competition for entry to the profession of officer in the Army, it had become necessary to ask not less but more from the would-be entrant. In other words, we have to seek primarily an improved type of entrant and to provide adequate opportunities for this type, rather than to reduce standards. Another consideration also presented itself. The pay of the young officer has at last been raised to a level at which he can manage, if he is keen enough, to live on it. There is accordingly a larger field to draw on for candidates. In these days it is neither necessary nor desirable to confine the selection of officers to any one class of the community. The type of education in the secondary schools available for the children of parents in comparatively humble circumstances is now higher than it has been at any time in the past; and barriers, social and intellectual, have been and daily continue to be broken down. We mention this cardinal fact in the early paragraphs of our report because it is one that has been constantly borne in upon us at all stages of our enquiry.

4. Our first aim, therefore, was to ensure that the supply of officers for the Army should be drawn from more available sources, and that with this in view, a higher standard of intelligent interest and intellectual curiosity among cadets should be attained and maintained. . . .

5. The problem of efficiency depends on securing the right types of candidates in sufficient quantity, and on the provision for these of satisfactory education at colleges where military instruction is given. Of these conditions the first is as important as the second. Excellence in subsequent education at cadet colleges or elsewhere cannot make up for deficiencies in the quality and the quantity of the candidates coming forward. We think, therefore, that the primary problem is concerned not merely with education subsequent to entry, but with the attraction of suitably educated candidates.

6. There is a second consideration which is hardly less important. It is much to be desired that first-rate brains should be attracted into the Army. It is not necessary, nor is it wholly desirable, that all, or even the majority, of regimental officers should be intellectuals.

In the case of all, however, it is necessary that there should be certain qualities of character, of which the capacity for leadership is the most obvious example. In consequence, a very difficult problem has to be solved in part by attracting a certain number of boys of high intellectual ability and in securing the proper opportunities of further education for these, and for the rest by attracting and educating a large number of boys in regard to whom stress is laid on character rather than on high intellectual qualifications.

7. The evidence that has been submitted to us makes it clear that the present mode of supply cannot be relied on as likely to prove sufficient in the future. . . . The causes which appear to have operated in diminishing the number of candidates are:

(*1*) *Frequent moves of regiments on account of the variety of the nation's commitments all over the world – involving long separation from families and service in unsettled and expensive stations.*

(*2*) *The unpopularity of service in India.*

(*3*) *The recent cuts in establishments, involving the compulsory retirement of officers and the fear that other cuts are imminent, and the consequent uncertainty.*

(*4*) *The reductions of pay to be effected in 1924.*

(*5*) *The reaction after the War.*

(*6*) *The heavy fees at the Military Colleges. These have recently been increased.*

(*7*) *The fact that some teachers are definitely anti-militarist and recommend their best boys not to take up a military career. . . .*

8. Any adequate improvement in the quality and quantity of candidates must depend upon a larger number of parents being induced to regard the Army as an attractive career for their sons. This implies the necessity of convincing parents that the Army provides openings for brains and character comparable with those provided in the Civil Service or in the other professions. The task of convincing parents may in the end become a matter of propaganda; but propaganda will be valueless unless the system can fairly be said to have been so adjusted as to make it true that such openings exist in fact. Nor is this all. Conviction is only likely to be secured on a sufficient scale by changes in the present system which will not only provide such openings, but which will also make them sufficiently striking to attract attention.

9. It has been represented to us by the many authorities that we have consulted that if it is desired to make the Army attractive as a profession to men of good intellectual attainments, certain conditions are essential –

(*1*) *Work must be provided of sufficient intellectual interest.*
(*2*) *There must be real opportunities for advancement by merit.*
(*3*) *The remuneration must be adequate.*

16. We understand that military rates of pay are under consideration at the present time. We in no way desire to pre-judge this question, but we hope that whatever rates may eventually be decided upon, they will be based on the principle that higher rates must be paid for higher intelligence and more arduous work. It is not for us to go into details on this subject, and we will confine ourselves to expressing the opinion that, while there may be advantages in a uniform rate of pay for officers of all arms and services, supplemented by a system of corps pay, it is desirable that the rates of corps pay should be fixed in such a manner as to give adequate additional remuneration for professional or technical qualifications.

18. In this connection we cannot too strongly emphasize that rates of staff pay should be adequate to attract officers of ability, and we view with favour a proposal that we understand has been made to enable p.s.c. officers to draw a substantial rate of additional pay during the periods when they are employed at regimental duty.

19. It is evident that the Army Council is not without sympathy for the policy of giving special remuneration for exceptional ability, since they have provided in the very early stages of an officer's career a system of prize-cadetships . . . and the granting of antedates to university candidates who have taken an honours degree. We feel, however, that an extension of this system is necessary, and we would recommend a system of scholarships taking the form of increments of pay (say £50 per annum for 5 years), which might be given to suitable candidates on their receiving commissions in order to help to tide over the difficult period on joining for a young officer of ability whose parents can give him little or no allowance. . . .

20. We attach the greatest importance to the whole question of providing at every stage adequate rewards for exceptional capacity. We believe liberal provision in this direction to be essential with a view to encouraging able boys to become officers, and we are unanimous in our opinion that a great opportunity exists at the present time to initiate the suggested reforms. It is not too late to convince the public that the lessons of the war are being taken seriously to heart by the military authorities, and that it is their

firm intention to make the Army an attractive career for men of talent. If we wait much longer the public will feel that the Army is such a hopelessly conservative institution that no vital change is possible in the principles on which the post-war army is organized.

7·8 THE COMPANY OF A CRACK REGIMENT

From the Duke of Portland, Men, Women and Things, *1937, pp. 25–6.*

A pen portrait of a photograph – reproduced in the book – of the followers of the Regimental Drag Hounds (of the Coldstream Guards) at Windsor during the season 1878–9.

Taking the names in the lower group from left to right, Edgar Sebright was afterwards the twelfth Baronet, and died in 1933; Mr Oliphant was a farmer; A. C. Jervoise, afterwards Sir A. Clarke Jervoise, third Bt., of Idsworth, Co. Southampton, died in 1902; Sutton, nicknamed 'the Stalk', died during the Sudan campaign in 1885. Of Colonel Julian Hall and the Hon. H. Legge (Whip), I have already written at length. Colonel Waller-Otway was the Master and Huntsman; A. B. Myers, commonly known as Jimmy Myers, was the Regimental Doctor; standing behind him is 'Coddy', now Lt.-General Sir A. E. Codrington, G.C.V.O., K.C.B., D.S.O., Colonel of the Coldstream; and next to him is myself. . . .

Continuing up the staircase, Colonel Follett, who took a First in Law and Modern History at Oxford before he joined the Army, commanded the 2nd Battalion of the Coldstream; 'Taffy' Wynn, nephew and heir of Sir Watkin Wynn, was unfortunately drowned in the Thames two years later, when attempting to shoot the weir below Windsor Bridge in a punt; Lady Julia Follett was a daughter of the second Lord Ailsa; Harry (Toby) Wickham married Lady Ethelreda Gordon, and was sometime Master of the Fitzwilliam Hounds; Charlie Wise was a very well-known horse-dealer at Eton, from whom we hired our hunters; and the Messrs. Headington were farmers, both very kind supporters of the Drag Hounds.

Captain the Hon. Miles Stapleton, afterwards the tenth Lord Beaumont and Lt.-Colonel commanding the 20th Hussars, was known as 'Inches' – an obvious nickname from his extreme want of them.

7·9 WORLD WAR II: THE NEW ARMY AND THE OLD SCHOOL TIE

Letter to The Times, *16th January 1941.*

MAN MANAGEMENT, *Junior Officers of the New Armies*

TO THE EDITOR OF THE TIMES

Sir, – The authorities who govern the Army and, indeed, all senior officers, are rightly and justly worried about one of the aspects of life in our new armies. That aspect is known as man management, and man management is chiefly the responsibility of the junior officers – the company and platoon commanders. The subject embraces not only the physical but the mental and moral welfare of the soldier – and the word moral is not here used in the customary 'goodie-goodie' sense.

Two or three weeks ago a Sunday newspaper published an address by the Prime Minister given to Harrow School on the subject of the character training acquired by the boys at the older public schools and completely justifying the human product which cheap music-hall artists have jeered at and labelled the old school tie. Never was the old school tie and the best that it stands for more justified than it is today. Our new armies are being officered by classes of society who are new to the job. The middle, lower middle, and working classes are now receiving the King's commission. These classes, unlike the old aristocratic and feudal (almost) classes who led the old Army, have never had 'their people' to consider. They have never had anyone to think of but themselves. This aspect of life is completely new to them, and they have very largely fallen down on it in their capacity as Army officers.

It is not that they do not wish to carry out this part of their duties properly, but rather that they do not know how to begin. Man management is not a subject which can be 'taught'; it is an attitude of mind, and with the old school tie men this was instinctive and part of the philosophy of life. These new young officers will be just as brave and technically efficient, but they have been reared in an atmosphere in which the State spoon feeds everybody from cradle to grave, and no one feels any responsibility for his fellow men. This, Sir, is a sad reflection on our educational system.

I am, Sir, your obedient servant,

R. C. BINGHAM,
Lieutenant-Colonel,
168 O.C.T.U.

7·10 THE REPRESENTATIVE FUNCTION OF THE ARMY

From the Minutes *of Evidence of the Select Committee on Estimates 1948–9. Parliamentary Papers 1948/9, vol. VII.*

Entertainment in the Armed Forces has changed much in the last hundred years, but as the following shows the Army is still expected to carry out a certain amount of ceremonial entertainment and the Air Force was expected to follow in the same footsteps.

1289. Yes? [*Sir Ralph Glyn (Chairman)*] – The second item in the Memorandum . . . is official entertainment in the Armed Forces, the expenditure on which in the aggregate in the year 1948–49 amounted as we told the Committee to, as much as £285,500. This entertainment, of course, takes a variety of forms. It is a long standing and perhaps natural tradition of the Services that they are responsible for some aspects of overseas relations, and it is necessary and certainly is traditional for, instance, for the Commander-in-Chief of an overseas station in the Navy, or the Army or Air Force Commanders in the Mediterranean or the Far East, or whatever it may be, to offer as well as receive a certain amount of entertainment which is not dissimilar in character from that which is carried out by the Government Hospitality Fund. The Commander-in-Chief Mediterranean takes his 'travelling hotel' about with him, and if he visits Greece or Alexandria or wherever it may be, it is necessary for him, as a representative of His Majesty's Government, to offer as well as to receive a certain amount of official hospitality; and allocations to senior officers of the Armed Forces account for a fairly substantial proportion of the total sums involved in expenditure of this kind. In addition of course, officers in command, even in the less exalted commands in the Armed Forces are required and expected to maintain official contacts not only with their own forces but with the people in the locality in which they may be serving, and with of course the other forces, They do receive a good many visitors both from overseas and from within this country and have to be in a position to offer certain entertainment as part of their job to these visitors. There used to be made to officers in command various allocations which were partly in the form of what was called table money or its equivalent, and partly in the form of special pay; but, as I think the Memorandum informed the Sub-Committee, as a result of the review of conditions of service in the Armed Forces which took place in 1945–46, this element of entertainment expenditure in the remuneration of officers in command was segregated out and treated, as it was in fact, as a separate and additional item to their general emoluments; and a scale of payments, going by rank for officers in command, was laid down in a White Paper which was presented to the House in March, 1946. . . .

1592. [*Chairman*] Then, as to the expenditure in the hands of individual officers, are there rules governing this expenditure? – [*T. Padmore*] None at all. In the case where an officer receives an allowance for the purpose of entertainment, it is his business to use it as he deems appropriate for entertainment purposes, but there are no rules governing the people to whom he may offer entertainment, or the scale on which he shall offer it.

1593. And this allowance is made to him, and if he does not expend it, what happens? – From time to time, of course, there is a review of the amount of these allowances, and officers are asked to give budgets of their expenditure on this kind of thing, and those budgets are examined. It is one's universal experience, I think, that officers in command spend more on entertainment than the allowances that are granted to them. I do not know whether an occasional case may arise in which an officer proves to have spent less than his allowance or would have given practically no entertainment at all, but in the case of an officer in a senior command who gave no entertainment at all, it could hardly be held that he was doing his job. . . .

1598. . . . [*Selwyn Lloyd.*] On the Navy and Army figures here, really the relationship they bear to the pre-war expenditure seems reasonable: they are up by about 50 per cent. That is, I imagine, because we must have rather more Generals than we had before the war, and, that being so, it does not seem excessive. But in the case of the Air Force it would seem to be a very big increase?

1599. The position with the Air Force is that in this matter the Air Force was to some extent the Cinderella Service before the war. I think it would be agreed that really rather inadequate provision was made in the case of the Air Force, and what has happened since the war is that the Air Force has been brought more into line with the other two Service Departments.

1600. You think that would explain their rather striking increase? – [*A. H. Clough*]. The system was quite different before the war. The Army Commander-in-Chief had a rate of pay of £9 1s. od. a day, if he were a full General, compared with £6 6s. 8d. a day; and £9 1s. od. is roughly another £2 15s. od., which was taxable, and that represented what he was given for entertainment. That was the Army system. . . . The Air Force people did not have the 'In Command' rates of pay. They had the basic rates of pay of their rank . . . and the Air Ministry were given a lump sum grant each year by the Treasury, which they distributed among their people holding Command jobs, according to the number of them and according to the amount which they were able to persuade the Treasury to allocate to them. In the year 1926, for example, we gave them £5,000, and that £5,000 was divided among 17 Air Officers, including Group Captains. . . . Well, you appreciate that the Air Officers and Group Captains, who had between them £3,500 out of the £5,000 (and there were only 17 of them) got rather a bigger share each than, say, in the year 1937, when we distributed to the Air Ministry a total of £7,250, of which £4,400 was used for these Senior Commanders, the total number of Senior Commanders being 28. What really took place is that, as the years went on from 1926 onwards, the Air Ministry did persuade the Treasury to give them more money each year for entertainment, but the number of Senior Commanders increased more rapidly than the funds available, so the average rate of the entertainment grants received by these officers became progressively less. After the war they persuaded us that it was only fair that their Senior Commanders should have practically the same as a corresponding Senior Commander in the Army. The reason we had taken a different view before was that we thought that, say, the General Officer Commanding Southern Command, an Army Commander, had a lot of standing commitments that had grown up traditionally that he just could not get out of; he was expected, as G.O.C. Southern Command, to entertain such and such a party each year, or to throw a garden party for somebody else each year. The Air Commanders were new and had not those obligations. That was the underlying principle of treating the Air Ministry less favourably.

8   The clergy

8·1 A WEALTHY WORLDLY CLERGY

From J. Wade, The Black Book, *an exposition of abuses in Church and State, new ed. 1835, pp. 59–61, 20–21, 24–7.*

While the author of the *Black Book* was ostensibly concerned in discovering and exposing abuses, he based his data on evidence which had emerged from Parliamentary Returns and investigations.

Everything in this country is formed upon an aristocratic scale. Because some noblemen have enormous incomes, *ergo* the bishops must have enormous incomes, to be fit and meet associates for them. Thus, one extravagance in society generates another to keep it in countenance; because we have a king who costs a million a year, we must have lords with a quarter of a million, and bishops with fifty thousand a year. . . . But why should the income of a bishopric so far exceed that of the highest offices in the civil department of government? A Secretary of State has to show his 'front in courts and palaces', as well as a bishop; he is in constant intercourse with dukes and princes, yet his salary does not exceed £6000 a year. The bishops have their private fortunes as well as others, and there is no just reason why their official incomes should be so disproportionate to that of a lord of the Treasury, or Chancellor of the Exchequer.

An *Archdeacon* is considered the deputy of the bishop, and assists in the discharge of the spiritual duties of his diocese. As such, we think the deputy ought to be paid out of the income of his principal, and the revenues of the archdeaconries applied to a fund to be raised, in lieu of tithes. Many bishops are not over-burthened with duty, and have little need of assistants. One bishop of the United Church, it is well known, spent all his time in Italy, where he dissipated the revenues of an immensely rich see. Some English bishops do not reside in their dioceses. We knew a bishop who resided, within the last eight years, not more than a mile from St. James's Palace; he lived till he sunk into a state of dotage and imbecility; he was in fact left to the care of a wet-nurse, who treated him like an infant: we never heard the church sustained any injury from the suspended services of this right reverend prelate, and he, or someone for him, continued, till his death, to receive the revenues of his see.

The *Dean and Chapter*, consisting of canons and prebendaries, are considered the *council* of the bishop. ... One of the most important offices of the dean and chapter, is to *elect* the bishop; that is choose the appointee of some court favourite, and in the exercise of which franchise, they discharge as virtual functions as the electors of Cockermouth or Ripon, who adopt the nominees of Earl Lonsdale and Miss Lawrence. The deaneries, prebends, canonries, and other cathedral dignities, are in fact honorary offices of great value; they are endowed with vast estates, numerous manors, and other good things, and have valuable livings in their gift; all of which advantages are so much public income idly squandered. ...

Next in order come the *Aristocratic Pluralists*. These are so many clerical sinecurists who receive immense incomes, without render-ing any service to the community. They are mere men of the world, whose element is the race-course, the ball-room, and billiard-table. They seldom see their parishes: their residence is in London, at Paris, Naples, or Florence. If they visit their benefices, it is not in the capacity of pastor, but of surveyor or tax-gatherer, who comes to spy out improvements, to watch the increase of stock and extension of tillage, and see how many hundreds more he can squeeze out of the fruits of the industry and capital of the impoverished farmer. The poor parishioner, who contributes his ill-spared tithe to the vicious indulgence of these spiritual locusts, is neither directed by their example, instructed by their precepts, nor benefited by their expenditure.

From the preceding table, it is evident that about 2152 incumbents, and 4254 curates, discharge nearly the entire duties of the established religion; that their average income is £301. . . .

It is further evident that the Bishops, Dignitaries, and Non-resident incumbents, amounting to 6,025 individuals, receive £7,485,062 per annum, or seven-ninths of the revenues of the church; that these classes hold either merely honorary appointments, discharge no duties, or are greatly overpaid; that, in consequence, by abolishing non-residence, stalls, and other sinecures, and by reducing the salaries of the higher clergy to a level with those of appointments in the State, . . . several millions of public income might be saved, to be applied either to the establishment of a fund for the maintenance of the operative clergy, in lieu of tithe and other ecclesiastical imposts; or, it might be applied, as a great portion of it was originally intended, as a provision for the maintenance of the poor; or, as a substitute for those public taxes whose pressure on 'the springs and sources of industry' tends to produce national poverty and embarrassment. . . .

Preferment in the Church is as regular a subject of sale as commissions in the army; and a patron would as soon think of rewarding an individual for his learning and piety with the gift of a freehold estate as a church living. Hence, the door of the church is open to all, whether they have *a call* or not, provided they possess a *golden key*; and, in the Metropolis, offices are openly kept in which spiritual preferment is sold as regularly as offices in the East Indies, medical practice, or any other secular pursuit. . . . In short, church patronage is dealt with as a mere commodity, and the produce of tithe and glebe, instead of being employed as the reward of religious zeal and service, is bought, like a life annuity, as a provision and settlement for families. . . .

All the offices of the Church being professedly of a spiritual nature, and executed for spiritual objects, an American bishop, Dr Hobart, during his sojourn in this country, felt much scandalized by reading the following details of secular traffic in the Morning Chronicle, July 13.

'The church livings in Essex, sold on the 1st instant, by Mr Robins, of Regent-street, were not the absolute advowsons, but the next presentations contingent on the lives of Mr and Mrs W. T. P. L. Wellesley, aged thirty-six and twenty-five years respectively, and were as under:–

Place	Description	Estimated Annual Value	Age of Incumbent	Sold for
Wanstead	Rectory	£653	62	£2,440
Woodford	,,	1,200	58	4,200
Gt. Paindon	,,	500	63	1,600
Fifield	,,	525	59	1,520
Rochford	,,	700	62	2,000
Filstead	Vicarage	400	50	900
Roydon	,,	200	46	580

The biddings appeared to be governed by the age and health of the incumbents, residence, situation, and other local circumstances, with which the parties interested seemed to be well acquainted'.

One of the greatest abuses in the disposal of patronage is *monopoly*, in a few individuals, of influence and connexion, sharing among them the most valuable emoluments of the church. In all spiritual offices and dignities, there is a great difference in value, and also in patronage; and the great object of ecclesiastical intrigue is, to secure not only the most valuable, but the greatest number of preferments. Hence arises the present disposition of church property. Scarcely any preferment is held *single*; the sees, dignities, rectories, and vicarages, being mostly held with other good things, and the most valuable monopolized by the relations and connexions of those who have the disposal of them; namely, the Crown, the Bishops, and Aristocracy. The bishops are frequently archdeacons and deans, rectors, vicars, and curates, besides holding professorships, clerkships, prebends, precentorships, and other offices in cathedrals. Their sons, sons-in-law, brothers, and nephews, are also pushed in to the most valuable preferments in the diocese. We shall give an instance of the manner of serving out the loaves and fishes of the church in particular families, from the example of SPARKE, bishop of Ely, who owed his promotion to the circumstance of having been tutor to the duke of Rutland. The exhibition is limited to the two sons and son-in-law of the bishop, without including appointments to distant relatives. In the shiftings, exchanges, resignations, movings about, and heaping up of offices, we have a complete picture of the ecclesiastical evolutions which are constantly being performed in almost every diocese of the kingdom.

1815. The Rev. John Henry Sparke, the eldest son, took his degree of
B.A.; he was then about 21; he was immediately appointed by
his father to a bishop's fellowship in Jesus College, Cambridge.
1816. He was appointed steward of all his father's manorial courts.
1818. He took his degree of M.A., and was presented to a prebendal
stall in Ely Cathedral, on the resignation of the Rev. Archdeacon
Brown, who had been holding it one year: he was also presented
to the sinecure rectory of Littlebury, and in the following month
he was presented to the living of Streatham-cum-Thetford, by an
exchange with the Rev. Mr Law for the living of Downham,
which last living had been held for three years by the Rev. Mr
Daubeny, the bishop's nephew, who now resigned it in favour of
Mr Law, and retired to the living of Bexwell.
1819. The Rev. J. H. Sparke had a dispensation granted him from the
archbishop of Canterbury, permitting him to hold the living of
Cottenham with his other preferments.
1818. The Rev. Henry Fardell, the bishop's son-in-law, was ordained
deacon.
1819. He was presented to a prebendal stall in Ely, the degree of M.A.
having been conferred on him by the archbishop of Canterbury.
1821. He was presented to the living of Tyd St Giles.
1822. He was presented to the living of Waterbeach, on the resignation
of the Rev. Mr Mitchell.
1823. He resigned Tyd St Giles, and was presented to Bexwell, on the
resignation of the Rev. Mr Daubeny, the bishop's nephew, who
was presented to Feltwell; but in a few weeks, when the value of
Feltwell was better understood, Mr Daubeny was required to
resign Feltwell and return to Bexwell. This, it is said, he did with
great reluctance; he was, however, presented to Tyd as well as
Bexwell, and the Rev. Mr Fardell was then presented to Feltwell.
1824. The Rev. J. Henry Sparke was appointed Chancellor of the
diocese, and this year he resigned the prebendal stall he held, and
was presented to the one which became vacant by the death of the
Rev. Sir H. Bate Dudley; the house and gardens belonging to the
latter stall being considered the best in the College.
1826. The Rev. Edward Sparke, the bishop's youngest son, took his
degree of B.A., and was immediately presented by his father to a
bishop's fellowship in St John's College, Cambridge, on the
resignation of Charles Jenyns, Esq. a friend of the family, who
had been holding it three years. He was also appointed Register
of the diocese.
1827. The Rev. J. Henry Sparke resigned the livings of Cottenham and
Stretham, and was presented to the rich living of Leverington.
1829. The Rev. J. Henry Sparke was presented to Bexwell.

1829. The Rev. Edward Sparke took his degree of M.A. and was presented to a prebendal stall on the resignation of Rev. Ben. Park (another friend of the family) who had been holding it three years.

He was also this year presented to the living of Hogeworthingham, and to the living of Barley.

1830. He resigned Hogeworthingham, and was presented to Connington. This year he resigned Barley also, and was presented to Littleport.

1831. He resigned Connington, and was presented to Feltwell, at the same time he resigned his prebendal stall, and was presented to the one become vacant by the death of the Rev. George King – the rich living of Sutton being in the gift of the possessor of the latter stall.

1831. The Rev. Henry Fardell resigned Feltwell, and was presented to the rich living of Wisbech.

Bishop Sparke is not the only prelate who has shown regard to the temporal welfare of his family. . . . The late archbishop Sutton is an eminent instance of the perversion of ecclesiastical patronage. The Suttons remaining in the church are very numerous; among seven of them are shared sixteen rectories, vicarages, and chapelries, besides preacherships and dignities in cathedrals. Of the *eleven* daughters of the archbishop, several had the prudence to marry men in holy orders, who soon became amply endowed. Hugh Percy, son of the earl of Beverly, married one daughter; and, in the course of about as many years, was portioned off with eight different preferments, estimated to be worth £10,000 per annum; four of these preferments were given in one year, probably that of the nuptials, and intended as an *outfit*. This fortunate son-in-law is now bishop of Carlisle, to which see he was translated from Rochester. According to law he ought to have resigned all the preferments he held at the time of being promoted to a bishopric; but somehow he has contrived to retain the most valuable prebend of St. Paul's, worth £3000 per annum, and also the chancellorship of Sarum. Another daughter of the archbishop married the Rev. James Croft, who is archdeacon of Canterbury, prebendary of Canterbury, curate of Hythe, rector of Cliffe-at-Hone, and rector of Saltwood – all preferments in the gift of the archbishop.

Archbishop Sutton kept a favourable eye towards *collaterals* as well as those in a direct line. A sister married a Rev. Richard Lockwood, who was presented, in one year, with the three vicarages of Kessingland, Lowestoft, and Potter-Heigham: all these livings are valuable, and in the gift of the bishop of Norwich, and were presented by his grace when he held that see. . . .

The Sumners, Blomfields, and Marshes are growing thick in the church calendar, but . . . they have been too recently planted to have yet struck their roots wide and deep in the Lord's vineyard. The death of a bishop causes a movement in the church, like a change of ministers in the state. Expectations are excited, numerous removes follow, the adherents and connexions of the deceased are got out of the way as fast as possible, and all vacancies filled with the followers of the new diocesan.

8.2 THE GULF BETWEEN BISHOPS AND CLERGY

From S. G. Osborne, Letters to the Editor of 'The Times', *2 vols 1890, 1, pp. 380–5.*

The author was himself a clergyman of the Church of England. In a letter written in 1852 he describes the consequences the Bishop's elevated social position had for his work as administrator of his diocese and leader of the parochial clergy.

Nothing can be more unsatisfactory or prejudicial to the real usefulness of the Established Church than the present relative positions of her bishops and clergy.

Once in three years we have a visitation; we are summoned to a neighbouring town to meet the bishop; we follow him to a morning service in the church, and hear one of our brethren preach a controversial sermon; our names are then called over; we stand before the communion rails, within which the bishop sits; he, from his chair, proceeds to read a long essay on Church matters in general, his own views regarding them, and the particular legal measures on Church matters which have been passed since the last visitation, or which may be expected before the next. We receive his blessing, and disperse – until the hour of dinner. . . .

The bishop in the meantime sees some half-dozen curates or new rectors, to whom he wishes to put some commonplace inquiries, or, perhaps, to administer some gentle rebuke; he then takes up the inn 'Times', and waits with patience the hour of the next stage of the visitation – the dinner. At last all are seated who intend to dine with the bishop; poor curates and indifferent rectors are gone home – the former cannot afford to dine – the latter it would bore; they know the routine by heart, and gladly avoid its repetition in their own presence. The chaplain and the preacher, and some of the rural deans, are the bishop's neighbours; the dinner is an inn dinner, and in general a very good one. . . . The bishop's health is drunk, and he is thanked for his admirable charge, and requested to print it; he is modest in his reply, and acquiesces. . . . After some small ecclesiastical talk at the episcopal end of the table, and some good stories from the secretary at his end, relished by his less awed neighbours, a petition or two for or against something is handed round, and gets a few signatures; the bishop rises, bows to all, and goes away for another three years. A neat London-built brougham, with his lordship and the chaplain inside, the episcopal mace in the swordcase, and his butler, who has acted as macebearer, on the box, soon takes out of the sight of the assembled clergy and the boys in the street their right reverend chief and counsellor. . . .

The next episcopal appearance among the clergy is at the confirmations. This is a hurried affair; eleven o'clock at Pumpford, three o'clock at Market Minster, and so on for a week or two in each year; travelling some twenty-five miles a day, being so hurried that he is forced to transgress the rubric by saying that to four children at a time which he is ordered to say to each one: it is no wonder that his clergy see but little of him on these occasions. Some few may meet him at dinner, wherever he may stay to dine and sleep; but they find him fatigued, and he has to play the guest to his host's family; he could hardly be expected to do more. . . .

A palace – house in town – seat in the Lords – the metropolitan charity sermon duty of each London season – a large income, with its attendant snares and cares, – these are elements in the present episcopal position which seem to me to defy the bishop being to the clergy what he ought to be, and what he must be, if the Church is ever to be active and yet at peace within herself. The bishop of our day is far too elevated above the heads of his clergy. Superior as many even of the curates of his diocese may be to him in general scholarship, and especially in theological learning, they can never feel quite at ease in his company. If they call upon him at the diocesan palace, or at his house in Belgravia, or his suite of rooms at —

Hotel, they are uncomfortably awed. The spiritual peer is too obvious to them; they cannot at their ease venture on the homely parochial topic on which they would seek advice. . . .

I am willing at once to admit that, considering the grounds on which, in bygone years, bishops have been appointed by the Crown, the Church has fared well in that she has fared no worse. To have been a bold and unscrupulous advocate of an unpopular measure; to have had a relative who had spent 10,000*l.* in contesting an important county on the ministerial side; to have been tutor to a Minister, or to his son; to have been an active partisan, on the right side, in a university election; to be an actual relation of the Minister – these, and such like, it is well known, have been the claims most powerfully acknowledged in the appointment of bishops. We have had, and may have still, bigots bad and bold in their bigotry. The bench has, even of very late, shown in some of its members a deplorable mercenary spirit. A spirit of nepotism has at times been very rife, and we have had very worldly men, but I cannot call to mind one offensively bad man.

What we really need, Sir, is *more bishops*, but of a *very different worldly position*. . . . Divide the dioceses into manageable districts, and have what I will call 'gig bishops'; men of learning, of piety, of some parochial experience, whose incomes should be, say, 1,500*l*, per annum; men who would visit the clergy in their own houses, keep up a regular acquaintance with them, become known, in some measure, to the congregation of each village church; men who would come to the rectory on a Saturday in their gig or four-wheel, stay the Sunday with us, wish for nothing better than the rectory's best room, and what the rector's limited establishment could afford, *without fuss*; preaching in our churches on the Sunday, going to the Sunday-school to encourage our wives and daughters in their task there. . . . The Monday would give time to the 'gig bishop' to look in at the day-school, to delight and encourage the teachers; to call on and also delight the churchwardens; carefully to inspect the church, and all this without preventing him moving on by an easy drive to the next scene of an episcopal kindly visit. He would thus gain a real knowledge of the state of his diocese, and the peculiarities of character among his clergy. He could make himself their confidential friend, and gaining, as he would, so much practical experience, he would become a valuable adviser. He would get a pride in his clergy, and they would be the more easily ruled as they would be reproved in private, and affectionately advised in a pious and humble spirit, and dealt with in a way which must win their love.

I feel satisfied that to some such ruling machinery as this we must come, if the Church is ever again to have any episcopal supervision in which the laity will have confidence, and to which the clergy would give allegiance. Thus, I should hope we should get rid of scandals which attach to the bench, to the hurt of the whole body of the clergy. My 'gig bishops' would be working men, practically acquainted with their work, and in a condition to follow it out under far less temptation to error or to idleness than now besets the spiritual peers with their 8,000*l*. a year.

8·3 CLERICAL RANK AND SECULAR HIERARCHY

From the Memorials from the Dean and Chapter of Lincoln and Salisbury Cathedrals to the Commission appointed to consider the state of the Established Church, *1837, Parliamentary Papers, 1837, XLI.*

The Commission was concerned among other matters with the claim that Cathedral Establishments were too large and the stipends and patronages which the Cathedral Clergy enjoyed were excessive. The latter defended themselves with reference to the antiquity of their property rights and to the social values which the system upheld.

ex Lincoln

We state thus broadly our conviction that individuals bearing a certain rank and outward appearance in the Church are, in various ways essentially beneficial to the community, because we fear that there is moving abroad a mischievous disposition to magnify, at their expense, the pastoral office and ministerial industry of those who are invidiously called the working clergy . . . (the Cathedral Clergy) form a connecting link between the higher and lower grades in the ministry, raising the latter in importance . . . while their regular attendance upon the choral services of the Church secure to the public the full preservation of the most beautiful and striking solemnities of Christian worship together with the more substantial comforts of daily prayer and thanksgiving.

ex Salisbury
We are deeply impressed with the value of cathedral establishment
to the cause of true religion, by maintaining a well-ordered gradation in an ecclesiastical institution, by providing a suitable reward
for which learning and distinguished professional character . . . by
giving tone to the morals and setting an example of propriety of conduct to all classes, by supporting the various charities and assisting
the local pecuniary resources of the respective Cathedral towns. . . .
We maintain . . . that our right to our patronage during our lives is
quite as strong and indubitable as our right to our incomes and
that to deprive us of it would be to shake to its very foundation the
security of title to all property and would amount to little short of
dissolution, on the part of the government, of the social contract.

8·4 BISHOPS AS BULWARK OF TRADITION

From James Hurnard, The Setting Sun, *abridged ed. by R.
Hamilton, Cambridge, 1946.*

Hurnard's autobiography in verse, ten thousand lines of it, was
originally published in 1870. A brewer by trade, a radical by
conviction, a poet by self-confidence, he gives us an admittedly
somewhat 'simpliste' view.

Have not the bench of Bishops always voted
For every cruel, every unjust law,
Until repentance ceased to be a virtue?
Have they not basely voted for the slave trade?
Have they not voted heart and soul for slavery?
Opposed the amelioration of all laws
That bore oppressively upon the people –
The Criminal Law, that strangled men by hundreds;
The Corn Law, which most surely starved its thousands; –
And Parliamentary Reform, which sought
To rectify the clumsy old machinery
By which the laws of England were enacted?
The Bishops have done this, and more than this,
And drawn their tens of thousands from the land,
Living in princely luxury and state;
Not like the bishops of the early ages –
Plain fishermen, who fished for souls, not mitres.

vi. 815–837

8·5 *PARSONS AS PRESERVERS OF ORDER*

From Augustus J. C. Hare, Memorials of a Quiet Life, *2 vols., 1872, I, pp. 58–9.*

Writing 40 years later Augustus Hare reproduces a letter by his mother which in turn quotes from a letter by her son Julius, himself a future clergyman.

Nov. 30. [*1830*] – I must copy for you part of Julius's letter about the riots:– 'The gentry, the farmers, the clergy, the citizens, the tradesmen of the towns must assemble and form constitutional associations for preserving peace and order. By active energy we may still avoid the danger, which if we are supine will crush us. Most now are weak and yield to intimidations, for it requires an inordinate degree of courage to resist a mob with such fearful weapons, and so unscrupulous in having recourse to the most fiendish measures. Surely, too, if people are but active, many a poor harmless peasant may be saved from joining the wicked hordes, many may be saved from the snares they have already fallen into. Surely the clergy still have an influence over their flocks: they should preach from the pulpit, they should speak in every cottage of the blessings of peace and order, of the intolerable, inevitable calamities that must fall on every class from a system like the present. Surely our nobility and gentry, in spite of the pestilential watering-places and other temples of vanity and frivolity that draw them away from their estates, may still marshal faithful tenants and peasants, if they will but appear among them and at the head of them. Surely the charity which the ladies of England have bestowed so liberally and almost prodigally, has not altogether fallen on stony ground, but will produce some good fruit even for themselves here. The heart of England I am convinced is still sound, in spite of all that has been done to poison it. But it must be appealed to strongly and honestly. We are trying at Cambridge to organize a kind of body for the protection of the country round, in the hope that our example may be followed, though there are many who say there is no need of it yet.'

8·6 BISHOP'S MOVES

From *Samuel Butler*, The Life and Letters of Dr Samuel Butler, *2 vols., 1896, vol. 2, pp. 167–9.*

Butler was appointed to the see of Lichfield and Coventry on 13 June, 1836, by Lord Melbourne. He had previously been head-master of Shrewsbury School. The following two letters reached him as the result of his appointment.

From John Herford, Esq.
Manchester, June 20th, 1836.

'My Lord Bishop, – Although I am sensible of the small value which can attach to any expression of the feelings of so unimportant a person as myself, I cannot resist the desire of assuring you the high gratification I experienced at the confirmation Saturday's *Gazette* afforded of an appointment which does far more honour to those from whom it has proceeded than to the distinguished individual upon whom it has been conferred.

'Although a Dissenter, I earnestly desire to see the Church of England placed upon a basis which shall secure it from all danger and render it truly a national Church. I sincerely rejoice therefore at every circumstance which tends to its prosperity and to its increased usefulness and popularity, and nothing appears to me better calculated to effect this object than the appointment of those to its highest offices who are alike distinguished for harmony, liberality, and a constitutional regard for the rights and liberties of the people. Let a fair proportion of the dignitaries of the Church be found amongst the supporters of a popular Government, friendly to the advancement of knowledge, and promoters of every scheme having for its object the real welfare and happiness of the people, and there will soon be an end of the absurd desire for their removal from the House of Lords. Living as I do amongst the Dissenters, and well acquainted with their views and feelings, I have no hesitation in saying that the Church has far less to apprehend from their hostility than from the mistaken zeal of its professed friends.

'The day is gone by when religious establishments might depend alone upon their antiquity and splendour. All institutions are now tested by their utility, and can only be maintained by their conformity with the spirit of the age, and the wants and feelings of the people.

'Your Lordship will I trust excuse these remarks, offered in a spirit of profound respect for yourself and of sincere anxiety for the permanence and increasing usefulness of that Church of which you are so distinguished an ornament. In the hope that you may live many years to strengthen and adorn it, and that your high reputation may advance as your sphere of honour and usefulness becomes more extended, I remain, my Lord Bishop, very respectfully yours,

'*JOHN HERFORD*.'

From the Bishop of Durham (Dr. Maltby).
28 Curzon Street, June 29th, 1836.

'Who could look into the Book of Fate, and conjecture that, when you and I were dining with Lord Berwick forty-four years ago, we should go to Court on the same day, you for the See of Lichfield, I for that of Durham? I am sure you are thankful, as I am, to a gracious Providence who has thus been pleased to notice (beyond *my* deserts) our honesty and independence.

'Now to business. Do you go to Court alone? If you do, will you take my son, who is not going to the Levee, but wishes to see the humours of it, as my Chaplain attending me when I do homage?

'My reason for asking is, that Lord John Russell has offered to call for me in his carriage; therefore I shall have mine to come for me, but not to carry me. Lord John is to call for me quarter before two; therefore if you set off at two you will be in good time.

'If you prefer that my carriage shall take you and him, we can squeeze home together, as my son's spareness will not make him a great addition to the weight and robes of two Bishops.

'Pray send me a frank of yours to Mrs A. Urquhart, St. Colme Street, Edinburgh; and if you want one of mine to Mrs Butler or any of your family today or tomorrow you shall have it.

'Wishing you an increase of health to enjoy your well-merited honours, I am, my dear Bishop, yours most sincerely,

'*E. DUNELM*.'

'I think you should put on your two cards:–
Bishop of Lichfield *elect*,
on his appointment.
Presented by Lord Melbourne (I suppose).
Remember, that is *extra metrum*'.

8·7 *CLERICAL JUSTICES*

From Hansard, *1875, 3rd Series, vol. 223, columns 765–6.*

One of the strongest ties which linked the clergy as a group to the ruling class was their frequent inclusion in the roll of the Justices of the Peace. They were thus allied to the landed classes who sat on the bench as the result of the property qualification which formed the basis for the magistracy.

The Earl of Albemarle, in moving that the Bill be now read the second time, said, that its object was to amend the Act of 18 Geo. II., by which it was declared that no person should be eligible to be a justice of the peace who did not hold land of the annual value of £100. By his Bill he proposed to enact that an income of £300 a-year from personal estate should be deemed equal to an income of £100 a-year from land. The noble Earl said that in the few remarks he desired to offer to the House, it would be his object to show that the restriction instituted by that Act was bad legislation – vicious in principle and obstructive in operation; that it was one of the last remnants of class legislation, and one by which the efficient administration of justice was rendered subservient to the social elevation of a class: – for by necessary inference, it was declared that landed proprietors alone were competent to administer justice in the rural districts of England and Wales – to the exclusion of vast numbers of gentlemen of rank, wealth, education, and intelligence who might reside within the counties, and to the exclusion even of that learned profession from which all other Judges were taken. The period when a property qualification was first affixed to the magistracy dated 450 years back; and at that time the object contemplated was to restrict the magistracy to the landed class. Subsequently, the Act of George II., by virtue of the tithe rent-charge, qualified incumbents of livings became eligible for the office of justice, and thus clergymen became sharers in that offensive monopoly, and stood in the invidious position of holding

lay appointments to the exclusion of the main body of the laity. He
wished to speak with all respect of the clergy of England and Wales;
but, in his opinion, they were not the most fit persons to administer
justice, and he expressed a very common view of the subject when
he said that clergymen should not be placed on the Commission of
the Peace, except where laymen of proper status could not be
found for the performance of magisterial duties. And here he
would call attention to a Return which had been laid on the Table
by which their Lordships would see how that clerical element in
the county magistracy was spread over the length and breadth of
the land. It was a Return of the number of clergymen of the
Established Church who acted on the Commission of the Peace in
each county; and it told them that in 51 out of the 52 counties into
which England and Wales were divided, the scarcity of lay magistrates was supplemented by beneficed clergy. When he moved
for the Return, he expected to be able to show that in the two
counties with which he was best acquainted, there was too great a
number of clergymen; the Return fully answered his expectation,
Norfolk and Suffolk being the counties in which clerical magistrates were most employed. If they took the contiguous counties –
the counties bordering on the German Ocean – namely, Essex,
Lincolnshire, and Yorkshire – and if they would make him a present of Herefordshire, in which also the clergy were very numerous
– they would find that in those six counties there was a greater
number of clergymen acting as magistrates than in any 14 other
counties. He had been told, in fact, that there was scarcely a
county in which an extension of the area whence lay magistrates
were taken would not be a positive boon; but if it would benefit
only the counties he had named, it would fully justify him in
asking their Lordships to pass the Bill before them. Why, by
excluding the laity from the magisterial Bench, should they create
an artificial scarcity of magistrates, when the demand was so much
greater than the supply? Was it right that these reverend gentlemen
who received stipends from the State, should be regarded as qualified; when men of culture and intelligence, and men well versed in
the criminal law, were debarred from rendering assistance on the
Bench in consequence of the civil disabilities inflicted on them by
the law?

8·8 THE CHURCH AND THE CROWN

From J. G. Lockhart, Cosmo Gordon Lang, *1949, p. 405*

The significance of this central passage from the broadcast which
the Archbishop of Canterbury made after the Abdication of
Edward VIII lies not only in the view of the nature of kingship
which it implied – there is little doubt that Lang's view on this
was widely shared – but also in the fact that the broadcast took
place at all. Baldwin apart, there was no other broadcast after the
King had made his own abdication speech over the air.

What pathos, nay what tragedy, surrounds the central figure of
these swiftly moving scenes! On the 11th day of December, 248
years ago, King James II fled from Whitehall. By a strange coinci-
dence, on the 11th day of December last week King Edward VIII,
after speaking his last words to his people, left Windsor Castle,
the scene of all the splendid traditions of his ancestors and his
Throne, and went out an exile. In the darkness he left these
shores.

Seldom, if ever, has any British Sovereign come to the Throne
with greater natural gifts for his kingship. Seldom, if ever, has any
Sovereign been welcomed by a more enthusiastic loyalty. From
God he had received a high and sacred trust. Yet by his own will
he has abdicated – he has surrendered the trust. With characteristic
frankness he has told us his motive. It was a craving for private
happiness. Strange and sad it must be that for such a motive, however strongly it pressed upon his heart, he should have disappointed
hopes so high and abandoned a trust so great. Even more strange
and sad it is that he should have sought his happiness in a manner
inconsistent with the Christian principles of marriage, and within
a social circle whose standards and ways of life are alien to all the
best instincts and traditions of his people. Let those who belong to
this circle know that today they stand rebuked by the judgment of
the nation which had loved King Edward. I have shrunk from
saying these words. But I have felt compelled for the sake of
sincerity and truth to say them.

Yet for one who has known him since his childhood, who has
felt his charm and admired his gifts, these words cannot be the last.
How can we forget the high hopes and promise of his youth; his

most genuine care for the poor, the suffering, the unemployed; his years of eager service both at home and across the seas? It is the remembrance of these things that wrings from our hearts the cry – 'The pity of it, O, the pity of it!' To the infinite mercy and the protecting care of God we commit him now, wherever he may be.